SOUTHEAST ASIA IN THE EYES OF EUROPE

Southeast Asia

IN THE EYES OF EUROPE

The Sixteenth Century

———

DONALD F. LACH

PHOENIX BOOKS

THE UNIVERSITY OF CHICAGO PRESS

CHICAGO AND LONDON

THE UNIVERSITY OF CHICAGO PRESS, CHICAGO 60637
The University of Chicago Press, Ltd., London W. C. 1

Preface to the Phoenix Edition

For this early period in the history of Southeast Asia there are but few indigenous accounts which can be used with confidence by the serious student. Although the extant native sources for the continental countries are better than those for the archipelago, they are all entirely unchronological or written so long after the event as to be suspect. And both the written records and the oral histories are so replete with legend that they can be used only in conjunction with the more reliable Chinese, Indian, Muslim, and European sources. Consequently, the history of the region in the sixteenth century has been painfully reconstructed almost in its entirety from archeological deductions and foreign literary materials.

The best reports on Southeast Asia written in European languages during the sixteenth century were prepared by the Portuguese and the Jesuit missionaries. Their accounts can also be checked in certain instances by reference to writings by Italian, Spanish, English, and Dutch explorers and merchants. Since the best sources were written in European languages that are less well known, they have been rather badly neglected by Asian specialists until recently. As a consequence, our knowledge of Southeast Asia in the first century of its discovery by Europe has remained fragmentary and very imperfect.

In this work an effort has been made, on the basis of the extant printed sources, to depict what Europeans of the sixteenth century reported home about the various countries and islands of Southeast Asia. The picture which emerges is far from complete and it is not always sharp, perhaps because the reporters were sometimes unclear about their own observations and delineations, or perhaps because of the difficulties we find today in visualizing and interpreting what these writers were trying to make their contemporaries see and understand. But it is possible to discern clearly, even from this partial depiction, the universal prominence of the Chinese and Muslims in the life of the region, the preponderant position of Malacca in its commerce, the relatively high degree of political independence enjoyed by its continental states, and the isolation and primitive condition of some of its insular areas.

This book is an exact reproduction of Part III, Chapter VII, from Volume I of my *Asia in the Making of Europe* (Chicago and London, 1965). It is being published separately in the hope that students will find it a useful supplement to the materials on Southeast Asia's history derived from other sources. While the European view is but one of several, it can be stated unequivocally that in the present state of scholarship the European sources provide the most continuous and detailed record obtainable on the history of Southeast Asia in the sixteenth century.

A few notes on the use of this book need to be recorded. Because it was originally prepared as a chapter for my larger work, the reader will occasionally find cross references in the text and footnotes which allude to materials not reprinted here. It was thought wise to retain these cross references to give the enterprising student the opportunity to locate easily those items in my original work on which he might like to have further clarification. With regard to the footnotes it should also be observed that a full bibliographical reference is given on the first occasion when a source is cited. Thereafter, when the same source is cited again, a reference to the footnote number of its first mention appears in parentheses after the *op. cit.* or *loc. cit.* This device, it is hoped, will make for easier consultation of the numerous and extended footnotes.

Finally, I wish to thank some of my friends and colleagues for the help they gave me in preparing this work. It owes much to the specialized knowledge of C. C. Berg of the University of Leyden, to J. A. B. van Buitenen of the University of Chicago, and to Evett D. Hester, formerly associate director of Chicago's Philippine Studies program.

Introduction

Asia's image, as it gradually evolved in Europe during the sixteenth century, retained shadings from the past but became sharper and more definite in its outlines and divisions. The vague geographical terms inherited from the Ptolemaic and medieval traditions (India before and beyond the Ganges, Further India, and Cathay) were gradually replaced in Europe by names similar to those then in use in Asia itself. India, Southeast Asia, Japan, and China were recognized for the first time as being distinct and different parts of Asia, and Europeans came to think of them along roughly the same lines that we do today. And, as Europeans of the sixteenth century came to understand that Asia was not simply of one piece, they also learned that its parts and peoples were as numerous and different from one another as were the various parts and peoples of Europe itself.

By 1600 a literate European might easily have known a good deal about the East from the published writings of merchants, travelers, and missionaries, and from the printed maps of the cartographers. Dimensions of depth and increased realism were added to the European impressions by the regular appearance of Asian merchants, emissaries, and goods in the commercial, administrative, religious, and intellectual centers of Europe. During the course of the century, images of the four parts of Asia and a new and composite picture of Asia as a whole emerged from Europe's great experience in the East, and this new conception became and remained a permanent part of Europe's view of the world.

Contents

1. The Printed Sources in Review   493
2. Malaya, the Crossroads of Asia   505
3. Siam   519
4. Burma   539
5. Indochina   560
6. Sumatra, Borneo, and Java   571
7. The Spiceries   592
8. The Philippine Islands   623

Illustrations

FOLLOWING PAGE 608

Southeast Asia in the late sixteenth century (according to European sources)

The map of southeast and eastern Asia in Ramusio's *Navigationi* (2d rev. ed.; Venice, 1554), Vol. I

Ortelius' map of southeast and eastern Asia

The map of Sumatra in Ramusio, *op. cit.*

The map of Java inserted into the Madrid edition (1615) of João de Barros' *Décadas da Ásia*

"Inhabitants of Malacca, who surpass all other Indians in courteous and amorous behavior"

Natives of Pegu, the Moluccas, and St. Thomas

Pigafetta's list of Malay words learned from the inhabitants of Tidore Island in the Moluccas

Illustrations

FOLLOWING PAGE 100

Southeast Asia

In our definition, southeast Asia divides into two vast geographical groupings: the continental peninsulas east of Bengal and south of China, and the insular world which lies within a vast triangle that has Sumatra, the Philippines, and New Guinea at its vertices. Life in the mainland states follows the rivers and flows in a north-south direction; communication and trade along the sea lanes of the archipelago run along east-west lines. In 1500 most of these lines intersected at Malacca, a hub of commerce for both the mainland states and the archipelago. A few places unrelated to this complex, such as the Ladrones (Marianas) will be mentioned collaterally. Australia is omitted because there are no certain references to this continent in the contemporary printed materials. It should be noticed, however, that Portuguese historians have claimed on the basis of evidence in sixteenth-century maps that voyagers touched on Australia in about 1522 and brought back to Europe word of its existence. The absence of additional references to Australia is attributed to Portugal's policy of secrecy and desire to conceal from the Spaniards whatever information it may have possessed on the continent down under.[1] But the evidence for Portugal's discovery of Australia in the sixteenth century is still much too vague and tenuous in our estimation to warrant more than mere mention.

I

THE PRINTED SOURCES IN REVIEW

There is no question that the Portuguese jealously guarded every scrap of information which might have led potential competitors to the sources of the spice trade. And, so far as the published accounts and printed maps show, they

[1] R. H. Major, *Early Voyages to . . . Australia* (London, 1859), pp. v–vi. For a statement of the claim that Australia was discovered by the Portuguese in 1522 see Armando Cortesão, "A expansão portuguesa através do Pacífico (Australásia, Macau, Japão)," in Antonio Baião (ed.), *História da expansão portuguesa no mundo* (3 vols.; Lisbon, 1937–39), II, pt. 3, chap. xi.

were successful for a time in keeping from others the authoritative information in their archives on routes, marts, prices, and methods of trade. Spies and the agents of foreign governments and commercial houses were naturally able to acquire copies of maps and rutters, and some of the interested outsiders, like Peutinger in Augsburg, collected a significant number of these documents.[2] But, it is worth repeating,[3] that no accounts of the East Indies by responsible Portuguese authors were in print before 1550. All of the rutters and pamphlets on the spice trade which appeared before mid-century were the work of foreigners who had been employed by the Portuguese or who had derived their information either from participating themselves in the voyages or by interviewing those sailors fortunate enough to return. The exception to this generalization is, of course, the general announcements by the crown of Portuguese successes in Asia.

The first printed material on southeast Asia was included in the *Itinerario* of Ludovico di Varthema which appeared in 1510. Though there is some doubt whether Varthema himself actually got east of Ceylon,[4] we may conjecture that his vague material on Tenasserim (Mergui), Pegu, Malacca, Sumatra and the Spice Islands should be dated approximately as 1505–6.[5] Nothing more was published in Europe on this region until after the return of the "Victoria" to Spain. The survivors of Magellan's expedition were courted and interviewed by a number of scholars, diplomats, prelates, and kings in an effort to learn from them the secret of the Spiceries. In 1523, Maximilian of Transylvania's *De Moluccis insulis*... was printed at Cologne and Rome, and it gave to Europe, on the basis of the author's interviews with the survivors, the first concrete information on the location of the Moluccas and the conditions prevailing there. Two years later, a truncated version of Pigafetta's story was published for the first time at Paris under the title *Le voyage et nauigation faict par les Espaignolz es isles de Mollucques*.[6] Pigafetta was the only participant in Magellan's expedition who left a written account. His work is particularly important for its vocabularies of Bisayan and Malayan words as well as for the author's deliberate and thorough investigation of trading practices in southeast Asia. After Pigafetta's story had been told in Venice, it was not until the publication in 1543 of the *Viaggi fatti alla Tana* that fresh news of Malacca, Sumatra, and the Moluccas appeared in print at the spice center on the Adriatic.

An aftermath of the successful circumnavigation of the world by a remnant of Magellan's crew was the dispatch of two more Spanish expeditions via the Pacific to the Spice Islands. These voyages, while unsuccessful in themselves, helped Charles I to establish a claim to the Moluccas which he finally abandoned

---

[2] A. Cortesão and A. Teixeira da Mota, *Portugaliae monumenta cartographica* (Lisbon, 1960), I, 15.

[3] See above, p. 181.

[4] See above, p. 165.

[5] A table with approximate dates is given in Sir Richard C. Temple (ed.), *The Itinerary of Ludovico di Varthema of Bologna from 1502 to 1508* (London, 1928), p. xxv.

[6] Translations of this French version into Italian and English were reproduced later in the century by Ramusio and Eden, respectively. See above, pp. 207, 210.

to Portugal in 1529 at Saragossa in return for a cash payment. While this arrangement officially brought an end to the contest for the Moluccas, the Spanish, particularly those in the New World, continued to hope and plan for a trading and missionary foothold in southeast Asia. The chronicles of Oviedo (Book XX, which deals with the East, was first published in 1548) and Gómara (published in 1552) summarized the information on the Spiceries obtained through the Spanish voyages and provided Europe with its first comprehensive accounts of the Philippines, Borneo, and the Spiceries.

In the first volume of Ramusio's *Navigationi* published in 1550, much of the data available at mid-century on southeast Asia was put between two covers for the first time. The Italian collector printed in the same volume the *Periplus of the Indian Ocean*, then ascribed to Arrian, along with the fifteenth-century travels of Nicolò de' Conti. He reproduced from manuscripts the letters on the spice trade prepared early in the century by Tomé Lopes, Giovanni da Empoli, and Andrea Corsali. He republished the *Itinerario* of Varthema in a new Italian version. The original text, Ramusio contended, was too full of errors to warrant reproduction. He included some of the available accounts of the Spanish circumnavigation of the globe by translating into Italian the Latin text of Maximilian of Transylvania and the French text of Pigafetta. He also published, apparently for the first time, the narrative of Juan Gaetano (also written, Ivan Gaetan) who described the expedition of 1542 headed by Ruy Lopez de Villalobos which sailed from Mexico across the Pacific to the Moluccas. Though he included in Italian translation a large part of the *Suma oriental* of Tomé Pires, Ramusio was unable to acquire the prize portion on the archipelago and Malacca which went unpublished until 1944. Ramusio's version, however, did include Pires' short accounts of Cambodia, Champa, Cochin-China, Burma, Siam, Pegu, and Arakan, as well as collateral references to the trade between Malacca and the Spice Islands with India, Pegu, and other parts of continental southeast Asia. The slighter and less authoritative summary of southeast Asia contained in the *Book* of Duarte Barbosa, who probably never got east of India, was acquired by Ramusio and is included in its entirety in Italian translation in his first volume.

In the 1554 augmented edition of Volume I, Ramusio added a map of the East Indies (probably drawn by Giacomo Gastaldi), Italian translations of two Jesuit letters from Malacca, and a brief narration on the Spiceries by a Portuguese who had returned on the "Victoria" from the Moluccas. In his second volume, which deals with the land travels into Asia, Ramusio included in the first edition (1559) his version of Marco Polo and in the second edition (1574) the travels of Odoric of Pordenone. The third volume of the *Navigationi*, first published in 1556, deals primarily with America but in it he included some authors, like Oviedo, who had remarks to make about the Pacific ventures of the Spanish, and also the discourses of Pierre Crignon on the French voyage of 1529 to Sumatra.[7]

[7] George B. Parks (comp.), *The Contents and Sources of Ramusio's Navigationi* (New York, 1955).

The major Portuguese sources on southeast Asia, which began to appear contemporaneously with Ramusio's compilations, are six in number: Castanheda's *História*, Albuquerque's *Commentarios*, Barros' *Décadas*, the materials of António Galvão in the *Tratado . . . dos descobrimentos* (Lisbon, 1563), Damião de Góis' *Chronica do felcíssimo Rey D. Manoel* (Lisbon, 1565), and Jorge de Lemos' *Historia dos cercos que em tempo de António Monis Barreto, Governador que foi dos estados da India, os Achens, e Iaos puserão â fortaleza de Malaca, sendo Tristão Vaz da Veiga capitão della* (Lisbon, 1585). All but the last of these books deal with events in southeast Asia during the first half of the sixteenth century. The Portuguese chroniclers, like the Jesuit historian, Maffei, characteristically confine their attentions to the empire during its zenith. It was not until the seventeenth century that Diogo do Couto and Manuel de Faria e Sousa, both of whom were employed by the Spanish, endeavored to write general histories of the empire's decline and even they were forced from lack of information to leave a gap for the five years from 1575 to 1580.[8]

Castanheda, who was resident in Asia from 1528 to 1538, may possibly have journeyed to Malacca and the Moluccas. In his book he makes the general claim to have visited the places which he describes; Do Couto, keeper of the Goa archives in the later sixteenth century, records in his *Ásia* that Castanheda traveled extensively east of India and even to the Moluccas.[9] The eight books of Castanheda's *História* were published between 1551 and 1561, but it is mainly in Books II through VI (published in 1552–54) that he takes up southeast Asia in connection with Portuguese activities there for the period from 1511 to 1542. While his first book was translated a number of times into various languages during the sixteenth century, the books (II–VI) pertaining to southeast Asia were translated only into Italian and that did not occur until 1577–78 (Venice).

In his treatment of southeast Asia, Castanheda follows closely the enterprises of the Portuguese but pays little attention to local conditions. He has less interest in geographical description than Barros and pays only passing deference to the pre-European history of the peoples in the regions discussed. Malacca, the Móluccas, and Pegu are described and commented upon in considerable detail, and his discussion of Pegu is clearly his best effort. It is probable that Castanheda used Barbosa for some of his data on the trade and ports of southeast Asia, though without acknowledging it. His narrative, which is generally prosaic and dry, begins to take on life when he comes to describe the struggles at

---

[8] See I. A. Macgregor, "Some Aspects of Portuguese Historical Writing of the Sixteenth and Seventeenth Centuries on South East Asia," in D. G. E. Hall (ed.), *Historians of South East Asia* (London, 1961), p. 196.

[9] *Década* IV, Book 5, chap. i. Many students of Castanheda seem not to have known about this possibility, or, if they did, dismissed it as being improbable and insufficiently documented. Certainly such travels were possible, even though we do not have contemporary documentation to clinch the matter. J. H. Harrison, "Five Portuguese Historians," in C. H. Philips (ed.), *Historians of India, Pakistan and Ceylon* (London, 1961), p. 163, has no hesitation in asserting unqualifiedly that "the great value of Castanheda lies in his personal acquaintance with Malacca and the Moluccas."

Malacca, Ternate and Tidore—perhaps another indication of the fact that he may have actually been in those places.

The *Commentarios de Afonso Dalboquerque* (Lisbon, 1557; rev. ed., 1576), prepared by the great captain's son on the basis of his father's letters written from the East, contains a mixture of firsthand observations and secondhand reports. Albuquerque's only direct experience in southeast Asia came during the siege and conquest of Malacca in 1511. While most of the description naturally relates to Malacca and its immediate vicinity, Albuquerque also comments on the initiation of relations with Siam and the dispatch of an expedition to explore the Moluccas. He also makes brief references to Sumatra, Pegu, Java, and Pahang. The abbreviated *Commentarios* includes rich detail on Malacca's history under the Malay sultanate. On the siege and capture of Malacca, there is considerable disagreement between the *Commentarios* and the letter of Giovanni da Empoli published by Ramusio. The account in the *Commentarios* is particularly valuable, no matter what Braz de Albuquerque might have done to his father's report, because the original is no longer extant.[10]

While references to various parts of southeast Asia are scattered throughout the *Décadas* of Barros, it is only the third decade (relating to the years from 1515 to 1525, not published until 1563) which deals extensively with the region. Since he never traveled to Asia, Barros' work is necessarily based exclusively on the reports of others, a fact which probably helps to account for his acceptance of several tall stories. But he more than compensates for his critical failings by his thoroughgoing researches into the official and unofficial sources available in his day. Barros' survey is more systematic for the region as a whole than any of the others produced in the century. While his description of Sumatra remained unsurpassed until the eighteenth century, Barros' information on Java and Indochina was not extensive and his narrative consequently is not always as clear and informative on these two territories as the reader might reasonably expect from an author of his competence and erudition.[11] But, unlike Pires and other writers who report from the scene, Barros seems to get his proportions better. He realizes that the intermediate world between India and China is similar to both but different from each. Always hostile towards the Muslims, Barros points out that Pegu and Siam are dominated by heathens and that they are rich and powerful states. While conscious of the wealth of the Indies, he does not overestimate, as do so many of the Portuguese, the importance of the archipelago and Malacca in the economy and politics of the entire region.

After the appearance of Lemos' book in 1585, the Portuguese secular writers provide no more sources of significance. Once again, the books which appear

10 Academia das sciencias de Lisboa, *Cartas de Afonso de Albuquerque* (7 vols.; Lisbon, 1884–1935); although invaluable on Albuquerque's activities, the collection does not include his report of the siege. For the translation of his remarks on Malacca see Walter de Gray Birch (trans. and ed.), *The Commentaries of the Great Afonso Dalbaquerque* ("Publications of the Hakluyt Society," Old Series, Vols. LXII and LXIII [London, 1880]), Vols. III and IV.

11 See Zoe Swecker, "The Early Iberian Accounts of the Far East" (Ph.D. dissertation, University of Chicago, 1960), pp. 113–14.

between 1585 and 1601 are from the pens of outsiders. These later sources may be divided into three groups: the accounts of two Spaniards who obtained their information about the East by way of the Philippines and Mexico; the narratives of the commercial travelers and explorers from Italy and northern Europe; and the Jesuit letterbooks and histories.

The two Spanish books, which first appeared respectively in 1585 and 1590, are the work of religious writers with experience in America and hence are only collaterally concerned with southeast Asia. The first of these was from the pen of the Augustinian friar, Juan González de Mendoza and was called *Historia de la cosas mas notables, ritos, y costumbres, del gran reyno de la China* (Rome, 1585).[12] While this famous book deals primarily with China, as the title indicates, it also includes in its last chapters some interesting materials on Malacca, Indochina, and the Philippines. Mendoza depends for these comments on the experiences there in about 1579 of Martin Ignatius de Loyola, a relative of the first Jesuit general and a Franciscan missionary himself. The second book by a Spaniard was the work of the famous Jesuit Humanist, José de Acosta, who sojourned for a long period in Mexico and learned about eastern Asia at this crossroads of the Spanish empire. Acosta's volumes first appeared in Latin (1588–89), and, in their complete form, were published in 1590 at Seville under the title *Historia natural y moral de las Indias*. While Acosta's work centers on the New World, it also includes scattered comments on the East Indies. From the viewpoint of the scholar interested in southeast Asia, Acosta's work illustrates strikingly how a Humanist of the late sixteenth century with overseas experience mentally wrestled with himself to integrate his knowledge of Asia inherited from antiquity with the newer information.

The Italian, Dutch, and English merchants who comment on southeast Asia had their narratives published between 1587 and 1599. The *Viaggio* (1587) of the Venetian, Fedrici, records that he was east of India on at least three different occasions, on the last two of which he was engaged in the opium traffic between Cambay and Pegu. On his first and most extended trip into southeast Asia, he visited from 1566 to 1569 in northern Sumatra (Achin), Malacca, Tenasserim (Mergui), Tavoy, and Martaban. His second voyage, which seems to have been restricted to Pegu, probably occurred in 1572–73. His third voyage, which again seems to have been limited to Pegu, possibly took place as late as 1577–78.[13] On the basis of these experiences it is not surprising, when we consider that Fedrici probably kept a diary, that he was able to provide the fullest and most accurate account of Burma (Pegu) prepared by a European in the sixteenth century.[14]

Gasparo Balbi, another Venetian, published his *Viaggio* in 1590. It is clear, because the author is precise in dating his peregrinations, that Balbi was in

---

[12] For a full analysis of this book see below, pp. 743–45.

[13] Since he gives so few dates in his record, it is difficult to determine exactly when he was at a given place and how long he stayed there. The above dates are based on the estimates given in Jarl Charpentier, "Cesare di Federici and Gasparo Balbi," *Indian Antiquary*, LIII (1924), 53–54.

[14] "Fredericke . . . has left us the best description of Burma that we have from a European source." See D. G. E. Hall, *Early English Intercourse with Burma (1587–1743)* (London, 1928), p. 18.

Pegu for more than two years (1583 to 1586). While Balbi pirated many of his comments on India from Fedrici, his record of events and his description of Pegu are the most independent and best part of his book.[15] It is also clear that Balbi's contemporaries in Europe valued the *Viaggio* most for its detailing of affairs in Pegu. Though Hakluyt probably knew Balbi's work, he never published it. When it finally appeared in English translation in Purchas' collection,[16] his account of India, except for materials on St. Thomas and Negapatnam, were omitted while the portion on Pegu was included in its entirety.

Linschoten, who was in western India from 1583 to 1588, published his *Itinerario* in its complete form in 1596. Though he never traveled east of India, Linschoten managed to reconstruct, from informants in Goa and from the books and maps at his disposal after he returned home, a comprehensive survey of the places in southeastern Asia known to the Portuguese. In his disquisitions on the flora and fauna of the East, Linschoten remarks on curiosities such as the elephants of Pegu, the great shellfish of Malacca, and the valuable camphor of Borneo. In 1597, the year after Linschoten's book appeared, an account of the first Dutch voyage to Java was published at Middelburg and in the following year it came out in an English translation.[17] While this narrative mainly recounts the problems of the voyage and the strife between the Dutch captains, it also includes comments on conditions affecting trade in Java.

Ralph Fitch was the first Englishman to visit southeastern Asia and record his experiences there. The account of his peregrinations which Hakluyt published in 1599 is based in part upon Fedrici and in part upon his own experiences. Fitch arrived at Pegu in 1586 and in the following year he made a journey to Chiengmai in the Siamese Shan states. After returning to Pegu, he left for Malacca in 1588 to collect information on the trade there. Then he made his way back to Pegu by way of Martaban, and, after a short respite in Pegu, began the long journey back to England. Since Fitch kept no diary or notes, his recollections are hazy and his descriptions much less precise than those recorded in the accounts of Fedrici and Balbi. Still, his experience of about three years in southeast Asia gave him a genuine understanding of certain features of life there, particularly of Pegu where he spent the most time. His independent picture of the Buddhist monastic system of Burma is still respected as a faithful representation.[18]

When Drake circumnavigated the world in 1577–80, his ship, the "Golden Hind," called at Ternate in the Moluccas, at Roma Island, and at Java. Notices of these places appeared in books and on maps prepared in northern Europe

[15] Charpentier, *loc. cit.* (n. 13), p. 61.

[16] As reproduced in Samuel Purchas (ed.), *Hakluytus Posthumus; or, Purchas His Pilgrimes* ("Publications of the Hakluyt Society," Extra Series, Vol. X [Glasgow, 1905–7]), pp. 143–64.

[17] The original is entitled *Verhael vande Reyse by de Hollandtsche Schepen gedaen naer Oost Indien* (Middleburg, 1597). The English version, translated by William Phillip, is entitled *The Description of a Voyage Made by Certaine Ships of Holland into the East Indies* (London, 1598). See above, p. 202n.

[18] D. G. E. Hall, *Europe and Burma. A Study of European Relations with Burma to the Annexation of Thibaw's Kingdom (1886)* (London, 1945), p. 15.

beginning in 1582. Of particular importance is the narrative compiled by Hakluyt from documents written by participants in the Drake enterprise. The final version, the last of several earlier and less complete compilations, appeared in 1600 in the *Principal Navigations*[19] and was entitled *The Famous Voyage of Sir Francis Drake into the South Sea . . . begune in the yeere of our Lord 1577.* This short narrative is particularly rich in its description of the garb and court ceremonies of Ternate. It also gives a few notes on the political conditions prevailing in the Moluccas in the crucial year of 1578 when the Portuguese established themselves at Tidore, and it also provides a few references to the rulers of Java in 1579. The first voyage ·to the East of James Lancaster, an Englishman with long experience in Portugal, took place in the years 1591 to 1594. He was sent out by a group of London merchants to make a reconnaissance of the Portuguese route to Malacca. Two narratives of these voyages of pillaging and surveying were acquired and published by Hakluyt.[20] These documents contain fascinating data on Portuguese trade, but very little material on Asia itself. The English narratives are especially important because they refer to times for which we have very few other contemporary sources on the eastern archipelago.

The Jesuit letters published in Europe give scattered runs of information on various parts of southeast Asia from 1552 to the end of the century. Most of the Xavier letters from Malacca and the Moluccas were not published until the Tursellinus collection appeared in 1595–96. The early letterbooks, published mainly in Portugal and Italy, frequently include letters from his followers in southeast Asia. But, as in the case of India, a sharp break in published versions of the letters occurs beginning with the letters penned in the period from 1564 to 1568.[21] Several of the letters written before 1564 were republished beginning in 1569. Over the entire period (1552–1600) ten of the letters dated from southeast Asia were published three or more times. It is not until the last decade of the century, however, that new and substantial additions were incorporated into the letterbooks. Most of the letters dated from the islands give information on native customs and the problems being faced by the Jesuits in the Moluccas and in Amboina before 1570. Not a single Jesuit letter from the Moluccas was published during the last generation of the century. Those dated from Malacca are ordinarily concerned with matters far removed from the

[19] III, 730–42; also see XI, 101–33.

[20] Barker's narrative is in Vol. II, Pt. II, pp. 102–3; May's narrative is in III, 571–72. For recent, edited versions of these documents see Sir William Foster (ed.), *The Voyages of Sir James Lancaster to Brazil and the East Indies* ("Hakluyt Society Publications," Second Series, No. LXXXV [London, 1940)], pp. 1–51.

[21] C. Wessels, S. J., *Histoire de la mission d'Amboine . . . 1564–1605* (Louvain, 1934), p. 9, asserts that as far as he can determine not a single letter from Amboina or the Moluccas was printed in the period from 1570 to 1600 which had been written during that time. He accounts for this by referring to the complete dependence of the mission upon the crowns of Spain and Portugal. He also points out how slow Rome was to publish Teixeira and Valignano's surveys of Xavier's activities in the East; from the context into which he puts this discussion he seems to imply that the papacy was also under pressure from the Iberian powers to keep detailed information on the Spiceries out of print.

local scene. The Jesuits at Malacca, like the merchants, were usually in transit, and mostly write about the places from which they came or about what they have heard of the place to which they are going. As a whole, the Jesuit letters are much less valuable for southeast Asia than they are for Japan.[22]

The first author to use the Jesuit letters extensively, as well as many secular sources, was Maffei whose *Historiarum Indicarum libri XVI* appeared at Florence in 1588. In his scattered sections on the various parts of southeast Asia, Maffei includes more from the Jesuit letters than he does when commenting on India. As he recounts the expansion of the Portuguese and the Jesuits to about 1557, Maffei interrupts his narrative at appropriate points to present thumb-nail sketches of what he knew from his researches about such places as Sumatra, Siam, and Pegu. The Spanish Jesuit, Guzman, in his *Historia de las missiones* (1601), likewise gives occasional vignettes of those parts of southeast Asia where the Jesuits were active. Since Guzman depends more than Maffei upon the letters and Spanish sources, and less upon the Portuguese historians who wrote almost exclusively about the first half of the century, he recounts political events in a slightly less stylized manner and without too much regard for the sensibilities of the Portuguese. His detailed descriptions of the wars going on in southeast Asia during the last quarter of the sixteenth century and the amount of information he possessed on Cambodia reflect the fact that some of his sources came to him from the missionaries in the Philippines. In short, Guzman is particularly useful for the history of southeast Asia during the last generation of the sixteenth century, a period when firsthand accounts, aside from Jesuit letters, are in short supply. Neither Maffei nor Guzman had traveled to Asia and both based their narratives on the materials available to them in Europe.

The European sources generally tend to consider southeast Asia as a part of "further India," even though they bring out clearly how important the Chinese, Japanese, and Muslims were at Malacca and in the islands. The Moluccas, always of interest for its cloves and other spices, receives the attention of most of the writers, including the Jesuits. As the place where the Spanish and Portuguese empires met in the East, the Spice Islands in the sources receive radically different treatment on a number of relatively simple matters. The sources are especially contradictory on the exact location of the Moluccas and the Philippines, important questions in the debated question of ownership. The Portuguese historians and other Europeans who traveled in Portuguese India are especially authoritative on Pegu, Siam, the Malay Peninsula, and Sumatra. The Spanish writers are best on the Philippines, Borneo, and Cambodia.[23]

[22] Based on a study of Robert Streit, *Biblioteca missionum* (Aachen, 1928), IV, *passim*.

[23] While Portuguese adventurers and the Dominican missionary Gaspar da Cruz were in Cambodia by 1555–56, it is not until the last years of the century that concrete information begins to appear on Cambodia in European published works. It was mainly in connection with the Spanish efforts to get a continental foothold that Europeans became aware of Cambodia. In 1601, the first description of the ruins of Angkor was included in F. Marcello de Ribadeneyra, O. F. M., *Historia de las islas del archipielago, y reynos de la gran China . . .* (Barcelona, 1601), pp. 173–87. For an excellent summary of the discovery of Cambodia by the Iberians see Bernard P. Groslier, *Angkor et le Cambodge au XVIe siècle d'après les sources portugaises et espagnoles* (Paris, 1958), chap. ii.

Java is the territory most slighted and the Javanese are the people viewed most hostilely by the Iberian authors, perhaps because of the sporadic wars in which they engaged the Portuguese, who sought to replace them as the great international traders of the region.[24] That the Portuguese were ultimately unsuccessful in their effort to eliminate the Javanese is brought out by the voyage of Lancaster which transgressed the Portuguese monopoly and by Linschoten when he writes to his countrymen: ". . . men might very well traffique [to Java] without any impeachment [hindrance], for that the Portingales come not thether, because great number of Iava come themselves unto Malacca to sell their wares." [25]

It was in the Byzantine versions of Ptolemy's *Geographia* that the first general description of southeast Asia became available before the fifteenth century.[26] Book VII, chapter 2 of the principal extant version lists the coastal features, riverine divisions, and the inland towns of the Golden Khersonese (Malay Peninsula). But no effort is made by the compiler to describe its countryside, people, or products. If the stylized Ptolemaic co-ordinates are abandoned when evaluating the data on southeast Asia, a clearly recognizable delineation of the coast of peninsular southeast Asia from the Bay of Bengal to Indochina emerges from the *Geographia*.[27] While modern scholars are not agreed on the identifications of the many rivers, gulfs, and inland towns mentioned in the *Geographia*, it is clear that the Byzantine compilers were aware of the strategic importance of the emporiums of the Malay peninsula in the trade of southeast Asia.[28]

Not until the late thirteenth century did the entrepôts, capitals, islands, and states of southeast Asia begin to be heard about in Europe under the names by which we know them today. Marco Polo refers by name to Champa (which corresponds roughly to modern Cochin-china), the Great Island of Java (Java or Cochin-china) and to Java the Less (Sumatra), while describing many other islands, towns, and peoples more difficult to identify. Significantly neither Polo nor Odoric of Pordenone, who returned to Europe in 1330, mentions Malacca. This may be accounted for by the fact that Malacca had not yet become a great merchandising center.[29] Odoric discourses on "Nicuveran" (the Nicobar Islands), but gives nothing more than some legendary information about them.[30] Other European travelers of the fourteenth century also refer to Champa, Java, and Java the Lesser (Sumatra), possibly based on the traditional yarns told to them by the Arab sailors with whom they voyaged. Nicolò de'

---

[24] The Javanese are usually described by the Iberian writers as fierce warriors who are base and unreliable in their business dealings. For an independent, and similar judgment see I. A. Macgregor, "Notes on the Portuguese in Malaya," *Journal of the Malayan Branch of the Royal Asiatic Society* XXVIII (1955), 24.

[25] A. C. Burnell and P. A. Tiele (eds.), *The Voyage of John Huyghen van Linschoten to the East Indies* ("Hakluyt Society Publications," Nos. LXX and LXXI, Old Series [London, 1885]) I, 112.

[26] Paul Wheatley, *The Golden Khersonese* (Kuala Lumpur, 1961), pp. 138–40.

[27] For a map showing the Ptolemaic coastline superimposed on a modern map of southeast Asia see *ibid.*, p. 146.

[28] See *ibid.*, pp. 151–52.

[29] Probably founded *ca.* 1400. *Ibid.*, pp. 306–7.

[30] D. G. E. Hall, *A History of South-East Asia* (London, 1960), p. 189.

Conti, the Venetian who returned home in about 1444, calls Sumatra by the classical name of "Taprobana" and refers to "Andamania" (the Andaman Islands) and the city of "Panconia" (Pegu), the capital of the Mon kingdom of Pegu in Burma. Girolamo da Santo Stefano, the Genoese merchant, who visited Pegu in 1496 gives its name more correctly, tells about setting out on a trading expedition to Malacca, and of finally having ended up on Sumatra.[31] From this brief recapitulation of Renaissance travel accounts it can be observed generally that the few Europeans who traveled into southeast Asia before the opening of the sea route included in their summaries some information on Champa, Java, Sumatra (though not under this name until Santo Stefano's visit there in 1497), Pegu, and the Nicobar and Andaman Islands. Many other places and peoples in "further India" they also referred to under designations which are not so readily identifiable.

Varthema, whether or not he actually traveled east of India himself, was the first writer formally to introduce Malacca to Europe, though the Portuguese and those who sailed with them had heard about it shortly after landing at Calicut.[32] The merchant from Bologna also comments in some detail on Tenasserim (Mergui) and Pegu, and he seems vaguely to understand that the religion of Burma (Buddhism) is different from Hinduism.[33] Like Santo Stefano, he calls Sumatra by the name which we use today, and like Conti, he identifies it with Taprobane.[34] He also sailed eastward to Banda and to the Moluccas "where the cloves grow," and was the first European writer who even made an effort to describe the Spice Islands. Varthema then began his return westward and stopped on his way at an island which he calls "Bornei." It is not clear from his brief description whether or not he is referring to Borneo, the great island which derives its name from one of the chief Malay states (Brunei) existing on it when the Europeans first arrived there.[35] If we assume, as I do, that he is referring to Borneo, it can then be concluded that most of the major islands of the archipelago and some of the leading cities of continental southeast

---

[31] R. H. Major (ed.), *India in the Fifteenth Century* ("Hakluyt Society Publications," Old Series, Vol. XXII [London, 1857]), Pt. IV, p. 7.

[32] In the Dutch work *Calcoen* (1504), "Melatk" is mentioned as the place from whence come the spices. The Nuremberg newsletter of 1505 (*The Right Way to Travel from Lisbon to Calicut*) gives the distance from Quilon to "Mellacka" and to "Scharmarttar" (Sumatra?). But, the famous letter from King Manuel to Castile (1505) makes no mention of Malacca. See above, pp. 160–61.

[33] Temple (ed.), *op. cit.* (n. 5), p. lxix.

[34] Conti also says that it is known locally as "Sciamuthera." But as far as its name is concerned, "even to the present day, it is like the other large islands of the Archipelago, Java perhaps excepted, without a name familiar to the inhabitants." (John Crawfurd, *A Descriptive Dictionary of the Indian Islands and Adjacent Countries* [London, 1856], p. 413.) For its derivation from "Sumātrabhūmi" rather than "Samudra" see N. J. Krom, "De naam Sumatra," *Bijdragen tot de taal-, land-en Volkerkunde van Nederlandsch-Indië*, C (1941), 5–25. Linschoten (in Burnell and Tiele [eds.], *op. cit.* [n. 25], I, 107–8) continues to call it Taprobane at the end of the century, even though Barros had earlier insisted upon Taprobane's identification with Ceylon.

[35] It may be that he actually is referring to the island of Buru, south of the Moluccas. See Temple, *op. cit.* (n. 5), pp. lxxv–lxxvi. Crawfurd (*op. cit.* [n. 34], p. 63) believes that he is talking about Borneo, and is simply giving one spelling of the Malay city or state which later European writers render as "Brune," "Brunai," "Burne," or "Burnai."

Asia were known in European literature (and some of them on maps) before the Portuguese captured Malacca in 1511.[36]

Mention of Cambodia in a printed work probably first occurred in a letter written by King Manuel in 1513 to Pope Leo X telling of the visit of Cambodian envoys with Albuquerque at Malacca.[37] Though additional information on the archipelago (especially the Philippines) was made available in Europe by the writings of Maximilian of Transylvania and Pigafetta, it was only at mid-century with the publication of Ramusio's first volume that the Portuguese authors, Pires and Barbosa, were in print for the first time. The great collector also included Empoli's letter to his father in Florence describing conditions at Malacca when he was there with Albuquerque in 1511–12. Though Barbosa discourses briefly on many parts of southeast Asia, his information, collected in India, is uneven in quality and his notions of geographical relationships are hazy. It was not until the appearance of the great histories of Castanheda and Barros that a comprehensive description of southeast Asia was attempted by a European author. And, of the two general pictures sketched by the great historians of the discoveries, the portrait by Barros, who had never been on the scene himself, is the more vivid and comprehensible.[38]

In his first *Década*, the great Portuguese historian divides the Orient, or the entire area between Arabia and Japan, into nine large sections. Southeast Asia falls into his sections numbered five, six, and seven. The area between the Ganges and Malacca is embraced within section five, the region from the tip of the Malay peninsula to the Menam River falls within section six, and the last section extends from the Menam delta "to a famous cape which is at the easternmost of the firm land which we now know about."[39] Each of these sections he breaks down into smaller components, and specific places are located by their distance from the equator and from one another.

In discussing the archipelago Barros gives a particularly full description of the placement, dimensions, and topographical features of Sumatra.[40] The Moluccas, which he locates south of the equator, are said to be five in number and to lie in a north–south line parallel to a large island called "Batochina do Moro" (Halmahera).[41] While he discusses the relations of the Moluccas to the neighboring islands (and he knows about many of them), Barros fails to give a completely clear depiction of Java. In a number of cases, Barros dismisses geographical description almost entirely from his considerations and refers the reader to his *Geografia* which was never published or found.

As a visual aid to the reader who had no map at hand, Barros conceived of an

---

[36] Varthema's *Itinerario* was first published in 1510. For a bibliographical survey see above, pp. 165–66.

[37] Groslier, *op. cit.* (n. 23), p. 142.

[38] Maps were not added to the *Décadas* until the revised and augmented version appeared in Madrid in 1615.

[39] Hernani Cidade and Manuel Múrias (eds.), *Asia de João de Barros . . .* (Lisbon, 1945), I, 353.

[40] *Ibid.*, III 231–32.

[41] *Ibid.*, pp. 257–59.

ingenious device to help picture the complicated geographical configurations and relationships of continental southeast Asia. By placing his own left hand, turned palm down with the fingers pointing in towards the body, the reader can see in front of himself a rough picture of the coastline from eastern India to Indochina. The thumb, spread apart from the index finger, represents India, and the space in between stands for the Bay of Bengal. The index finger which is in turn spread apart from the remaining fingers represents the Malay peninsula. These three digits, pressed together and slightly drawn up underneath the palm represent the Indochinese peninsula and indicate its more northerly placement and its northward slant. Specific localities and their relationship to one another are brought out by referring to the nails and knuckles of the fingers and to the nerves of the hand. The body of the hand is even used to help the reader get a rough idea of the placement of interior areas and of their relationship to each other and the coast.[42]

Through his references to this finger-map, Barros quickly locates for the reader the political divisions of India, the island of Ceylon, the three Burmese states of Ava, Arakan and Pegu, as well as Siam, "Jangoma" (Chiengmai), the three kingdoms inhabited by the Laotians, Cambodia, Champa, the various vassal states of Siam, Sumatra, Malacca and other cities, the Menam and Mekong rivers, and various mountain ranges. No other general description of southeast Asia was again attempted in the sixteenth century until the appearance of Linschoten's *Itinerario* in 1595–96.[43] And Linschoten's discussion, based on traders' reports which came to him in Goa, is generally inferior to Barros' though it does include more recent materials, especially on Java. A short but accurate survey is also included in Guzman's *Historia de las missiones* (1601) and it brings in a few additional geographical details garnered from the Jesuit letters and the Spanish reports from the Philippines.[44]

2

MALAYA, THE CROSSROADS OF ASIA

Though the Malays were certainly a civilized people when the Portuguese first arrived at Malacca, the history of the peninsula before 1500 has had to be painfully reconstructed from oral traditions, archaeological evidence, and foreign sources. The earliest extant record in the Malay language is the *Sĕjarah Mĕlayu* (*The Dynasty of Mĕlayu*) which is usually dated between 1500 and 1550.[45]

[42] *Ibid.*, III, 76; my explanation is adapted from the summary in Swecker, *op. cit.* (n. 11), p. 79.

[43] Burnell and Tiele (eds.), *op. cit.* (n. 25), I, chaps. xvii–xxii.

[44] Luis de Guzman, *Historia de las missiones* (Alcalá, 1601), I, 4–5.

[45] Sir Richard Winstedt, "Malay Chronicles from Sumatra and Malaya," in D. G. E. Hall (ed.), *op. cit.* (n. 8), p. 24, dates it from "the end of the fifteenth or beginning of the sixteenth century." Wheatley, *op. cit.* (n. 26), p. iii, attributes it "to a date no earlier than the middle" of the sixteenth century.

Chinese histories, encyclopedias, geographies, and travel accounts, supplemented by Arab and Persian records which begin in the ninth century, provide the most continuous and concrete data on early Malay history. Other dimensions are added to the story from scattered references found in Indian writings, the classical authors of the West, and in Siamese and Javanese accounts. The European chronicles, travelogues, and letters are consequently significant additions to this heterogeneous corpus of literature, because they incorporate native traditions current in the early sixteenth century as well as more specific materials recorded from personal experiences in the peninsula.[46]

The only Europeans to publish on the basis of personal experience in Malacca were Varthema (possibly), Empoli, Albuquerque, Castanheda (possibly), Fedrici, Balbi, Fitch, and the Jesuit correspondents. Barbosa and Linschoten largely base their accounts on materials which they gathered in India. Barros, Góis, Maffei and Guzman were never in the East, consequently their histories are founded exclusively on the oral and written reports of others. Barros, however, was not content to depend upon European sources. In his narrative he often prefaces his remarks with a cryptic aside to the reader explaining that what follows is "according to the natives." It is also possible that he obtained some of his information from the Persian, Indian, and Chinese materials which he is known to have had at his disposal. On the early history of Mělayu (pre-Portuguese Malaya) we will generally follow Barros' comprehensive account[47] and modify it with appropriate observations from the others, especially Albuquerque, who concern themselves with the pre-European period.

The Humanist Barros, after noting that Malacca is situated on the peninsula called the Golden Khersonese by the Ptolemaic geographers, discourses learnedly but briefly on the true meaning of "Khersonese." He observes that he was not able to locate written records pertaining to the founding of the city or its earliest inhabitants. But, according to ideas current in the East, Malacca was supposedly founded a little more than 250 years before the Portuguese arrived

[46] The *Suma oriental* of Tomé Pires, which was written in Malacca from 1512 to 1515, gives one of the earliest and best accounts of the city's history, environs, administration, and trade. Unfortunately, however, this section was one of those omitted from the Ramusio version published in 1550. Hence, Pires' account did not become available until its discovery in the twentieth century and its publication in Armando Cortesão (trans. and ed.), *The Suma Oriental of Tomé Pires . . .* ("Hakluyt Society Publications," 2d Ser., Nos. 89–90 [2 vols.; London, 1944]). A few of Pires' references to Malacca's troubles with Siam were published by Ramusio from the section on continental southeast Asia. Apparently, Pires' work as a whole was not even generally available in manuscript during the sixteenth century for it seems not to have come to the attention of later writers or cartographers. See Swecker, *op. cit.* (n. 11), pp. 42–43. However, it is possible that Barros may have gotten some of his information on Malaya's early history from it.

[47] Cidade and Múrias (eds.), *op. cit.* (n. 39), II, 249–59. This account is in his second *Década*, first published in 1553, which deals with Portuguese activities in the East from 1505 to 1515. For a French translation of Barros' historical discussion, as well as excellent editorial comment, see Gabriel Ferrand, "Malaka, le Mālayu et Malāyur," *Journal asiatique*, Series XI, Vol. XI (1918), pp. 431–38. Because of its indispensable editorial comment, we will use Ferrand's version of Barros and Albuquerque.

there, or sometime shortly after the middle of the thirteenth century.[48] In earlier times the leading settlement of Mĕlayu was "Singapura" (in Sanskrit, Singhapura or City of the Lion)[49] where traders from east and west came to conduct their affairs. According to Barros, it was this city which Ptolemy called "Zaba," but recent scholars place Zaba as an island off the coast of Indochina.[50]

At the time when Singapore flourished (probably in the fourteenth century) as a great mart at the tip of the peninsula, its ruler, according to Malay tradition, was a king called "Sangesinga" (lord of Singapore)[51] and he owed vassalage to Siam. In the time of Sangesinga, one of the kings on the island of Java died and the care of his two sons was confided to his brother. This regent-uncle, coveting the kingdom for himself, killed the older of his nephews. The assassination of this prince touched off a revolt among the leading lords of the land. From the outset the rebels fared badly and many of them were forced to flee the country and settle elsewhere. Among these émigrés was one named "Paramisora" (Paramesvara, which means supreme lord)[52] who was graciously received at Singapore by Sangesinga. Paramesvara repaid his host by treacherously killing him and taking over his city with the aid of other Javan refugees. The king of Siam, hearing of the death of his vassal and son-in-law, attacked the usurper by land and sea. Unable to stand off the elephants and ships of Siam, Paramesvara, after ruling five years, retreated from Singapore with two thousand men and took up a position on the Muar River at Pago, a spot in the hills northwest of the site where Malacca came to be located.

Paramesvara was accompanied into exile by a people called the *Cellates*[53] who lived constantly on the sea and maintained themselves by fishing and piracy. The Cellates, who had aided Paramesvara in his conquest of Singapore and in his fight against Siam, now aroused the fear of the weakened Javan exile

---

[48] Diogo Lopes de Sequeira, the first Portuguese emissary to arrive in Malacca, anchored there in 1509. Subtracting 250 years from this date would place the founding of Malacca around 1259. Wheatley *op. cit.* (n. 26), p. 306, asserts incorrectly that Barros "proposed the *first* half of the thirteenth century." Albuquerque's son, on the basis of his father's letters, fixed the date at about 1421. While disagreement still reigns, most modern scholars are inclined to place the founding date around 1400; for their documentation they lean heavily on the account which Pires gives on the basis of Javanese materials (see Cortesão [ed.], *op. cit.* [n. 46], II, 229–35). It should also be noticed, though most modern scholars have failed to do so, that Varthema remarks (in Temple [ed.], *op. cit.* [n. 5], pp. lxxi and 84) about it being built eighty years before his visit there, or in about 1426.

[49] Barros and Albuquerque say that in the local language the word *Singapura* means a "treacherous delay." But modern scholars believe that *Singapura* is one of several "lion cities" so designated by the adherents of Buddhism in the Majapahit period. See Wheatley, *op. cit.* (n. 26), p. 304. For references in the Chinese sources see Hsü Yun-ts'ia, "Notes on the Historical Position of Singapore," in K. G. Tregonning (ed.), *Papers on Malayan History* (Singapore, 1962), pp. 226–38.

[50] Ferrand, *loc. cit.* (n. 47), p. 432, n. 6.

[51] *Ibid.*, p. 433, n. 5, associates "*Sange*" with *Sang i*, a designation often affixed to divine and royal names; "singa" (for *singha*, also found in Singhapura or Singapore) means "lion."

[52] Translation of Professor C. C. Berg. For modern scholarship on Paramesvara as founder of Malacca see D. G. E. Hall, *op. cit.* (n. 30), pp. 179–80. After 1331 he was known as Ādityawarman, king of Mĕlayu.

[53] From *Sĕlatĭ*, an Arabic-Malay word meaning "people of the strait," and referring to the people of Malacca. Also see Ferrand, *loc. cit.* (n. 47), p. 434, n. 3, and S. R. Dalgado, *Glossário Luso-Asiático* 2 vols.; Coimbra, 1919), I, 245.

and he refused to receive them at Pago. The sea-rovers then merged with the half-savage, indigenous inhabitants and established a settlement of their own on the site of Malacca. Such an affiliation was made possible by the common use of the Malay language and by the intermarriage of the Cellates with local women. Still, each group retained its own customs, and the Cellates continued to make their living from the sea while the Malays continued to farm the land. Their joint village with its balanced economy soon began to prosper and become overcrowded. The villagers then moved to a hill nearby which they called "Beitam" (Bertam),[54] a name which they also soon applied to the plain beneath it. Since this new place was spacious and fertile, and since they knew that Paramesvara was living in the hills in poor circumstances, the villagers invited the Javan prince and his followers to abandon the fortress at Pago and join them. Here, at this burgeoning town, Paramesvara lived out his few remaining years in fear of the Siamese governors at Singapore. On his death he left the ruling of the new city to his son, "Xaquem Darxa" (Sikandar Shah). His followers intermarried with the Cellates and the native Malays, and it was from this amalgam of peoples that the population of Malacca originated. Sikandar Shah gave the name Malacca to this new city in memory of his father's exile, because it means "an exile" in the Malay language. The people of the city henceforward called themselves "Malays," a word meaning to Barros the inhabitants of Malacca and its environs.[55]

Once the Javanese took over leadership, the plain of Bertam was put under cultivation and "duções" (plantations)[56] began to grow up in the countryside. At certain times of the year the townsmen took their wives to visit the "duções" for an outing. Though the Cellates were men of low extraction and the natives only half civilized, they both proved to be faithful servitors. Paramesvara and his son, knowing their worth, permitted these lowly people to intermarry with Javans of the highest rank and even conferred titles of nobility upon them. It is from these unions among the earliest inhabitants of the city that all the *mandari* (councillors) are descended. Sikandar Shah, the first to take the title of king, began to build up Malacca which soon rivaled Singapore as the entrepôt of the peninsula. With the death of the Siamese king who had defeated his father, Sikandar sent out fleets of ships manned by Cellates to patrol the straits and to force passing vessels to call at Malacca. As this policy succeeded, the merchants began to emigrate from Singapore to the new mart at Malacca, and the king of Siam began to feel pinched by the consequent loss of revenues. When it became clear that the Siamese ruler was about to mount an attack against Malacca, Sikandar Shah sent emissaries to him offering vassalage and promising to pay

[54] In the *Commentarios* this place is called Bintão. For a discussion of the name see Ferrand, *loc. cit.* (n. 47), p. 435, n. 1. Possibly Bertam district about eight miles north of modern Malacca. See Wheatley, *op. cit.* (n. 26), p. 307.

[55] This etymology, also given in the *Commentarios*, is not accepted by modern scholars. Ferrand, *loc. cit.* (n. 47), p. 148, n. 2, categorically asserts, and others agree with him, that "Malacca" is the Sanskrit-Malay name for the myrobalan (*Phyllanthus emblica*), a dried fruit of astringent flavor.

[56] From Malay *dusu* meaning farm, village, or country house. See Dalgado, *op. cit.* (n. 53), I, 371.

tribute equal to what he lost in revenues from the decline of Singapore. The king of Siam accepted this offer and confined the area of Sikandar's jurisdiction to ninety leagues of the western coast stretching from Singapore to "Pullo-cambilam" (Pulaw Sembilan). The growing commercial prosperity of the city led the successors of Sikandar Shah to repudiate gradually the suzerainty of Siam, particularly after Moors from Persia and Gujarat converted them to Islam along with other rulers in the neighboring states of Sumatra and Java. Siam nonetheless continued to claim Malacca as a vassal state, and in 1500, just nine years before Diogo Lopes de Sequeira arrived there, the Siamese made an unsuccessful effort to take the city by sea. And, even after the Portuguese themselves got to Siam, they learned that preparations were underway for other assaults against the "city that was made for merchandise." [57]

The account of Malacca's early history in the *Commentarios* of Albuquerque is generally similar but differs in many particulars from that given by Barros. Paramesvara is identified as the pagan king of Palembang, probably a city in northwestern Java,[58] who was married to the daughter of a Majapahit ruler of eastern Java and paid a fixed tribute to his father-in-law. In the struggle which ensued when Paramesvara refused to pay his tribute, the vassal was defeated and forced to flee with his family and retainers to Singapore. Barros and Albuquerque essentially agree on the seizure of Singapore, but give quite different versions of Paramesvara's eviction. Barros attributes his defeat to the actions of the king of Siam, while Albuquerque credits the lord of Patani, a petty prince on the northeastern side of the peninsula, with dispossessing him. Two years after Paramesvara went to Malacca, Albuquerque claims that the population of the town had increased from a handful to two thousand. Seven years after his arrival in Malacca, the founder died and left the city to his son, Sikandar Shah. Shortly thereafter Sikandar married a princess of Pasei (in Sumatra) and, at her request, became a convert to Islam. After several sons had been born to his wife, Sikandar reportedly went on a three-year visit to China as a tribute-bearing vassal.[59] There is no doubt that the rulers of Malacca had close relations with China, even though this particular voyage may not have been undertaken. Sikandar, according to Albuquerque, had a Chinese wife with whom he had a son called "Rajapute" (the white rājā).[60] From this son, according to tradition, were descended the kings of Kampar, a Malay state on the northeast coast of Sumatra, and the kings of Pahang, a Malay state on the eastern side of the peninsula.

Shortly after his return from China, Sikandar died and was succeeded by his son, "Modu faixa" (Muzaffar Shah). The new ruler ratified the treaties concluded

[57] Pires in Cortesão (ed.), *op. cit.* (n. 46), II, 286.

[58] On the confusion over the two Palembangs of Java and Sumatra see Ferrand, *loc. cit.* (n. 47), pp. 412–14, n. 3.

[59] Not substantiated elsewhere. See Hall, *op. cit.* (n. 30), p. 180.

[60] According to C. C. Berg, marriages between Javanese rulers and Chinese women are commonly recounted in Indonesian stories. Berg suggests that *Rajapute* may be derived from *Daraputih* rather than *rajapuari* or white rājā.

by his father with China, Siam, and Java. He also seized control over Pahang on the peninsula, over Kampar and over Indragiri on the east coast of Sumatra, forced their royal families to accept Islam, and required their kings to marry three of his nieces. He was succeeded by his son, "Marsusa" (Mansur Shah), who began at the beginning of his reign to build large houses on Malacca's hill. In the belief that his uncle, Rajapute, was fomenting a revolt, Mansur visited him at Bertam and killed the old man. When the kings of Pahang and Indragiri learned of this assassination, they rose in insurrection against Malacca. Mansur attacked and defeated them, forced them to pay double tribute and to marry two of his sisters; he forced the king of Pahang to give him his daughter as wife. By this woman he had a son who died of poison. Thereafter he married a daughter of his "lassamane" (admiral)[61] by whom he had a son called "Alaodim" (Alā' uddin).[62]

On the death of Mansur, Alā' uddin became sultan, married a princess of Kampar, and enjoyed great material prosperity from the revenues collected at Malacca. He then decided to make a pilgrimage to Mecca and ordered the kings of Kampar and Indragiri to accompany him. As these two Sumatran rulers were inclined to resist this demand, he induced them to come to Malacca, held them there in custody, and took over their realms. In Alā' uddin's reign Malacca became more prosperous and powerful, and its population, which reportedly numbered forty thousand, included people from all over the world. The sultan married a daughter of his "bendará" (treasurer)[63] who had been a "quelim" (judge)[64] during the previous reign and by her he had a son named "Sulayman," who was legally the heir apparent because he was descended from kings on both sides.

Just when he was finally prepared to depart for Mecca, Alā' uddin was poisoned, presumably at the instigation of the kings of Pahang and Indragiri. His death was followed by a succession battle between the advocates of his two sons: Pahang and Kampar favored Sulayman, while Muhammed, the nephew of the incumbent "bendará," received support from the powerful and wealthy commercial interests of the city. Muhammed's party won the day, and upon becoming sultan he completely severed Malacca's vassalage to Siam and Java and declared that he recognized China as his only suzerain. Among other things, Muhammed was determined to take over control of the tin-producing districts subject to Kedah, another of Siam's vassal states.[65] Upon learning of its assertion of independence, the king of Siam sent a fleet of one

---

[61] Adapted from the Malay, *laksamana*, meaning admiral or fleet commander. See Ferrand, *loc. cit.* (n. 47), p. 427, n. 2.

[62] An Arabic name meaning "the highness of the faith." *Ibid.*, p. 422, n. 2.

[63] From Malay, *bendahāra*, meaning treasurer or minister of finance. See *ibid.*, p. 427, n. 1.

[64] Identification with judge is not entirely certain. See *ibid.*, p. 423, n. 2. Professor Berg believes that this title is from Malay *Kĕling*, often written "Kling," and refers to natives of India, especially from its eastern coast. Also see above, p. 412.

[65] According to Pires in his section on Siam, published by Ramusio in 1550. See Cortesão (trans. and ed.), *op. cit.* (n. 46), I, 108.

hundred sails to attack Malacca. The Siamese fleet was intercepted near the island of "Pulopicão" (Pulaw Pisang in the Riau archipelago, south of Singapore)[66] by a Malaccan force in 1489 and was completely vanquished.

From this time until Albuquerque's conquest of Malacca in 1511, no further Siamese efforts were made to punish the Malay sultan. But Muhammed was personally very proud and arrogant and contributed to his own undoing. He ridiculed his father for wanting to make a pilgrimage to Mecca by asserting that Malacca itself was the true Mecca. He had his brother Sulayman assassinated along with seventeen other nobles who were his relatives. He even killed his own son and heir because he asked for expense money (the Moors claimed that he was punished for this crime by Albuquerque's seizure of the city). The properties of the dead he seized for himself, and took their wives and daughters, about fifty of them, for his own concubines. When speaking with his nobles, he always required them to stand off at a distance of five or six paces.

Justice, it is reported, was traditionally administered in independent Malacca by the sultan himself or through the office of the "bendará" (minister of finance and ofttimes chief minister).[67] Nobles condemned to the death penalty possessed the right to die by the kris at the hand of their nearest relation. Should an ordinary man die without heirs, his property passed to the crown. No marriages could be celebrated without permission from the sultan or the "bendará." If a man caught his wife commiting adultery within his own house he might legally kill both parties (but he was not legally permitted to take the life of just one). If he was not able to kill them both, he had to bring charges against them (or the survivor) before a judge.[68] Whenever a person was required by law to pay damages for injuring another, half of the fine went to the injured party and the other half to the crown. Capital punishments prescribed by law varied according to the nature of the crime. Some criminals were thrust upon spits, others had their chests crushed; some were hanged or boiled in water, while still others were roasted and eaten by cannibals whom the king imported from Aru in Sumatra for this purpose. The property of those condemned to death was divided equally between the heirs and the crown; if there were no heirs the crown received everything.

In Muhammed's time there were five chief functionaries at his court. The first minister, or viceroy, was called the "pudricaraja" (*putrikarāja*).[69] The "bendará" normally controlled the treasury, and often held the portfolio of the "pudricaraja" as well, "for two separate persons in these two offices never agree well together."[70] The "lassamane" (admiral) obviously occupied an important post in government because of Malacca's reliance upon keeping the sea

[66] Ferrand, *loc. cit.* (n. 47), p. 423, n. 7.

[67] Albuquerque in Birch (ed.), *op. cit.* (n. 10), III, 87.

[68] For further clarification of this passage, which is also obscure in the original *Commentarios* of Albuquerque, see the French translation by Ferrand, *loc. cit.* (n. 47), p. 426.

[69] *Ibid.*, p. 426, n. 3.

[70] Albuquerque in Birch (ed.), *op. cit.* (n. 10), III, 87.

lanes open and defending itself against maritime invasions.[71] A military official called the "tamungo"[72] was in charge of maintaining control over and administering justice to the numerous foreigners in the city. The fifth office was staffed by four "xabandars" (harbor masters),[73] nationals of the following states: China, Java, Cambay, and Bengal. The foreign merchants of their own states, as well as some from other unrepresented countries, were assigned to the jurisdiction of each of these four port authorities. In turn, they were responsible to the "tamungo" in his capacity as the superintendent of the customs and of the foreign merchant communities. When the Portuguese took over Malacca in 1511, they retained much of this administrative structure and left most problems of local government and justice in the hands of native authorities who upheld the traditional law.[74]

While Muhammed's rule was hard, Malacca prospered during his reign. At the time of Albuquerque's conquest the city and its immediate territory had a population of one hundred thousand and stretched along the coast for a distance of about four miles. Beyond the city itself, the jurisdiction of Malacca extended east to Pahang, north to Kedah, and inland to the territories subject to Siam. Thus, in a short period of ninety years (1421–1511), from its founding to its capture by the Portuguese, Malacca is pictured by the conqueror's son as having developed from a backward fishing village into a bustling commercial and administrative metropolis with a tiny empire of its own. The state, which was primitive at the beginning of the century, possessed by 1500 a well-defined hierarchy charged with administering a body of law and custom for natives and foreigners alike. While Albuquerque's chronicle of the sultans of Malacca is certainly faulty, he renders a picture of the past which could not be found in other Portuguese books printed in his day and preserved data which are even yet valuable in reconstructing Malayan history.

The printed books of the sixteenth century contain no single narrative describing the development of Malacca under Portuguese rule. Modern scholars, even when writing about the Portuguese themselves and their way of life in Malacca, are forced to piece together the story from a vast number of printed and manuscript sources of varying degrees of reliability.[75] Aside from Barros, who has surprisingly little to say on the European period of Malacca's history, sixteenth-century Europeans had available the printed reports on conditions in Malacca for the following years: Varthema (*ca.* 1506), Albuquerque and

[71] For his other duties, such as chief of the harem, see the translation from the code of Malacca in Ferrand, *loc. cit.* (n. 47), p. 427, n. 2.

[72] Probably from the Malay *temengung*, a term which is now used to designate a military rank. See *ibid.*, p. 415, n. 1, and p. 427, n. 3.

[73] *Shāh-bāndar*, a Persian term used generally in maritime Asia which literally means "king of the port." See *ibid.*, p. 428, n. 1.

[74] On Albuquerque's decision about retaining traditional government see Barros in Cidade and Múrias (eds.), *op. cit.* (n. 39), II, 283; for confirmation by recent scholarship see I. A. Macgregor, *loc. cit.* (n. 24), pp. 23–24.

[75] See, for example, the excellent summary in I. A. Macgregor, *loc. cit.* (n. 24), pp. 5–47.

Empoli (1511), Barbosa (*ca.* 1515), Castanheda (between 1528 and 1538), Fedrici (*ca.* 1566–69), Lemos (1574–75), Mendoza (*ca.* 1579), Linschoten (1583–88), and Fitch (1582). As can readily be observed, the greatest gaps in the printed reports are for the middle (*ca.* 1538–66) and final years (1588–1600) of the century. Fortunately, the Jesuit letters from Malacca, while as a rule not overly informative on local conditions there, are especially numerous and detailed for the middle and end years of the century.[76] So, on the basis of these materials alone, it was theoretically possible for a contemporary of Hakluyt to fit together in sketchy outline a picture of both the permanent and changing features of life in Portuguese Malacca during the sixteenth century.

On the physical features of Malacca the European sources are essentially in agreement. Its port is described as being better and safer than the harbor at Singapore. No ships within it are ever lost from storms, and the harbor is easy to reach, particularly from the west. The city is situated at the mouth of a tiny stream and the surrounding territory is unproductive, even though jungle vegetation is profuse and luxuriant. Malacca has a plentiful supply of good water and delicious fruits (grapes, chestnuts, figs, durians, and other fruits), but most of the other food has to be brought in by sea from abroad.[77] Though the land is not fertile, it yields valuable woods, gold, and tin. Wild animals are numerous.[78] Castanheda reports that the city is divided into two parts by a river which is spanned by a connecting bridge. In the southern section of the city the king and his nobles reside and here the chief mosque is also located. On the northern side of the river live the merchants. The houses in both the administrative and mercantile sections of the city are constructed of wood and stone.[79] Merchants come to Malacca from all over the world, but nobody stays there longer than necessary because its climate, though temperate, is reported to be hot, damp, and unhealthy for natives and foreigners alike. Apparently the only Portuguese who resided permanently at Malacca during the sixteenth century were the few soldiers who manned the fortress, the crown officials, and occasional priests and missionaries.[80]

The cosmopolitan population of the city includes merchants and sailors from all the lands between Arabia and China, whether Moors, Jews, or heathens. Especially numerous are the Islamic Gujaratis from Cambay, the Klings and

[76] For additional data on the middle years see J. Wicki (ed.), *Alessandro Valignano, Historia del principio y progresso de la Compañia de Jesús en las Indias Orientales (1542–64)* (Rome, 1944), pp. 85–93.

[77] M. L. Dames (ed.), *The Book of Duarte Barbosa* (London, 1921), II, 178; also see Linschoten's remarks in Burnell and Tiele (eds.), *op. cit.* (n. 25), I, 105.

[78] Varthema in Temple (ed.), *op. cit.* (n. 5), p. 84.

[79] Pedro de Azevedo (ed.), *História do descobrimento e conquista da India pelos Portugueses* (Coimbra, 1924), I, 458. For a description of Malacca based on all available sources (not only those printed in Europe during the sixteenth century) see Wheatley, *op. cit.* (n. 26), pp. 311–12. Also see Barros in Cidade and Múrias (eds.), *op. cit.* (n. 39), II, 173–74.

[80] Malacca was clearly a hardship post for officials of the Portuguese crown. For additional comment see Macgregor, *loc. cit.* (n. 24), pp. 6–8. Some of the Jesuits went to Malacca to recover from asthma, but others complain about the inland winds which make everyone ill with the fever. See J. Wicki (ed.), *Documenta Indica* (Rome, 1962), VII, 33, 46, 86.

Bengalis of the east coast of India, the men of Java, the Chinese, and the "Gores" (Japanese). The Siamese, because of their political differences with the sultans of Malacca, are conspicuous by their absence.[81] When Albuquerque took the city, two powerful Javanese communities were resident in Malacca who controlled the rice trade with their homeland. The more powerful group lived on the northwestern side of the river at "Upi" (Upeh) and the other on the southeastern side at "Ilher" (Hilir).[82] The Portuguese had considerable difficulty controlling these rich mercantile groups of Javans and ultimately ejected them from the city. Many of the Javan mariners lived with their families on their ships and never went ashore except to trade. The Javans, in Barbosa's time, clearly controlled most of the shipping between Malacca and the archipelago, including the Spice Islands. Apparently, the Javans were also known in Malacca for their tendency to run amuck when sufficiently agitated.[83] The Moors and the Javans were clearly the spoilers of Malacca as far as the Portuguese were concerned. With the other foreign groups, especially the Chinese and Indians, the Portuguese, except for occasional incidents, normally had peaceful and profitable relations. The Hindu merchants were especially friendly to the Portuguese and helped them to obtain an understanding of the prevailing business practices.

To European eyes the natives of Malacca are "white," well-proportioned, and proud. The men normally wear cotton garments (sarongs) which cover them only from the waist down, but a few of the more distinguished wear short, silk coats, "after the fashion of Cairo,"[84] under which they carry daggers called krises. Their women, who are olive-colored, comely, and brunette, usually wear "fine silk garments and short shirts. . . ."[85] Nobody but the king may wear yellow colors without special permission under pain of death.[86] The faces of the natives are broad with wide noses and round eyes.[87] Both sexes are well-mannered and devotees of all forms of refined amusement, especially music, ballads, and poetry. The rich pass life pleasantly in their country homes at Bertam which are surrounded by bountiful orchards. Most of them maintain separate establishments in the city from which they conduct their business. They especially take delight in cultivating the arts of love-making and war. They take offense easily and will not permit anyone to put his hand on their

---

[81] Albuquerque in Birch (trans. and ed.), *op. cit.* (n. 10), III, 85. Pires, who includes discussion of the political troubles of the Malays and Siamese in his section on Siam, most of which was published by Ramusio in 1550, asserts that the Siamese had not traded in Malacca for twenty-two years (since about 1490). See Cortesão (trans. and ed.), *op. cit.* (n. 46), I, 108.

[82] Barros in Cidade and Múrias (eds.), *op. cit.* (n. 39), II, 257. For their subsequent difficulties with the Portuguese see Macgregor, *loc. cit.* (n. 24), p. 24, n. 72.

[83] Barbosa in Dames (ed.), *op. cit.* (n. 77), II, 174–77. On running amuck in Malacca also see Varthema in Temple (ed.), *op. cit.* (n. 5), p. lxxi.

[84] Varthema in Temple (ed.) *op cit.* (n. 5), p. 84; for comment see also p. lxxi. One of the Venetians who contributed information to the *Viaggi fatti alla Tana* (1543) from his experiences in India notes that the people of Malacca are small and ruddy, wear long, black turbans, fight with murderous poisoned arrows, pay tribute in cloves to Portugal, and purchase porcelain from China.

[85] Barbosa in Dames (ed.), *op. cit.* (n. 77), II, 176.

[86] Albuquerque in Birch (ed. and trans.), *op. cit.* (n. 10), III, 86.

[87] Varthema in Temple (ed.), *op. cit.* (n. 5), p. 84.

heads or shoulders.[88] Often malicious and untruthful, they take pride in their ability to wield the kris adroitly against their personal enemies. In larger engagements they fight in bands with bows and arrows, spears, and krises.[89] In their beliefs they are devout Moors. Their language called Malayan "is reported to be the most courteous and seemelie speech of all the Orient."[90] It is readily learned by foreigners,[91] and is the lingua franca for the entire region. And, at this point it is interesting to remember that Pigafetta had supplied a short vocabulary to Europe of Malay commercial terms which was republished and made broadly available through its inclusion in Ramusio's collection (1550).[92] While Xavier was in Malacca in 1545, he translated with great difficulty into Malay the Ten Commandments, the General Confession and other articles of the faith. The following year he wrote to the European fathers from Amboina as follows:

The Malayan language, spoken in Malacca, is very common throughout this area. . . . It is a great handicap in these islands that they have no writings, and know only a little about writing; and the language they write is in Malay and the letters are Arabic, which the Moorish priests have taught them to write and still teach them at present. Before they became Moors they did not know how to write.[93]

While the European writers without exception comment on the international importance of Malacca, they have very little to say about conditions in the rest of the Malay Peninsula. They make clear that Pahang, as well as two Sumatran principalities, were vassals of Malacca and that the remaining states of the peninsula continued to be subject to Siamese governors. While occasional references occur to trade at other ports on the east and west coasts, nothing much is said about conditions in them. Except for Malacca, Barros asserts, the entire west coast has nothing but jungle, swamps, and a few villages of fishermen. The wild animals of the countryside, including huge and savage cattle, are so ferocious that people sleep at night in the highest trees and build huge bonfires to frighten the tigers away.[94] Even the towns themselves are sometimes invaded by the tigers which roam about everywhere.[95]

It is only by inference from the accounts of the Portuguese chroniclers concerning the capture of Malacca and the campaigns into other parts of the

[88] Albuquerque in Birch (trans. and ed.), *op. cit.* (n. 10), III, 86.

[89] Barros in Cidade and Múrias (eds.), *op. cit.* (n. 39), II, 258–59.

[90] Linschoten in Burnell and Tiele (eds.), *op. cit.* (n. 25), I, 106.

[91] Castanheda in Azevedo (ed.), *op. cit.* (n. 79), I, 458.

[92] *Delle navigationi et viaggi* (Venice, 1554), p. 408, extracts only a few sample terms from the total list.

[93] G. Schurhammer and J. Wicki (eds.), *Epistolae S. Francisci Xaverii aliaque eius scripta* (Rome, 1944–45), I, 333. Xavier is probably wrong in asserting that the Malays did not know how to write before learning the Arabic script. It is likely that they wrote in earlier times, and that they used a modified Indian script.

[94] Alfred Wallace, the great British naturalist of the nineteenth century, wrote of his trip to the interior behind Malacca that tigers were still found there and that he and his party kept a fire going throughout the night to frighten away tigers, elephants, and rhinoceroses (*The Malay Archipelago* [10th ed.; London, 1898], p. 26). See also Wheatley, *op. cit.* (n. 26), p. 317.

[95] Barros in Cidade and Múrias (eds.), *op. cit.* (n. 39), II, 258.

peninsula which followed it that bits of information emerge about the history of Malaya and the fortunes of the deposed sultan. Albuquerque's *Commentarios* naturally contains the classical account of the siege and it is the archetype for most of the later European versions of it.[96] Though Albuquerque describes the flight of Muhammed into the interior, the most detailed rendition of the emigrés' troubles printed in the sixteenth century is provided by Castanheda.[97] He records that the sultan, thinking that Albuquerque would withdraw after plundering the city, first retired with his followers and captives to his estates not far from the city. Muhammed then went further inland to the Muar River and left his son Ala' uddin behind in the camp near Malacca to await the withdrawal of the Portuguese. When Albuquerque learned that the prince was obstructing trade upriver, he sent out an expeditionary force which routed the Malays.[98] The sultan and his son, after seeking to re-establish contact with each other in the interior, finally met in Pahang. Muhammed, according to Castanheda, died in Pahang, and the prince returned to his father's stockade on the Muar River to continue putting pressure on the Portuguese. Another Portuguese force was sent out in 1512 to dislodge the prince and he finally fled to Bintan, an island in the straits south of Singapore.[99] Except for the death of the sultan, Castanheda's story jibes well with what modern scholars are able to learn from other sources.[100]

From their retreat on Bintan, the followers of the sultan preyed upon Portuguese and other ships participating in the Malacca trade. Castanheda reports that the defiant Malays were again on the peninsula in 1518 or 1519 and operating in the valley of the Muar River.[101] Then, he asserts that they were again driven out of the peninsula in 1520 and forced to return to Bintan for the next six years.[102] In 1526 the Portuguese captured Bintan and the refugees fled to Sumatra.[103] Subsequently, a remnant of resistance returned to the peninsula under Ala' uddin's leadership and established themselves in the upper reaches of the valley of the Johore River. In 1535–36, the Portuguese sent a force under Estavão da Gama up the river to root them out.[104] This enterprise was never completely successful, and so, around 1540, the sultan established a new capital at Johore Lama at the mouth of the Johore River directly across the strait from Bintan.[105]

---

96 Birch (trans. and ed.), *op. cit.* (n. 10), III, 101–37.

97 Azevedo (ed.), *op. cit.* (n. 79), II, 150–54.

98 Details of the river barricade are in G. Maffei, *L'Histoire des Indes Orientales et Occidentales . . .* (Paris, 1665), pp. 281–83.

99 For a description see Barros in Cidade and Múrias (eds.), *op. cit.* (n. 39), III, 253.

100 Albuquerque, Góis, and Maffei also claim that the sultan died shortly after the conquest. More recent scholarship avers that he continued to harass the Portuguese and finally took refuge in Kampar (in Sumatra) where he died late in 1527 or early in 1528. See I. A. Macgregor, "Johore Lama in the Sixteenth Century," *Journal of the Malayan Branch of the Royal Asiatic Society*, XXVIII (1955), 73–75.

101 Azevedo (ed.), *op. cit.* (n. 79), II, 436.

102 *Ibid.*, III, 61.   103 *Ibid.*, IV, 42.   104 *Ibid.*, pp. 340–41.

105 On the exact location the sixteenth-century printed materials are not clear. This is also the conclusion of Macgregor, *loc. cit.* (n. 100), p. 84.

Since the Portuguese chronicles published in the sixteenth century do not cover the period after 1540, little could have been known in Europe about the Johore sultanate (1540–97) except through the Jesuit letters. Though much of what they wrote was left unpublished, the Jesuits report on the sieges of Malacca of June–September, 1551,[106] and of January–February, 1568.[107] Lemos, in his description of the sieges of Malacca of 1574–75, asserts that Johore was secretly supporting the ruler of Acheh (in Sumatra) in his attacks upon the Portuguese bastion and that the Portuguese unsuccessfully attacked Johore in 1576.[108] While the Portuguese themselves published nothing on subsequent difficulties with Johore, Linschoten from his vantage point in Goa reported that in 1587 the Portuguese were again at war with Acheh and Johore, that Malacca was in danger, and that the entire eastern traffic of the Europeans was halted.[109] He also described the outfitting of the fleet of Dom Paulo de Lima and its return to Goa with news of the relief of Malacca, the razing of Johore Lama, and the reopening of the sea route to the east.[110]

The Jesuit, Fróis, paints a bleak and distressing picture of Christian life in Malacca in 1556.[111] The small site on which the Portuguese live is utterly dependent for food upon its imports: wheat and meat from India, rice from Java, and local fruits. There is no fresh water in the settlement and people have to bring it in from the surrounding bush. When foraging expeditions go out, the men arm themselves with muskets and other weapons to scare off thieves and to kill attacking wild animals: elephants, tigers, lions, wildcats, and panthers. The Portuguese in Malacca are ruled completely by sensuality and their desire for gain. The Christians are so concerned about trade and quick profits that they do business with Moorish merchants and even take them as passengers on board their vessels. *Casizes* (Muslim religious called *Lajji* in Arabic) disguised as merchants take advantage of Portuguese avarice to sail with them to many heathen lands where they constantly spread the nefarious teachings of the Prophet. These Muslim teachers are so "solicitious and industrious that they come from Mecca and Cairo and Constantinople to these remote regions to plant and propagate their poisonous sect."[112] To gain the confidence of the easily beguiled Portuguese, the Muslims contribute alms to the Christians. They have been so successful that many of them regularly embark on Portuguese

---

106 For example see Francisco Perez to Fathers in Goa (Malacca, November 24, 1551) in Wicki (ed.), *op. cit.* (n. 80), II, 204–20. Xavier wrote to King John III from Cochin in 1552 telling about the damage suffered by Malacca during the siege and requesting special grants for the Portuguese who had so nobly defended the city. This letter was not published in the sixteenth century. See Schurhammer and Wicki (eds.), *op. cit.* (n. 93), II, 302.

107 See the letter to Leão Henriques, Provincial of Portugal (from Lourenço Peres?), (Malacca, December 3, 1568) in Wicki (ed.), *op. cit.* (n. 80), VII, 519.

108 As quoted in Macgregor, *loc. cit.* (n. 100), pp. 86–87.

109 Burnell and Tiele (eds.), *op. cit.* (n. 25), I, 193–94.

110 *Ibid.*, pp. 198–99. For details of the Portuguese attack on Johore Lama see Macgregor, *loc. cit.* (n. 100), pp. 101–12.

111 To Fathers in Portugal (Malacca, Nov. 19, 1556) in Wicki (ed.), *op. cit.* (n. 80), III, 529–39.

112 *Ibid.*, p. 537.

vessels for Borneo and other heathen lands. In 1555 one of these Arab sailors arrived in Malacca from Japan where he had done as much as he could while there to infect the Japanese with Muslim doctrines. This threat to Japan, the pride and joy of the Jesuits, leads Fróis to a bitter denunciation of the Moors as "the most pestiferous and hateful thing there is in these regions." [113]

The merchant accounts of the late sixteenth century dwell almost exclusively on Malacca as a trading center and upon its connections to the east. Like their Portuguese predecessors, Fedrici, Balbi, Linschoten, and Fitch were clearly conscious of Malacca's role as a crossroads where the products of East and West were traded and where the spices of the archipelago were exchanged for the textiles of India. They were also aware of the dependence of Cambay and Malacca upon each other in maintaining trade with the West. But they were most interested in informing their readers about how the Portuguese used Malacca as a sentinel to keep watch and control over the trade to the Moluccas, China, and Japan. Fedrici, who had "not passed further than Malacca towards the East," [114] learned that licenses had to be obtained from the Portuguese for eastward voyages and that most of those granted went to the *fidalgos*. The cargos carried to China when he was there (*ca.* 1566) were largely made up of "drugs [opium?] of Cambaia" and silver. [115] The ships plying the route between Macao and Japan carried silk to Japan and returned with a load of silver. While the Chinese brought silk, porcelain, and ginseng by sea to Malacca, they also traded overland with Persia. Similar assertions are made by the other commercial spies, but none of them volunteers significant new information on affairs in Malaya itself. It is evident, both from these accounts and the published Jesuit letterbooks, that the Portuguese, despite occasional wars with Acheh, continue to be in control of the trade passing through Malacca. Of equal importance, however, is the fact that the Jesuits were letting it be known in Europe that Malacca was being bypassed by the Spanish who were going directly from the Philippines into the Moluccas, Indochina, China, and Japan. [116]

The published European writings of the sixteenth century bring out a number of the more persistent features about life in Malaya without divulging more than general data on trade. They emphasize the pre-European period of Malaya's history and picture Malacca as the center of the Malay world in the fifteenth century. There emerges clearly the great devotion of the sultans of Malacca to Islam, and the role which they assume of spreading the teachings of the Koran by the sword to neighboring states. Siam's place in the affairs of the Malay principalities, the close trading connections of Malacca and Java, and the distant but powerful influence of China are all present in the European accounts. The

[113] *Ibid.*, p. 538.

[114] In R. Hakluyt, *The Principal Navigations*... (Glasgow, 1904), V, 404.

[115] *Ibid.*, pp. 405–7.

[116] For a further discussion of the religious situation in Malacca see Guzman, *op. cit.* (n. 44), I, 175–76.

Malay language, depicted as the lingua franca of the archipelago and the peninsula, helps the European authors to explain why the Malays occupy the key position in the trade and diplomacy of the region. Malacca, which lives from trade almost exclusively, is shown as being situated in an unproductive area, dependent on food imports, and surrounded by jungle, swamps, and impassable country. A few details of the peninsula's internal geography, particularly the river valleys, emerge from the descriptions of those expeditions which were undertaken against the Malays who resisted Portuguese domination.[117] The Malay people, especially those of Malacca, are seen as indulging in frivilous pastimes and are considered to be warlike in their behavior; hence they are often used as auxiliaries by the Portuguese captains. The Malays, who resist the Portuguese throughout the century, are given only uncertain support at critical times by their coreligionists and fellow Malays of Sumatra and Java. It is nonetheless implicit in the reports that the Portuguese are not at all times firmly in command of Malacca. Careful readers in Europe might even have deduced from the published accounts that the Portuguese position in Malacca could be attacked most effectively (as it eventually was) from bases on Sumatra and Java with the aid of the anti-Portuguese rulers of those islands.

3

SIAM

Continental southeast Asia, with its high mountains and great rivers which run southward into the surrounding seas, has acted historically as a barrier to communication between India and China. The great land routes traversing the Eurasiatic continent generally circumvented its rugged and tortuous terrain.[118] East and west transportation within the area itself was mainly by sea. The Chinese, Muslims, and Portuguese, their maritime and mercantile interest being in the archipelago and the spice trade, had less direct contact with the people of the continent (except for those at Malacca) and knew correspondingly less about them. It was primarily as a result of the southward migrations of the early twelfth century that Thai peoples from China and Tibet began to settle this region. Thereafter, as civilization developed along the Tenasserim littoral and in the great and fertile river deltas of southeast Asia, people and ideas began to pour in from the outside world, especially from China and India.

---

[117] On the sparsity of geographical description see I. A. Macgregor, "Notes on the Portuguese in Malaya," *loc. cit.* (n. 24), pp. 5–6. Apparently there were no large Malay settlements away from the rivers.

[118] For a period in the second century A.D. one of the overland routes between China and the West crossed northern Burma. At a somewhat later date there was probably a road from Upper Burma into India. Pires (in Cortesão [trans. and ed.], *op. cit.* [n. 46], I, 111) reports hearing at Malacca that the Burmese and Siamese trade up the rivers and overland with China.

Buddhism, a bequest from India, was the dominant religious and civilizing force at work in continental southeast Asia when the first Portuguese got east of Bengal. Varthema in his comments on Tenasserim and in his references to "Christians of Sarnam" [119] seems to realize that he is in touch with a belief not to be found in India proper. At the time of Albuquerque's descent upon Malacca, Portuguese emissaries were sent to Siam because it was the traditional suzerain of the Malay sultanate; a mission was also sent to Pegu because of its reputation for wealth. Burma remained only of secondary importance to the merchants working out of India, but Portuguese freebooters took service in its armies and played an active role on both sides in the numerous wars fought between Burma and Siam. A few Christian missionaries also went into these continental lands, even though their lives were often in danger. However, Siam and its continental neighbors remained entirely outside of the Portuguese imperial design and charted their own destinies during the sixteenth century.

Albuquerque, even before he arrived at Malacca, knew that its Malay sultan was involved in a permanent war with Siam. The ruler of Siam, the Portuguese realized, still claimed suzerainty over the Malay Peninsula and much of continental southeast Asia. Upon arriving at Malacca, Albuquerque soon heard stories about the power and wealth of Siam and determined to find out for himself all that he could about this celebrated state and its king's attitude towards the new conquerors of Malacca. Even before completing the conquest, Albuquerque nervously dispatched his envoy, Duarte Fernandes, to the court of Rama T'ibodi II (reigned 1491–1529) [120] in the capital city of Ayut'ia. But Albuquerque need not have worried about T'ibodi's reaction, for he was at war with neighboring Chiengmai and was consequently in no position to interfere at Malacca. Fernandes was well equipped for his mission of peace and amity because he knew Malay, having previously learned it as a prisoner in Malacca. After a friendly reception in Ayut'ia, Fernandes returned to Malacca in the company of a Siamese envoy who was carrying gifts and letters for Albuquerque and the king of Portugal. Almost at once Albuquerque sent a reconnaissance mission to Ayut'ia under Antonio de Miranda de Azevedo. [121] One of its number, Manuel Fragoso, was to study Siam's location, markets, commercial practices, the other customs of the land, the depths of its ports, and collateral matters vital to the establishment of trade. Fragoso remained in Siam for two years to prepare a written report. He took it personally to Goa in 1513 accompanied by a Siamese emissary to the viceroy. [122] This report was sent immediately to Portugal, but it has never been published. It is likely, however, that Barbosa and Barros used it.

---

[119] Sarnam is another word for Siam. See below, p. 531, for further comment.

[120] For a description of Fernandes' reception see Albuquerque in Birch (trans. and ed.), *op. cit.* (n. 10), III, 152–55.

[121] *Ibid.*, pp. 156–59.

[122] See J. J. Gonçalves, "Os Portugueses no Sião," *Boletim da sociedade de geografia de Lisboa*, LXXV (1957), 435–37; J. de Campos, "Early Portuguese Accounts of Thailand," *Journal of the Thailand Research Society* (Bangkok), XXXII (1940), 3–5.

Portugal's relations with Siam remained for a time on an informal basis, though Siamese were encouraged to return to Malacca to replace many of the Muslim merchants who left when the Portuguese seized the city. A few Portuguese freebooters also found their way to Siam to take up service in the royal army. In order to formalize relations and to enlist powerful Siam on their side, the Portuguese sent another mission to Ayut'ia in 1518. Duarte Coelho, plenipotentiary of the king of Portugal, had previously made two visits to Siam, once in the entourage of Miranda and once when the ship on which he was sailing was forced by storms to take refuge up the Menam River. He was accompanied on this third occasion by a sizable retinue and carried letters and presents sent directly from King Manuel to Rama T'ibodi II to confirm the peace treaty earlier concluded by Miranda. In addition, Coelho was able to conclude a political-military agreement with Siam which was designed to help strengthen Portugal's precarious position in southeast Asia. The treaty of 1518 granted the Portuguese the right to trade and settle in Siam and to enjoy religious freedom. Trading was officially permitted at Ayut'ia, at Lugor (its Siamese name is Nakhon Sritammarat), at Patani, and in Tenasserim at its capital city of Mergui. In return, groups of Siamese were allowed to settle in Malacca, and the Portuguese promised to provide Ayut'ia with guns and munitions needed in the war then being fought with Chiengmai.

The pact effectively opened Siam to traders, mercenaries, and settlers from Malacca. Portuguese military advisers and instructors were attached to the Thai army shortly after 1518. Trading factories sprang up at the port towns of Lugor and Patani as commerce between Ayut'ia and Malacca became brisk. Though we have no records, it is probable that Catholic priests went into Siam at this same period to minister to the spiritual needs of the Portuguese settlers there.[123] Reports on trade and local conditions funneled back to Lisbon from the Portuguese in Siam. Some of these were used by Barros in his vivid account of Siam for the period before 1540.

In Siam itself the early years of the sixteenth century were comparatively peaceful and prosperous, particularly after Chiengmai had received a stinging defeat in 1515 with the aid of the Portuguese. Rama T'ibodi II then began a military reorganization of his kingdom which helped to preserve peace and stability for the next score of years. A succession crisis in Chiengmai, however, brought about a new and large-scale Siamese intervention in 1543. This event ended the relative calm of the earlier years, involved Ayut'ia in wars with its northern neighbors, and led to troubles with Pegu. Finally, in 1569, the forces of Bayin Naung from Pegu besieged, captured, destroyed, and depopulated Ayut'ia. For the next fifteen years Siam lived restively as a vassal of Burma. The accession at Pegu of Nanda Bayin in 1581 marked the beginning of a lengthy effort on the part of Siam to break the hold of the Toungoo rulers of Burma and to regain independence. Plagued with internal problems the Burmese rulers

---

[123] Gonçalves, *loc. cit.* (n. 122), p. 440.

were forced to fight on several fronts simultaneously and over a long period; in the meantime Siam became increasingly less easy to control. The situation going from bad to worse for the harassed Burmese, they were gradually forced out of the Thai country. The Thais, following up their advantage, continued to beleaguer their overlords, but the city of Pegu ultimately fell into the hands of the Arakanese in 1599. At the end of the sixteenth century, Siam held all of lower Burma south of Martaban and had regained its independence.[124]

Among the European writers whose accounts of Siam were published in the sixteenth century, the most important are those of Pires, Barbosa, Barros, and Pinto. A number of illuminating sidelights can also be gleaned from the narratives of Varthema, Pigafetta, Castanheda, Albuquerque, Fedrici, Balbi, and Fitch. Varthema, Pinto, and Fitch are the only ones among these commentators who almost certainly set foot on Thai territory. Varthema was probably in Tenasserim in 1505, and Fitch reports that late in 1587 he journeyed to Chiengmai about two hundred miles northeast of the city of Pegu. Pinto was the only one of the writers who actually lived in the capital of Siam. While the Portuguese sources are substantial on the period of Ayut'ia's ascendancy (before 1545), they give only scattered bits of information relating to the decline and resurgence of Ayut'ia in the latter half of the century. The European records, as uneven and spotty as they are, nonetheless have considerable value for the reconstruction of Siamese history. Most of the contemporary Thai writings were burned in the flames which swept and consumed Ayut'ia in 1767.[125] The only native history of significance which covers the sixteenth century is the *Pongsawadan* (*Annals of Ayut'ia*, 1349–1765) compiled in the eighteenth century from earlier writings. Unfortunately, the compilers issued several differing versions and failed to preserve the sources from which they wrote. Besides this, the only other sources are of foreign provenance and of contestable value. The Chinese records are clearly the best, because the annals of Siam's closest neighbors, whenever available, tend to be biased and to disagree on dating and chronology.[126]

Barros ranks Siam, along with China and Vijayanagar, as one of the three richest and most powerful continental empires with which the Portuguese have friendly relations.[127] Its vassal states appear to be so extensive that they would be considered great states in Europe. Apparently accepting the Siamese claim to suzerainty over almost all of continental southeast Asia, Barros includes under his description of Ayut'ia's empire a good portion of what we call Indochina today. To illustrate the complicated character of Siam's boundaries

---

[124] Hall, *op. cit.* (n. 30), chap. xiii.
[125] Campos, *loc. cit.* (n. 122), p. 2.
[126] On the types of available Asian sources (mainly Siamese) see Prince Damrong, "The Story of the Records of Siamese History," *The Siam Society Fiftieth Anniversary Commemorative Publication* (Bangkok, 1954), I, 82–98.
[127] Cidade and Múrias (eds.), *op. cit.* (n. 39), III, 75–77.

Barros reverts to the hand-map which we described earlier.[128] Starting with the Menam River (which is called "Mother of Waters"),[129] he explains that it runs through the center of the country from north to south and empties into the bay which originates at the place where the index finger and the other three join the hand. The north-south extension of the empire runs through twenty-two degrees of latitude, or, if we use sixty-nine miles for each degree, about 1,518 miles. The Mekong River to the east has a huge delta which divides the coastal states of Cambodia and Champa. In the extreme north, where all of these great rivers rise from a single lake,[130] there is a range of mountains as rugged as the Alps which is located on his hand-map at the point where the hand joins the wrist. In this mountainous hinterland live a barbaric people called the "Gueos." They border Siam only on a small part of its northern frontier, because the Laos states encircle Siam on the north and east and control the upper reaches of the Mekong River. South of the Laos states lie the coastal kingdoms of Cambodia and Champa. On the west and north Siam is bounded by the Burmese states.

The "Gueos," according to Barros,[131] are ferocious and cruel cannibals. They fight on horseback and descend periodically from their mountain strongholds to attack the Siamese and the Laotians. The "Gueos" tattoo themselves and brand their whole bodies with hot irons. Barros ventures the opinion that these may be the primitive people to whom Marco Polo refers as inhabiting the kingdom of "Cangigu" because their customs are so similar.[132] The Laos, who live along the Mekong, are technically vassals of Siam but they often revolt against their suzerain. Their territories are divided into three semi-independent kingdoms: Chiengmai, Chiangrai, and Lanchang (Luang Prabang).[133] Their only reason for accepting Siam's overlordship at certain times is to receive its protection from the depredations of the "Gueos." Were it not

128 See above, p. 505. Castanheda (in Azevedo [ed.], *op. cit.* [n. 79], II, 156) reveals nothing about Siam's geography. Apparently he knew about just a few coastal towns.

129 Me = Mother, Nam = Water.

130 This is a reference to the legendary lake of Chiamai supposedly situated at 30 degrees north latitude in the Tibetan plateau. Early maps show all of the rivers of continental southeast Asia as originating from it.

131 Cidade and Múrias (eds.), *op. cit.* (n. 39), III, 78.

132 Though they do not mention the opinion ventured by Barros, similar speculations may be found in H. Yule and H. Cordier (eds.), *The Book of Ser Marco Polo* (New York, 1903), II, 117 n. and 128 n. Campos, *loc. cit.* (n. 22), pp. 10–11, identifies these people with the Lawas and the Was of northern Siam who practiced ritual cannibalism like the Bataks of Sumatra (see below, p. 575). On these two primitive groups see W. A. R. Wood, *A History of Siam* (London, 1926), p. 41. Barbosa (in Dames [ed.], *op. cit.* [n. 77], II, 167–69) dwells on the details of ritual cannibalism as practiced in the hinterlands of Siam. Camoëns (X, 126), on the basis of this passage in Barros, wrote (Burton's translation):

> "See how in distant wilds and woods lie pent
> the self-styled Gueons, savage folk untamed:
> Man's flesh they eat: their own they paint
> and sear, branding with burning iron,—usage fere!"

On the map of Asia prepared by Sanson for Louis XIV in 1692 the "Gueyes" continue to be shown as living just to the southeast of the legendary "Lake of Chiamaj."

133 Cidade and Múrias (eds.), *op. cit.* (n. 39), III, 79. Actually, this description of the semi-independent status of the Laotian states coincides with what we know from other sources.

that the king of Siam keeps sending large armies against the hordes of the north, the "Gueos" would long ago have destroyed the Laos and conquered Siam. From the testimony of Domingo de Seixas, a Portuguese employed in the Siamese army for twenty-five years, Barros reports that the forces sent into the north numbered 20,000 cavalry, 10,000 war elephants, and 250,000 infantry, as well as carabao for cargo carriers.[134]

The king of Siam rules over nine kingdoms, just two of which are peopled by the Thai themselves.[135] The one which includes Ayut'ia, the capital, borders on the territory of Malacca and is called "Muantay" (Mu'ang Thai) meaning the southern Thai kingdom. Besides the capital, the southern kingdom includes many other cities and ports. Pires says that the Siamese control three ports on the Pegu side of the Malay peninsula and a great many others on its eastern side.[136] Barbosa discusses trade at just two of these western territories, Tenasserim and Kedah.[137] On the eastern side Siam controls the port cities of "Pangoçai" (Bang Plassoy), "Lugo" (Lugor or Lakon), "Patane" (Patani), "Calantao" (Kelantan), "Talingano" (Trenganu), and "Pam" (Pahang).[138] Each of these ports has a governor called an "oia" (*p'aya*) who is comparable to a duke in Europe.[139] At Lugor, there is a viceroy called "peraia" (probably *pra p'aya* meaning "lord governor"), who has charge of the entire coast from Pahang to Ayut'ia.[140] On the Pegu and Cambodia side the "aiam campetit" (p'aya of Kampengpet) acts as viceroy, is next to the king in power, has his own fighting force, and is evidently charged with maintaining the Siamese position on these unstable frontiers.[141] The northern kingdom under Ayut'ia's control is called "Chaumua" (Chau Nua, or peoples of the north), and, according to Barros, its inhabitants have a language of their own.[142] To the northern and southern kingdoms collectively foreigners have given the name "Siam" but it is not the appellation used by the Thai themselves.[143] In surveying the non-Thai states

[134] *Ibid.*, p. 78. Campos, without indicating why, says these figures are exaggerated (*loc. cit.* [n. 122], pp. 10-11).

[135] The first written reference to the Siamese as a historical people is found on the bas-reliefs of Angkor Wat and is dated from the twelfth century. The earliest mentions of the name Thai are dated from the late thirteenth century. See L. P. Briggs, "The Appearance and Historical Usage of the Terms Tai, Thai, Siamese, and Lao," *Journal of the American Oriental Society*, LXIX (1949), 65.

[136] Cortesão (trans. and ed.), *op. cit.* (n. 46), I, 103; later on Pires lists a number of ports under Siamese jurisdiction, but these names were unfortunately omitted from the version which Ramusio published. Pigafetta learned a few of the names of these port cities from his Javanese pilots and he records them. See James A. Robertson (ed.), *Magellan's Voyage around the World by Antonio Pigafetta* (Cleveland, 1906), II, 173.

[137] Dames (ed.), *op. cit.* (n. 77), II, 163-65.

[138] Barros in Cidade and Múrias (eds.), *op. cit.* (n. 39), III, 79.

[139] Among the higher officials, the p'aya ranks third. See C. H. Philips (ed.), *Handbook of Oriental History* (London, 1951), pp. 106-7.

[140] Pires in Cortesão (trans. and ed.), *op. cit.* (n. 46), I, 109.

[141] *Ibid.*

[142] Cidade and Múrias (eds.), *op. cit.* (n. 39), III, 79. For an ethnic and linguistic map of modern Siam see Wendell Blanchard *et al.*, *Thailand, Its People, Its Society, Its Culture* (New Haven, 1957), p. 58.

[143] "Siam" appears to be derived from the Malay, *Siyām*, an appellation which the Portuguese learned at Malacca. For a detailed etymology see Briggs, *loc. cit.* (n. 135), pp. 68-69, n. 62.

ruled over by Ayut'ia, Barros presents a confusing and indefinite picture. What emerges from studying his list is the fact that the Portuguese in Ayut'ia were probably told about a number of kingdoms over which Siam claimed suzerainty but which were actually semi-independent. Those non-Thai states listed which are identifiable are Chiengmai, Chiangrai, Lanchang, Cambodia, and several states in Burma.[144]

The fullest accounts which exist of a dependent province are those relating to Tenasserim (Mergui) and they are provided by Varthema and Barbosa. Tenasserim, a peninsular area facing on the Bay of Bengal, was not among Siam's tributary states for it was ranked, according to the law of King Boroma Trailokanat (reigned 1448–88), as a second-class province under the crown's direct jurisdiction.[145] Like many such territories remote from Ayut'ia, it probably enjoyed a substantial degree of independence. Still, it is clear from Barbosa's placement of Tenasserim in his chapter on Siam that he considered it to be a division of that empire. Actually, the references to Tenasserim are all to a city rather than a province and so most editors of these early accounts conclude that their authors are actually talking about the city of Mergui.[146] The governor of the city, who is referred to as its "king," is a pagan who always has a large army at his command.[147] Aside from being well supplied with fruits and animals, Tenasserim produces brazil-wood and a resin called benzoin.[148] Varthema reports that silk is woven in Mergui and that the people of the city use quilted cloth of silk or cotton on their persons and in their homes.[149] The adventurous Italian and his companions witnessed cockfights of the kind which are still a form of popular amusement in Thailand. One of his group, being a stranger in the city, was asked to deflower the sixteen-year-old bride of a merchant; this custom of premarital defloration by strangers seems to have been followed in the region of the Bay of Bengal long after Varthema's time.[150] At death the nobles and Brahmans of the city are burned on a pyre and their ashes are preserved in special earthen urns. Fifteen days after the death of her husband, the widow commits *sati*. A young man, in making overtures to a girl, reportedly makes his plea for love while placing a burning cloth on his naked arm as proof

---

[144] See Campos, *loc. cit.* (n. 122), pp. 11–12; Swecker, *op. cit.* (n. 11), pp. 82–83; and John Bowring, *The Kingdom and People of Siam* (London, 1857), I, 11–12.

[145] Ulrich Guehler, "The Travels of Ludovico di Varthema and His Visit to Siam, Banghella, and Pegu A.D. 1505," in the special volume of selected articles from the *Journal of the Siam Society* (Bangkok), VII (1959), 252.

[146] Conti (in Major [ed.], *op. cit.* [n. 31], pt. IV, p. 9) writes about "the city of Ternassari which is situated on the mouth of a river of the same name." Pires (in Cortesão [trans. and ed.], *op. cit.* [n. 46], I, 105) includes Tenasserim in Siam and identifies it as the port "nearest to the land of Pegu." Fedrici (in Purchas [ed.], *op. cit.* [n. 16], X, 115) reports on Tenasserim after it had fallen to Burma's control: "This Citie of right belongeth to the Kingdome of Sion, which is situate on a great Rivers side, which commeth out of the Kingdome of Sion: and where this River runneth into the Sea, there is a village called Mirgim. . . ."

[147] Varthema in Temple (ed.), *op. cit.* (n. 5), pp. 74–75.

[148] *Ibid.*, p. 75, and Barbosa in Dames (ed.), *op. cit.* (n. 77), II, 164.

[149] For comment see Guehler, *loc. cit.* (n. 145), p. 253, n. 3.

[150] *Ibid.*, pp. 257–58, n. 10.

of his sincerity and devotion. Murderers in Tenasserim suffer death by impale-
ment. The people of this part of the world write on paper,[151] not on palm
leaves as they do in Calicut. As a port, Mergui plays host to many Muslim and
pagan merchants from Bengal, Malacca, and Gujarat.

Barbosa also reports on trade at Kedah, another western port of Siam south
of Mergui, where pepper grows in abundance. He likewise notices that Siam
controls two or three other ports along the Malay coast between Mergui and
Malacca. Muslim merchants who want to trade at any of these ports are forced
to come unarmed.[152] It is clear from this remark and the confirmatory reports in
other Portuguese sources that the Siamese authorities were determined that
the Muslim merchants should not have an opportunity to take over political
control of the ports under Ayut'ia's jurisdiction as they had been doing in the
archipelago. Still, it appears that they were permitted to trade and settle in
Siam providing that they did not become a political menace.

Except for its frontier regions, Siam is mostly flat and this is especially true
for the valley of the Menam. The people of Siam devote themselves primarily
to agriculture and fishing; consequently, food is abundant. Very few of the
Siamese are craftsmen, and so the markets of the country are not thronged
with foreign traders competing to buy merchandise. The few native products
which attract business originate in Chiengmai. Silver comes from the Laos
territories. Much of Siam's trade with India is carried on through Martaban
and other ports of the Bay of Bengal where Gujarati and other Muslim trades-
men are freer from surveillance by the authorities. Part of Siam's difficulty in
participating in international trade apparently stems from the fact that Muslims
are not welcome; Pires bluntly asserts that the Thai "do not like them." [153]
Hindus, and especially Chinese traders, are commonly received well, but nobody
seems to make great profit from trading in central Siam. Six or seven junks from
Siam carry goods to China annually.[154] The gold from Pahang and the tin
from Kedah were being funneled into Malacca by the time the Portuguese
arrived there, and they tried to make certain that this movement would continue.
Even though Siam was not commercially attractive, Portuguese traders continued to go to the ports under Ayut'ia's control, for, in the practical words of
Pires, the Europeans "bear some things on account of profit . . . because otherwise there would be no trading." [155]

The king of Siam, whose title is "Peraia" (*P'ra Chao*, or Lord of All),[156] is
reputedly very powerful, wealthy, and tolerant of all foreigners except the
Muslims. Though he is formal with strangers, he is free and easy with his own

---

[151] On the cardboard type of paper used in Siam see W. A. Graham, *Siam* (London, 1924), I, 285.
[152] Dames (ed.), *op. cit.* (n. 77), II, 164–65.
[153] Cortesão (trans. and ed.), *op. cit.* (n. 46), I, 104.
[154] *Ibid.*, p. 108.
[155] *Ibid.*
[156] *Ibid.*, I, 109; for the taboo on the use of the king's personal name and the various titles used by
the common people to refer to "His Majesty" see H. G. Quaritch Wales, *Siamese State Ceremonies,
Their History and Function* (London, 1931), pp. 38–39.

subjects.[157] He rules justly, if absolutely, from his permanent capital in Ayut'ia. His harem includes more than five hundred women and he lives in sumptuous palaces surrounded by extensive orchards and gardens.[158] He frequently goes to the hunt on horseback accompanied by many greyhounds and other dogs.[159] On the death of a king, the crown usually passes to a nephew,[160] a son of the king's sister, providing that he is acceptable; if not, conclaves are held to determine which member of the royal family will succeed to the throne. Once a king is crowned, the lords follow his commands obediently and his ambassadors carry out his instructions to the letter. Like his brother monarch in Pegu, the king of Siam is partial to white elephants and will undergo the most severe trials to acquire as many of them as possible.[161]

The men of Siam have close-cropped hair and are tall, swarthy, peaceful, and temperate in eating and drinking like their neighbors in Pegu.[162] As a rule they wear a sarong from the hips down but go naked above the waist.[163] In their beliefs they resemble most of the other people of continental southeast Asia, because they all allegedly derived their religious notions from the Chinese. They are generally very much involved in religion and build many magnificent temples, some of stone and lime, and others of brick and lime.[164] To the Siamese, God, as the creator of Heaven and Earth, rewards virtue and punishes sins. Each man on this earth has two conflicting spiritual advisers, one who protects his soul and the other who tempts it. Both inside and outside their temples, the Siamese build idols in human forms and dedicate them to those among the departed who have lived worthwhile lives. They do not worship these idols, but cherish them simply because they serve to keep green the memory of the individuals whom they represent.[165]

Notable among their numerous images is one in clay which is about 225 feet long and depicts a man lying asleep on some pillows.[166] This holy image is called the "father of man," possibly Buddha. They believe that he was sent directly from Heaven and was not created of man. The original of this reclining image is said to be the vital force which put certain men into the world who were martyred for the sake of God. The largest and oldest of the Siamese images is

---

[157] Pires in Cortesão (trans. and ed.), *op. cit.* (n. 46), I, 104.

[158] Castanheda in Azevedo (ed.), *op. cit.* (n. 79), II, 157; this figure on the size of the royal harem is probably low. See Wales, *op. cit.* (n. 156), pp. 47–50.

[159] Barbosa in Dames (ed.), *op. cit.* (n. 77), II, 166–67.

[160] Pires in Cortesão (trans. and ed.), *op. cit.* (n. 46), I, 104; this seems to be utterly wrong, for most of the kings of the Ayut'ia dynasty were the sons of their predecessors. See list in Philips, *op. cit.* (n. 139), p. 135. The succession law of 1360 provided that the eldest son of the queen has precedence over all other members of the royal family. See Wales, *op. cit.* (n. 156), p. 67.

[161] Below, p. 548.

[162] Pires in Cortesão (trans. and ed.), *op. cit.* (n. 46), I, 103–4.

[163] Barbosa in Dames (ed.), *op. cit.* (n. 77), II, 166.

[164] For a discussion of Siamese temples and their properties, images, and shrines see Kenneth E. Wells, *Thai Buddhism, Its Rites and Activities* (Bangkok, 1939), pp. 23–38.

[165] Barros in Cidade and Múrias (eds.), *op. cit.* (n. 39), III, 80.

[166] See Swecker, *op. cit.* (n. 11), p. 83. For a discussion of this ancient artwork see Graham, *op. cit.* (n. 151), II, 156.

one cast in metal which is housed in a temple in the city of "Socotay" (Suk-hothai). This bronze image stands about sixty feet high.[167] Other idols are numerous and of various sizes, some of them no taller than a man. Their temples are large and next to them one often sees pyramid-like structures (Prachedi stupas, or Buddhist relic shrines)[168] topped by huge spires which are dedicated to the gods as ornaments. Ordinarily they are built of stone or brick and decorated with gilded wooden facings and moldings. The lower levels of these buildings are colorfully painted and at the tip of the spire, where the Portuguese usually put a weathercock on their churches, the Siamese hang a flat disc that looks like a hat around the edge of which they suspend many little bells which tinkle with the slightest movement of the air.

The priests of these temples are respected and venerated, for in their way they are genuinely religious. They are so chaste that no female of any sort, even a nun, may enter their dormitories in the temple compound. Those who bring women in are punished by expulsion. They wear a habit of yellow cotton, the sacred color being yellow because of its similarity to gold. Like the habit of the Portuguese priest, these yellow robes are so long that they touch their ankles. The Siamese priests, unlike the Europeans, keep their right arm bare and across the left shoulder they drape a long strip of wide cloth which is held against the habit by a belt.[169] It is this belt which indicates the order and rank of the wearer just as a vermilion mark indicates that a native of Malabar is a Brahman. Like the priests of Pegu, the Siamese shave their heads, go about shoeless, and carry a large paper fan to shade themselves from the tropical sun. They show great temperance in eating and drinking; if a monk drinks wine he is stoned by his fellows for violating the rules. During the year they observe many fast days, especially at one particular period when the people flock to the temples to hear sermons as Christians do during Lent. Their special holidays take place both at the beginning of the new moon and when it is full; on these occasions they pray in choirs by day and at certain hours during the night.[170]

All learning and tradition are in the hands of the priests. Aside from studying their religion, they devote themselves to investigating the revolutions of the Heavens and the planets as well as to problems of natural philosophy. In their cosmography they contend that a universal flood followed the creation and that this world will last for eight thousand years, six thousand of which have already passed. The end of this world will result from fire. Seven eyes will open in the sun, each one will successively dry up everything on land and sea. In the ashes left from the burning of the land, two eggs will remain, one male and one

---

[167] According to Campos (*loc. cit.* [n. 122], p. 12), this figure is probably called Phra Attaros and is not as tall as Barros says. If a taller image existed at Sukhothai, it was probably destroyed in 1563 when the Burmese sacked the city.

[168] For a description of the *Prachedi* (or *cetiya*) see Wells, *op. cit.* (n. 164), p. 30, n. 1.

[169] For a similar description see *ibid.*, p. 154.

[170] A reference to the rainy season retreat during which time the people retreat into their temples. The retreat lasts for three months and begins in July a day after the full moon appears. See *ibid.*, pp. 91–95, where this period of fasting is also compared to Lent.

female. From these two eggs the world will be reproduced. In this new world there will be no seas of salt water, but only rivers of clear, unbrackish water. These great rivers will make the earth so fertile that it will bring forth its bounty without man's labor. The human race will then be free to abandon itself to perpetual enjoyment.

The priests hold classes for boys in the temples. At these sessions the boys learn something about the liberal arts and how to read and write. Along with the rites and ceremonies of their religion, they are taught the colloquial language (Thai). The sciences, however, are taught in an ancient language (Pali) which is to them what Latin and Greek are to Europe. They write after our fashion from left to right.[171] Though the Siamese possess many books, they are all in manuscript because, unlike the Chinese, they have not developed the art of printing.[172] They are great believers in astrology and never act without consulting an oracle for the auspicious moment. They have no sundials, but rely on water clocks. Every hour they beat so hard on a kettle drum that the whole city resounds. With their astronomy and astrology, they mix heavy doses of geomancy and sorcery which they learn from the "Quelins" (Klings) of the Coromandel coast who are great adepts in these arts and highly esteemed in Siam for their mastery of them. The Siamese year has twelve months; the New Year begins with the first moon of November. As we assign to each month a sign of the zodiac, they designate the month by the name of an animal: November is the month of the rat, December the bull, January the tiger, February the hare, March the great snake (or dragon), April the little snake, May the horse, June the goat, July the monkey, August the cock, September the dog, and October the pig. Actually, Barros is badly mistaken in identifying these animal names with particular months. While he gives the correct names and in the right order, the animal names are actually used in the old Siamese system of dating to stand for the individual years of a sub-cycle of twelve years in the normal sixty-year cycle.[173]

The Siamese ruler is the most absolute on earth, because he owns all the land in a kingdom where all the wealth is in the soil. The whole of Siam, Barros avers,[174] is in effect a royal domain like the limited *reguengo* (crown land) of the Portuguese king. Every worker pays a share to the individual who possesses the right to the crown's land. The lords down to the "oya" (*p'aya*) level, as well as the officials and captains of the crown, are rewarded with gifts of land for their services. Such bequests are made mainly in return for military service, usually for a term of years, or for a lifetime, but never in perpetuity. All lords and officials must be prepared to give military service by participating themselves and by providing horses and elephants for wartime needs. Whenever a vassal contributes to the royal army, an entry is made beside his name in the

---

171 See Graham, *op. cit.* (n. 151), I, 265 for further discussion.
172 For a description of these manuscript books see *ibid.*, pp. 285–86.
173 On the traditional system of dating see Philips (ed.), *op. cit.* (n. 139), pp. 128–29.
174 Cidade and Múrias (eds.), *op. cit.* (n. 39), III, 82.

official ledger which is kept after the fashion of a chronicle so that all services may be remembered and justly rewarded. In addition to the levies which he raises by these means, the king has permanent garrisons stationed at the frontiers. Since the country is large and has many cities, the crown has no trouble in getting a large army together on short notice. The capital alone can readily furnish fifty thousand soldiers. If necessary, the king of Siam can raise soldiers in his vassal states, but ordinarily he avoids calling upon them because their forces might be too unreliable and because foreigners might thereby learn too much about Siam's military system.

In essence, Barros' brief account of the interdependent social and military organization of Siam is in harmony with what is found in other sources.[175] From the earliest records it is known that the ruler was sole owner of the kingdom and his subjects were chattels over whom the king had absolute control. In addition to the payment of an annual corvée, the principle of universal, obligatory military service for all able-bodied men was in force throughout Siamese history. Barros is almost certainly trying to describe the reformed version of this system which was put into effect beginning in 1518 by King Rama T'ibodi II. By its terms the whole kingdom was divided into military districts and every man upon reaching eighteen years of age was automatically enrolled on the military lists. This system with modifications remained in effect until 1899.

Officials who hold land, according to Barros.[176] are required periodically to show their skill in arms at festivals which are held at intervals in Ayut'ia. One of the most celebrated of their pageants takes place on the Menam River, where over three thousand boats congregate and divide into two contingents to stage a race. Once the race is over, the two groups fight a battle reminiscent of the mock naval combats put on in ancient Rome.[177] Tournaments are also held on land between men mounted on horses and elephants, and between individuals who engage in duels with swords and lances. Persons condemned to death are permitted to take part in these trials of strength and skill, and are pardoned if they emerge victorious. When not fighting in war or in mock combat, the lords of Siam spend their time in pleasure and debauchery. They are gourmands, very devoted to the fair sex, and zealous in guarding the women of their household. Like the men of Pegu, the Siamese are said to insert bells in their sex organs to please the women.[178]

The wars in which Siam became involved around mid-century are not reported on by the Portuguese chroniclers because their accounts end in about 1540. The only European to write about them was Fernão Mendez Pinto. He was asked, shortly after he joined the Society of Jesus in 1554, to set down the

[175] See Graham, *op. cit.* (n. 151), I, 235–38; Wood, *op. cit.* (n. 132), pp. 37, 99–100; and Blanchard *et al., op. cit.* (n. 142), p. 398.

[176] Cidade and Múrias (eds.), *op. cit.* (n. 39), III, 83.

[177] Possibly a reference to the *Kathina* ceremonies described in Wales, *op. cit.* (n. 156), pp. 200–12.

[178] Barros in Cidade and Múrias (eds.), *op. cit.* (n. 39), III, 83–84; also see Pires in Cortesão (trans. and ed.), *op. cit.* (n. 46), I, 104. See below, pp. 553–54, for details.

recollections of his experiences in the East. In a letter written from Malacca on December 5, 1554, Pinto summarizes his memories. The following year this letter in a truncated and censored version appeared in *Copia de unas Cartas* published by the Jesuits at Coimbra. Shortly thereafter it was translated into Italian and republished a number of times during the next decade.[179] The published portion deals mainly with Pegu, Siam, the Indochinese peninsula, and Japan, but the greatest detail is given on his experiences in Siam, probably in 1548–49. Though Pinto has often been called the Sinbad of Portugal because of his tall stories, enough solid data are included in this letter to make it worth analyzing. This is particularly true, not only because we have no other European materials which deal with the middle years of the century, but also because Pinto wrote this brief account just a few years following the events which he describes. His famous *Peregrinations*, written in his old age in Europe and not published until 1613, is the fanciful and unreliable narrative from which he gets his unsavory reputation.[180]

What follows is extracted from those portions of his letter actually published and circulated in sixteenth-century Europe.[181] Like Varthema, Pinto refers to Siam as "Sornao"[182] as well as using the more familiar "Sion" or Siam. According to his own testimony, he was twice in Ayut'ia, which like Venice is a city of canals where gondola-like boats are common. He claims to have been told that the city has two hundred thousand boats, but is cautious enough to admit that he does not know whether this figure is correct or not. Nonetheless he goes on to report that he has seen the river packed solidly with boats for a distance of about three miles. On all the rivers roundabout the city there are floating markets where as many as five hundred to one thousand boats congregate.[183]

The king calls himself "Precaosale" (P'ra Chao Chang Phenak or "Lord of the white Elephants"),[184] which means, according to Pinto, the person second

[179] For the full text of his letter see Wicki (ed.), *op. cit.* (n. 80), III, 142–55; and for a slightly different version see A. Silva Rego (ed.), *Documentação para a historia das missões do padroado portuguès do oriente* (Lisbon, 1949), V, 369–72.

[180] For thoroughgoing and damaging critiques of this book see G. Schurhammer, "Fernão Mendez Pinto und seine'Pergrinaçam'!" *Asia Major*, II (1926), 72–103, 196–267; and W. A. R. Wood, "Fernão Mendez Pinto's Account of Events in Siam," in selected articles from the *Journal of the Siam Society* (Bangkok), VII (1959), 195–209. But also notice that "the Siamese records for this period are so conflicting and obscure that it is almost impossible to check his [Pinto's] details." (Hall, *op. cit.* [n. 30], p. 210.)

[181] All references are taken from Anton Eglauer (trans.), *Die Missionsgeschichte späterer Zeiten; oder, gesammelte Briefe der katholischen Missionäre aus allen Theilen der Welt . . . Der Briefe aus Ostindien* (Ausburg, 1794), I, 245–57; this eighteenth-century compiler translated into German the truncated version generally circulated in the sixteenth century from *Diversi avisi particolari dall'India di Portogallia ricevute di 1551 al 1558 dalli Padri della Compagnia di Giesu* (Venice, 1559).

[182] Conti in the fifteenth century talks about "Cernove," and the routier of Vasco da Gama's voyage by Alvaro Velho refers to "Xarnauz." In both these cases, and probably in Pinto's as well, the authors seem to be using the term taught to them by Muslim sailors. See Campos, *loc. cit.* (n. 122), p. 3, n. 6. It may well be derived from the Persian name, *Shahr-i-nao* or "new city," referring to Ayut'ia when it was founded in the fourteenth century. See Wicki (ed.), *op. cit.* (n. 80), III, 149, n. 27.

[183] Eglauer (trans.), *op. cit.* (n. 181), I, 248.

[184] Cf. above, p. 526.

only to God himself. His palaces may never be visited by foreigners unless they are emissaries or slaves. Still, Pinto, who was neither emissary nor slave, claims to know something about them. On the outside the royal palaces are covered with tin and on the inside with gold. The ruler sits in one of them on an elevated and splendid throne which is encircled by artistically decorated platforms or stages. The daughters of his great lords dance on one stage, their sons on another, and their wives on a third. Twice each year the king leaves his palace to show himself in the city. This is a sight worth seeing, because the king is accompanied by a huge procession of elephants and bodyguards as well as his wives and concubines. While the people of the city disport themselves, the king sits comfortably in his splendid chair perched on the back of an elephant throwing coins to the spectators.[185]

Pinto also describes a regal procession which he saw on the river at Ayut'ia, probably an event similar to the *Thot Krathin* pilgrimages still made annually by the king to the riverside *wats* (Buddhist temples) of modern Bangkok.[186] The royal barges still in use are modeled on those of Ayut'ia, and Pinto's description of them in no way exaggerates the splendor of these magnificent craft. If anything, his word portrait is somewhat too restrained and unexcited to one who has seen the modern counterparts of these sleek vessels. He contends that they are much longer than a galley; the modern barges are about 160 feet long. He describes the royal barge as having a winged creature on it which looks like a siren, probably a reference to a towering figurehead on the prow representing a mythical animal. The stern he describes as being heavily gilded, and the rudder as being decorated with ornaments of great value. Twelve barges (probably guard-boats) precede the royal craft and twelve thrones of different kinds rest on each of them. While nobody sits on these thrones, the spectators make to them the same obeisances which they offer to the king. Over two hundred smaller boats surround the royal barge and these belong to the leading captains and lords of the realm. The rank of each of these lords is distinguished by the color of his barge and the costume worn by his steersman. A large ship with many youths and musicians aboard follows the royal barge and behind it throng the numerous crafts of all descriptions belonging to the spectators.

On another occasion Pinto witnessed the ceremonial bathing of a white elephant, a creature held in great esteem because, he thinks, its kind is not found elsewhere in the world.[187] This elephant is guided in a lavish procession to the river for his bath. The streets along the route which the procession follows are washed and gaily decorated with banners. The white elephant is preceded through the city by 160 small horses native to the land and 83 other elephants in

---

[185] For a more recent description of the pageantry attending the king's visit to a *wat* in the vicinity of the royal palace on the occasion of the *Thot Krathin* ceremony see Graham, *op. cit.* (n. 151), II, 243–45.

[186] Eglauer (trans.), *op. cit.* (n. 181), I, 249–50; Graham, *op. cit.* (n. 151), II, 245–47.

[187] Eglauer (trans.), *op. cit.* (n. 181), pp. 250–51; for a summary of the literature on the subject and a description of the great reception of the white elephant in Bangkok in 1927, see Wales, *op. cit.* (n. 156), chap. xxiii.

rich coverings on which sit some of the leading dignitaries of the realm; behind it ride 30 or 40 great lords on elephants. The white elephant wears a saddle of golden cloth and a chain of sterling silver. Other silver chains are fitted around its chest and neck to make a harness.[188] On the bank of the river a tent is erected into which the elephant walks for its ceremonial washing. Though Pinto was not allowed to see the bathing rites, he was told that they were elaborate. The elephant is so highly revered that when he stops walking in a procession nobody else may move. Even the other elephants hesitate to approach too close to him. When he urinates, they hold a golden basin under him and with this water the greatest lords of the kingdom wash their faces.[189] While some of Pinto's facts may not have been entirely correct, he managed to convey through his vivid description of the bathing ceremony a bit of the adoration which the Siamese undoubtedly displayed for this sacred white elephant.

The king of "Brama" (Burma or Toungoo) in an effort to become lord of the white elephant himself, decided, according to Pinto, to invade Siam and take the elephant.[190] This is certainly a reference to the expedition which Tabinshwehti of Pegu was preparing in the winter of 1547–48, one phase of which was to declare war by summoning the king at Ayut'ia to turn over the white elephant to him. Since no road large enough to accommodate a large army connected Pegu with Siam, Pinto asserts that the king of "Brama" with his force of 300,000 had to hack his way through the forests in order to reach Ayut'ia.[191] Then the Burmese stormed the Siamese capital several times without taking it. In this fruitless campaign, he contends, the Burmese expended 120,000 men and the Siamese losses amounted to 200,000, of whom some were killed and some taken in captivity back to Pegu. After living three years longer, the white elephant died amidst great lamentations. Ayut'ia went into official mourning for one month, Pinto was told by merchants who were there at the time, and the elephant was then burned on a pyre of costly, scented woods. Meanwhile another white elephant was captured in the mountains and wastes of "Innasarim" (Tenasserim) and was greeted in Siam with great thanksgiving and festivity. While Pinto gives no dates for the siege of Ayut'ia, it is generally agreed to have taken place in 1549. His story of the capture of a white elephant in Tenasserim is confirmed by the Siamese annals.[192] The rest of this account seems to do no violence to the facts as we know them from other sources.

---

[188] Cf. photograph of the white elephant of the sixth reign in *ibid.*, facing p. 275.

[189] Lest this rite be thought of as merely imaginative, see Wales' (*op. cit.* [n. 156], p. 279) testimony that he possesses a photograph "of a Siamese woman suckling a young elephant, probably a white one."

[190] Eglauer (trans.), *op. cit.* (n. 181), I, 251–52.

[191] For a description of Tabinshwehti's overland route from Moulmein to Ayut'ia see G. E. Harvey, *History of Burma from the Earliest Times to 10 March, 1824 . . .* (London, 1925), p. 159. In the *Peregrinations* Pinto greatly exaggerates the numbers involved, among other things he gives Tabinshwehti an army of 800,000 men. See for comment Wood, *loc. cit.* (n. 180), p. 206.

[192] O. Frankfurter, "Events in Ayuddhya," in the compilation commemorating the fiftieth anniversary of the *Journal of the Siam Society* (Bangkok), I, 54.

The ruler of Siam interferes with nobody's religious beliefs, for he claims to be only the master of men's bodies not their souls. Consequently, he forces neither the heathens nor the Moors to accept one faith or another but is tolerant of all beliefs.[193] And Siam, as Pinto saw it, was a nation full of believers in many strange gods and spirits. He tells about an esteemed idol who sits constantly before a banquet table with jaws open and is served by forty or fifty old women. This figure is called the god of the enlargement of the stomach because they can think of no more honorable name for him. The people also worship the elements: when a person dies who believes in the efficacy of water, they throw him naked into the river; if in fire, they cremate him; if in earth, they bury him; if in the air, they expose his body on a wooden frame near the river where the vultures and other birds of the air can eat him.[194] Every year at the end of the winter, the king bathes in the river to purify the water so that his subjects can drink it. An eclipse of the moon, which Pinto witnessed in Ayut'ia, is thought by the Siamese to be caused by a snake which tries to swallow the moon.[195] To force the snake to regurgitate the moon, the people shoot at the sky, pound on the gates of their houses, and yell at it from both land and water. When the Portuguese heard these thunderous noises, they thought a revolt had broken out in the city. Such stories are perfectly credible in light of the great concern which the Siamese people still have for spirits and natural phenomena.

The Moors have seven mosques in the city of Ayut'ia which are presided over by Turkish and Arab priests. The capital has thirty thousand Moorish families, and the followers of Islam are so firmly entrenched that free propagation of the Christian gospel will certainly be opposed by them. Fróis in 1556 writes a lament in which he claims that Muslim converts, when they assemble in Ayut'ia to hear the *casizes* speak, "keep their mouths open, fanning their mouths with their hands, saying that the air of those words entering their body will sanctify their hearts."[196] The king of Siam is so powerful that he will not formally receive an emissary from a foreign king who does not present him with appropriate presents as recognition of his greatness. Once an envoy has met this requirement, the king deferentially gives him a small golden cup and other presents. Though he is genuinely a great lord and suzerain over many lesser princes, the king of Siam is himself a vassal of China and each year sends a tribute-bearing mission to Canton. So you can see, Pinto informs his fellows in Portugal, what important gates Father Francis Xavier tried to open in his effort to penetrate China and to introduce Christianity there.[197] While Pinto, in his letter of 1554, may have occasionally drawn on imagination when

---

[193] Eglauer (trans.), *op. cit.* (n. 181), I, 253.

[194] On animism among the modern Siamese see Wales, *op. cit.* (n. 156), pp. 301–2.

[195] Professor C. C. Berg observes that this is a version of the Rāhu story (explaining eclipses) still current in Sumatra, Java, and Bali.

[196] To Portuguese Fathers (Malacca, November 19, 1556), in Wicki (ed.), *op. cit.* (n. 80), III, 538.

[197] Eglauer (trans.), *op. cit.* (n. 181), I, 253–54. Shortly before his death, Xavier had conceived the idea of sailing to Siam to join the annual mission for China and in that way gain entrance to the country. See Schurhammer and Wicki (eds.), *op. cit.* (n. 93), II, 499.

memory failed, there is nothing here which compares with the gross exaggerations and numerous fabrications contained in his *Peregrinations*.

The wars of the later years of the sixteenth century between Siam and Pegu are referred to occasionally in the narratives of the commercial agents, Fedrici, Balbi, and Fitch. Bayin Naung, the ruler of Pegu, assembled a huge army of 1,400,000 men and besieged the city of Ayut'ia for twenty-one months before taking it in 1567.[198] So reports Fedrici who was in Pegu six months after the king's departure on this campaign and remained there long enough to see Bayin Naung return in triumph to his capital. In this war the loss of life on both sides he tells us is high. The army of Pegu required 500,000 new recruits as replacements for those killed before the walls of Ayut'ia. The capital of Siam never would have surrendered, in Fedrici's view, if its defenders had not been betrayed by one of their number who left a gate open through which the besiegers entered by night. The ruler of Ayut'ia, realizing that he had been betrayed, reportedly poisoned himself, his wives, and his children.[199] Those people from the city who were not killed, or who had not fled to safer places, were carried back to Pegu along with all the loot that the elephants of Bayin Naung could manage to transport.

As a consequence of the Burmese victory, the city of Ayut'ia was badly depopulated and reduced in status to a small and defenseless frontier town in vassalage to the mighty rulers of Pegu. In the reign of King Maha T'ammaraja (1569–90), Siam's neighbors to the east, especially Cambodia, sought to take advantage of Ayut'ia's plight by attacking it and by refusing to honor its traditional suzerainty. The undeniable threat from the east provided the Siamese with a splendid opportunity again to erect the fortifications of Ayut'ia without arousing the suspicions of the ruler of Pegu. The task of gradually rebuilding the state was left primarily in the hands of Prince Naresuen, who was allowed to return to Ayut'ia in 1571 from captivity in Burma. Over the next decade this prince readied the armies of Siam for the day when an opportunity would come to break the hold of Pegu. The death of Bayin Naung in 1581 and the succession struggle at Pegu preceding the assumption of power by Nanda Bayin (reigned 1581–99) gave Naresuen precisely the opening he had been hoping for.

Gasparo Balbi, who kept a notably accurate diary of his activities in the East, reports that Nanda Bayin returned to Pegu on July 14, 1583, from his campaign against Ava only to learn that in his absence a Siamese contingent had arrived in Pegu under Naresuen to support their overlord but had returned home rather than going on to Ava. The king of Siam thereafter contended that Naresuen had been ignobly turned away by a slave of Nanda Bayin. After

---

[198] Translated in Purchas (ed.), *op. cit.* (n. 16), X, 110–11. This date is incorrect by two years. Both the Siamese and Burmese annals put it in 1569. See Harvey, *op. cit.* (n. 191), p. 169, and Wood, *op. cit.* (n. 132), p. 123–24.

[199] King Mahin, according to other reports, died while being taken as a captive to Burma. Wood, *op. cit.* (n. 132), pp. 124–25.

being so insulted, he felt that he could no longer recognize the suzerainty of Pegu.[200] An expeditionary force under the "great Brama" (the *Yuvaraja*, or crown prince) then undertook a new and costly campaign against Siam late in 1583. Though Ayut'ia was besieged, its new defenses thwarted the Burmese invaders. The only concession which King Maha T'ammaraja was willing to give was the vow that he would acknowledge Nanda Bayin's suzerainty if he would personally come to the front to accept homage. The Siamese king, who absolutely refused to pay homage to an inferior representative of Burma, was told that he would eventually have to acknowledge his vassalage before Nanda Bayin's lowest slave.[201]

When Ralph Fitch was in Pegu (*ca.* 1586), the war with Siam was still in progress and he reports that Nanda Bayin himself led an expeditionary force of three hundred thousand men and five thousand elephants against Ayut'ia.[202] The following year, Fitch made a side journey to "Jamahey" (Chiengmai) in the country of the "Langeiannes" (Lan-nas) who are called "Jangomes" (Yun?).[203] On a twenty-five-day trip to the northeast of Pegu, Fitch reports passing through "many fruitful and pleasant Countries" studded with poor houses constructed of canes and covered with straw. The city of Chiengmai, long contested by both Burma and Siam and fairly independent of both, is described as a pleasant and large town with wide streets and stone houses. Its men are "very well set and strong" and its women are much fairer than those of Pegu. They have no wheat, but seem to subsist mainly on rice and fruits. Copper and benzoin are found here in abundance, and Chiengmai is a great trading center for musk, gold, silver, and the products of China. Indeed, many Chinese merchants are to be seen in the marts of Chiengmai. The rites and customs of Chiengmai, such as public cremations, seem to be similar to those practiced in Burma and Siam.[204]

While merchants based on Pegu seem to have had relatively few difficulties moving about, the Christian missionaries who tried to penetrate into Siam through Ayut'ia had many bitter experiences. Pinto's prognostications about hardships for those carrying the gospel into Siam are borne out by the experiences of the Christian missionaries who actually tried to work there. The earliest missionaries to attempt the penetration of Siam were the Dominicans who had founded their first cloisters in India during 1548–49 and had then sent Gaspar da Cruz on a reconnaissance mission to southeast Asia.[205] It was Friar Fernando de S. Maria, General-Vicar of Goa, who sent two Dominicans to Siam in 1567 while he was making a visitation in Malacca. After a voyage of one month from

[200] Naresuen actually took advantage of Nanda Bayin's absence to attack Moulmein and Martaban and to carry off some of their inhabitants. See Hall, *op. cit.* (n. 30), p. 219.

[201] Balbi in Purchas (ed.), *op. cit.* (n. 16), X, 162–63.

[202] Fitch in *ibid.*, p. 819.

[203] Chiengmai was also called the Yun kingdom of Lan-na. See Briggs, *loc. cit.* (n. 135), p. 73.

[204] Fitch in Purchas (ed.), *op. cit.* (n. 16), X, 194–96.

[205] Benno Biermann, O. P., "Die Missionen der portugiesischen Dominikaner im Hinterindien," *Zeitschrift für Missionswissenschaft und Religionswissenschaft*, XXI (1931), 306–7.

Malacca, Friars Jeronimo da Cruz and Sebastião da Canto arrived in Ayut'ia. The Portuguese merchants, who escorted them there and at whose behest they had probably been sent, had prepared the ground for them in the Siamese capital. They were received by the Siamese with the greatest kindness and given a fitting house in the best quarter of the city. While the Buddhist monks and laity came along with the Portuguese to hear their sermons, the Muslims allegedly plotted to take their lives. In a fracas between some Portuguese and Muslim traders, Jeronimo was killed by the thrust of a spear and Sebastião wounded by a stone which hit him. The leading Siamese nobles apologized to Sebastião for the incident, and the king, Maha Chakrap'at, punished the guilty by having them trampled to death by elephants. The king graciously received Sebastião in audience and asked him not to leave the country without permission. Sebastião later returned to Malacca to recruit two additional missionaries with the king's permission.

It seemed at this point that the Christian enterprise, enjoying royal favor in Siam, was off to a good start. But all three of the Dominicans who worked there were killed when the Burmese captured Ayut'ia in 1569. Subsequently, other Dominicans were sent to Siam but they were all caught up in the whirlwind of the wars then going on and were fortunate when they escaped with their lives.[206] After the Portuguese Dominicans turned their efforts to more peaceful areas, Spanish Franciscans from the Philippines made an effort of their own in 1583–84. While they received a warm reception in Ayut'ia both from the Portuguese and the Siamese, the outbreak of war between Burma and Siam in 1584 rendered their efforts fruitless. Other Spanish missionaries from the Philippines, both Franciscans and Dominicans, were caught up in the wars between Cambodia and Siam around 1594 and were generally lucky if they survived the experience.[207] At Manila, meanwhile, both the civil and religious authorities were urging Philip II to take advantage of the war-torn conditions in Siam and Indochina to outfit a military expedition for the purpose of gaining a foothold on the Asiatic continent in one or another of these places. Siam, it was estimated by one overly optimistic hotblood, could be conquered and held by one thousand men.[208] In Europe, the Spanish Jesuit, Guzman, described Siam as a trouble spot where little could be hoped for from peaceful missionary activity.[209] In the sixteenth century the Christian mission had little but grief to record for the sporadic efforts made by its emissaries to Siam.

From the European sources it was possible even in the sixteenth century to obtain a sense of the importance of Siam in southeast Asia and the changing character of its role in the affairs of the region. The Portuguese writers are all

---

[206] *Ibid.*, pp. 319–21.
[207] L. Lemmens, O. F. M., *Geschichte der Franziskanermissionen* (Münster, 1929), p. 109. Also see below, pp. 568–69.
[208] Gregorio F. Zaide, *The Philippines Since Pre-Spanish Times* (Manila, 1949), pp. 280–81.
[209] *Op. cit.* (n. 44), I, 173–75.

agreed on the great strength and wide influence of the Ayut'ia monarchy in the first half of the century. They also bring out the complicated character of Siam's vassal relationships and the sketchiness of its political boundaries. There can be no question, however, about the authority which Siam maintained before the defeat of 1569 over the ports between Malacca and Martaban on both sides of the Malay Peninsula. It also may be inferred from these sources that most of Siam's trade with the nations to the west was carried on in the ports facing on the Bay of Bengal rather than in Ayut'ia itself. Such an orientation of trade was probably the natural result of Malacca's earlier refusal to respect the suzerainty of Ayut'ia and the consequent departure from Malacca of the Siamese traders.

Merchants from all the surrounding countries certainly called at Ayut'ia itself. The Muslim traders, however, clearly had to respect the wishes of the Siamese authorities and to live there on Siam's terms. These were not harsh conditions, according to the Portuguese, for the kings of Ayut'ia were tolerant of all different faiths even though they jealously guarded their political authority. In fact, the entire administrative, social, economic, and military life of the state, as it was understood by the Europeans, clearly centered in the person and authority of the king. They even bring out that land grants were never made in perpetuity and that service to the crown was the sole basis for all awards of land.

The Europeans also emphasize strongly the surface aspects of Buddhism with its countless temples, monks, and statues. The festivals, especially those involving boat processions on the Menam River, catch their fancy in particular. Barros takes more than a passing interest in Buddhist learning, education, and popular cosmology, even though he is sometimes misinformed or confused on details. The firsthand observers, such as Pinto and Fitch, freely cite figures on the size of armies, military losses, and population. Most of these figures appear in round numbers and are clearly intended to convey little more than the author's general impression of the numbers involved. But, perhaps in an effort to impress his religious superiors in the Jesuit order, Pinto becomes more precise and mentions, for example, that eighty-three (no more or fewer) elephants marched in a procession. Such calculated exactitude on minor and unimportant figures weakens rather than strengthens confidence in his honesty. But, even with this qualification, it is impossible to dismiss Pinto completely. His letter from Malacca is an important primary source for those trying to reconstruct a period of Siamese history which is notably deficient in all kinds of extant written records. On the wars between Pegu and Siam in the latter half of the century the writings of Pinto and the commercial interlopers provide helpful data to supplement and amplify the native accounts. While the European writers were often guilty of accepting legend and rumor as fact, they are generally no more gullible than the native annalists.

4

BURMA

Very little is known about Burma's history before a great Buddhist state was founded at Pagan in 1044 A.D.[210] Burmese inscriptions and chronicles, which only began to be compiled systematically in the eighteenth century, depend upon earlier writings of uncertain authority and preserve numerous stories from the oral tradition.[211] Much of the country's earlier history has consequently had to be reconstructed from Chinese travel accounts and annals, Siamese chronicles, Arabic histories, and European materials. The maps in Ptolemy's *Geographia* (probably from the thirteenth century) show Burma's coastline in a sketch which is roughly correct. The Arabian geographers, whose information likewise came mainly from traders, were not much better informed than the cartographers who prepared the Ptolemaic maps.[212] Marco Polo, who is responsible for so many "firsts," was the first writer to make Europe aware of Burma's existence by his graphic description of the Mongol invasion of 1277, the initial step in bringing about the collapse of the Pagan empire a decade later.

With the eclipse of Pagan, Burma split into numerous principalities which were generally under the control of Shan princelings. It was only in the fifteenth century that three of these states gradually became focal points of political power: Ava in the Irrawaddy Valley, Toungoo on the upper Sittang River, and Pegu in the delta of the Sittang River. It was this situation which those Europeans met who visited Burma in the fifteenth century. Conti stopped at Tenasserim, Arakan, Ava, and Pegu, and he comments on a few of his experiences in these places.[213] Santo Stefano, who stayed in Pegu for eighteen months in 1496–97, describes its ruler, Binnyaran II (reigned 1492–1526) as a rich idolater who was then engaged in war with Ava.[214] Most of the sixteenth-century writers likewise begin their discussions of Burma with reference to conditions in Pegu and the southern part of the country.

Portugal's relations with Pegu were generally friendly until the last years of the sixteenth century. At Malacca, in 1511 the merchants from Pegu had been the first to surrender to Albuquerque. He permitted them to leave for home freely and to take their possessions with them.[215] In response to Albuquerque's emissary to Pegu, Binnyaran II sent an envoy to the conqueror at Cochin in 1514. Five years later the Portuguese signed a commercial treaty with Pegu and set up a factory at Martaban. The name "Pegu" first appeared on a European

[210] For a summary of what is known see Hall, *op. cit.* (n. 30), pp. 119–24.

[211] An evaluation of these chronicles as sources is given by U Tet Htoot, "The Nature of the Burmese Chronicles," in Hall (ed.), *op. cit.* (n. 8), pp. 50–54.

[212] Hall *op. cit.* (n. 18), p. 10.

[213] Major (ed.), *op. cit.* (n. 31), Pt. IV, pp. 10–11.

[214] *Ibid.*, p. 6. For a few critical comments on these accounts see John C. Furnivall, "Europeans in Burma of the Fifteenth Century," *Journal of the Burma Research Society (Rangoon)*, XXIX (1939), 236–49.

[215] F. C. Danvers, *The Portuguese in India* (London, 1894), I, 238.

world chart in the Lopo Homem-Reinels atlas compiled in 1519.[216] In 1539, a Portuguese trading fleet from India helped Pegu to no avail in its losing war against Toungoo. With the capture of Pegu by the Burmans, the Mon kingdom came to an end and henceforward the new Toungoo dynasty aimed to unite the three kingdoms under its rule. While the Portuguese still visited Pegu and talk about it as such, they are really alluding after 1540 to a relatively united Burmese state under the Toungoos. The war between Burma and Siam which commenced in 1548 found Portuguese *condottieri* fighting on both sides. Many of these military adventurers were settled in lower Burma and Arakan and they continued throughout the century to live and work there. Around 1560 the Portuguese were permitted to build a fortress at Syriam, a port of Pegu. One of the Portuguese settlers in lower Burma, Felipe de Brito, soon acquired grandiose ambitions and tried unsuccessfully near the end of the century with help from the Portuguese in Goa and the kings of Arakan to transform the fort at Syriam into the base for a Portuguese colony. Almost a full century of good relations with Burma was brought to an end by this act, and hostilities followed. A consequence of the previous era of good relations was the acquisition of substantial information in Europe on events in Burma and continental southeast Asia.

Though Burma was not a leading international entrepôt, the sixteenth-century accounts of it are much more detailed and informative than those on the great islands of the archipelago. Besides a few missionary letters, ten substantial accounts were published in Europe between 1510 and 1599—by Varthema, Pires, Barbosa, Castanheda, Barros, Fedrici, Maffei, Balbi, Fitch, and Linschoten. Of these authors the only ones who wrote from personal experience were Varthema (possibly), Castanheda (possibly), Fedrici, Balbi, and Fitch. Even though none of the Portuguese writers (Castanheda possibly excepted) appears to have been on the scene, they are surprisingly well informed on local affairs and social customs. The fullest and best descriptions are given by Pires, Castanheda, Barros, and Fedrici. But most of the other writers have additional information to contribute of the kind which vitally enriches our knowledge. Those who wrote from their experiences with Peguans in India or Malacca (Pires, Barbosa, and Castanheda) would probably all agree with Linschoten, who argues that what he writes is true "for I doe not onely knowe it by the dayly trafficking of the Portingalles out of India thether, but also by the Peguans themselves, whereof many dwell in India, some of them being Christians. . . ."[217]

In the period before 1540 the kingdom of Pegu, which the natives themselves call "Bagou,"[218] is described as being bounded on the west by the sea and

[216] Cortesão and Teixeira da Mota, *op. cit.* (n. 2), I, 56–57.

[217] Burnell and Tiele (eds.), *op. cit.* (n. 25), I, 100.

[218] Barros in Cidade and Múrias (eds.), *op. cit.* (n.39), III, 128. The Burmese is *Bagó*; the Portuguese "Pegu" is derived from the Malay, *Paigu*. See H. Yule and A. C. Burnell, *Hobson-Jobson: Being a Glossary of Anglo-Indian Colloquial Words and Phrases* . . . (London, 1886), p. 525.

Arakan and on the east by the kingdoms of "Brema" (Burma or Toungoo) and "Davá" (Ava).[219] Arakan lies between Bengal and Pegu, faces toward the Bay of Bengal, and conducts most of its trade through the port of Myohuang.[220] War is often fought between Arakan and Pegu, but Pegu cannot readily defeat and occupy Arakan because of the high, wooded mountains (Arakan Yoma) which divide the two places.[221] The territory of Pegu commences at a point near Cape Negrais which is about 120 leagues (480 miles) southward down the coast from Chittagōng, the great port of call for the Portuguese which was constantly being vied over by the rulers of Bengal and Arakan.[222] The coastline of Pegu stretches through only four degrees of latitude (or 276 miles at 69 miles per degree), but it is much longer than this would suggest since it has many twists, turns, and deep indentations.[223] The littoral of Pegu is flat and marshy and the deltas at the mouths of its principal rivers are dotted with islands. The city of Pegu, from which the kingdom derives its name, is located in the valley of the "Cosmi" (a branch of the Irrawaddy River), a full day's journey upriver from the sea.[224] It is served by three major ports in the delta of the river: "Copymy" or "Cosmin" (Bassein),[225] "Dozõ" (Dagon, the early name of Rangoon), and Martaban.[226] In addition to these ports, Castanheda[227] lists the other towns known to him as "Dixara" (Henzada?),[228] "Dala" (Dalla), and "Sirião" (Syriam). Fedrici, who sailed from Chittagōng to Tenasserim and then up the coast to Pegu, indicates that in his day Tavoy was the southernmost port within Pegu's jurisdiction.[229] Balbi lists the names of an additional number of smaller towns and villages which he passed through as he made his way in 1583 across the delta through the Myaungmya creeks from "Cosmin" (Bassein) to Pegu.[230]

The hot, moist climate of lower Burma and the abundance of water in the delta supplied by the periodic floods of the great rivers help to make Pegu a highly productive kingdom. In foodstuffs, such as rice, "it is more plenteous

[219] Castanheda in Azevedo (ed.), *op. cit.* (n. 79), III, 15; also see the political divisions of sixteenth-century Burma given by Barbosa in Dames (ed.), *op. cit.* (n. 77), II, 148–61.

[220] Pires in Cortesão (trans. and ed.), *op. cit.* (n. 46), I, 95–96. Barbosa (Dames [ed.], *op. cit.* [n. 77], II, 150), on the contrary, claims that Arakan has no port.

[221] Cf. the statement in Harvey, *op. cit.* (n. 191), p. 137, which reads: "Shut off from Burma by a hill range, Arakan has a separate history, but it is the same in kind."

[222] Castanheda in Azevedo (ed.), *op. cit.* (n. 79), III, 15.

[223] Barros in Cidade and Múrias (eds.), *op. cit.* (n. 39), III, 128–29. Castanheda (in Azevedo [ed.], *op. cit.* [n. 79], III, 15) gives its coastline as 50 leagues (200 miles).

[224] Barbosa (Dames [ed.], *op. cit.* [n. 77], II, 153) places Pegu inland about seven leagues (28 miles) from the sea on the branch "of another river, very great, which flows through this Kingdom. . . ."

[225] Probably a corruption of the old Pali name, *Kusima*, by which the city now called Bassein (in Burmese, *Pathein*) was once known. See Philips (ed.), *op. cit.* (n. 139), p. 109.

[226] Cortesão (ed. and trans.), *op. cit.* (n. 46), I, 97–98, n. 1. Pires (*ibid.*, p. 99) calls Martaban a dangerous port, because of its rushing tides.

[227] Azevedo (ed.), *op. cit.* (n. 79), III, 16.

[228] On the west bank at the bar of the Irrawaddy River to the north of Dalla.

[229] Translated in Purchas (ed.), *op. cit.* (n. 16), X, 117.

[230] *Ibid.*, pp. 152–53.

than Siam and [has] almost as much as Java."[231] Cattle, sheep, hogs, birds, and fish, both the fresh and salt water varieties, thrive in the delta. In the forests and mountains of the interior roam many elephants and horses as well as wild cattle, pigs, and sheep. Gold and precious stones, especially rubies, are plentiful in the city of Pegu. Most of its gold supply is not from local deposits. In the mountains east of Arakan, at a place called "Capelan" in the vicinity of Ava, rubies, sapphires, and spinels are mined.[232] The principal product of the country is lac, a resin which is produced by a tiny ant that lives there.[233] Many junks are constructed in the port of Rangoon because of the availability of wood.[234] The chief exports of Pegu are rice and lac, though it seems also to have had a reputation for preparing and selling loaf sugar.[235] Cane sugar is grown in many places, but is mostly consumed domestically where it is used in cane form as food for humans and elephants and as outer coverings for temples and *pagodes* of earthen construction to protect them from the rains.[236] Musk from the civet cat is sent into Pegu from Ava. Martaban is renowned in trading circles for its glazed earthenware jars in which fruits, spices, water, and liquors are preserved and transported.[237]

On the political divisions of what we call Burma today, the European writers reflect in their narratives the changing conditions of the sixteenth century. Naturally the earlier authors know much more about Arakan and Pegu than the interior states. Barbosa, however, begins his account with a brief description of "Berma" (Toungoo) even though he admits that he really knows very little about it since "there is no means of sailing thither."[238] He reports on "the city and kingdom of Ava" in eastern Burma, particularly with reference to its precious stones and musk. Martaban he also treats separately but without

---

[231] Pires in Cortesão (trans. and ed.), *op. cit.* (n. 46), I, 97.

[232] References to these mountains occur repeatedly beginning with Varthema. It is hard to know precisely what is meant by these vague indications, for the real location of ruby production today is about seventy miles northeast of Mandalay. See Yule and Burnell, *op. cit.* (n. 218), pp. 121–22. The mines are actually large, open pits from which the "ruby-earth" is taken and the stones washed out. Spinels and sapphires are found along with the rubies. These stones and musk were apparently monopolized by the king of Ava for sale to foreigners until the king lost the mines to Pegu (Barbosa in Dames [ed.], *op. cit.* [n. 77], II, 159–60).

[233] For references to lac in a host of Portuguese authors see Dalgado, *op. cit.* (n. 53), I, 501–2. Lac is actually the coloring matter exuded from the female of a scale insect (*Coccus lacca*) and is found as a resinous incrustation on the twigs and young branches of various kinds of trees. See Yule and Burnell, *op. cit.* (n. 218), pp. 380–81. Lac is the principal ingredient in sealing wax, the base of some varnishes, and a valuable dye. The sixteenth-century writers are not always clear or in agreement on the details of lac production.

[234] Pires in Cortesão (trans. and ed.), *op. cit.* (n. 46), I, 98.

[235] Barbosa in Dames (ed.), *op. cit.* (n. 77), II, 153; ". . . for the sugar cane is cultivated to the north of Ava . . . and a very coarse article extracted from it, and made into flat cakes." See John Jardine (ed.), *The Burmese Empire a Hundred Years Ago as Described by Father Sangermano* (Westminster, 1893), p. 192.

[236] See Fedrici in Purchas (ed.), *op. cit.* (n. 16), X, 133.

[237] Martaban jars were used on Portuguese ships to carry water, oil, and wine. Evidently the jars were also imported for domestic use in Portugal. See Linschoten in Burnell and Tiele (eds.), *op. cit.* (n. 25), I, 101.

[238] Barbosa in Dames (ed.), *op. cit.* (n. 77), II, 149.

indicating whether or not it is politically a part of his Pegu.[239] Barros brings out clearly that the divided condition of Burma underwent changes shortly after the Portuguese began to trade at Martaban in 1519 and after both Pires and Barbosa wrote their accounts. He tells about the wars between the "Bramás" (Burmans) of "Tanga" (Toungoo) and the incumbent ruling house of Pegu. He explains that even with Portuguese assistance the Mon forces were finally not able to repel the "Bramás" and that the city and dynasty fell in the face of their onslaughts. In Barros' narrative, the king of Toungoo, Tabinshwehti (reigned 1531–50), is classified as being originally a vassal of the Wareru king. In 1539, the vassal revolted against his overlord, occupied the city of Pegu, killed off its leading officials, and made it his own capital. This ambitious usurper then extended his conquests to "Prom" (Prome), "Melitai" (unidentified), "Chalão" (Chalang?), "Bacão" (Bassein), "Mirandu" (unidentified), and "Avá" (Ava). After all these victories, the rebel ruler sought to extend his conquests into Siam. But events turned against him, particularly as he lost many men in his early campaigns while traversing the mountainous, wooded terrain between his kingdom and Siam. He returned to Pegu defeated in his efforts to take Ayut'ia, but still in control of all Burma except Arakan.[240] It is for this reason that the later European writers, such as Linschoten,[241] refer only to Arakan and Pegu in their discussions of Burma. In fact, it was during the mid-century wars between Pegu and Siam that Arakan began to be much more closely associated with the Portuguese, as its rulers derived great revenues from the traders at Chittagōng, and began to act more independently. Still, when the Europeans write about Burma, they refer primarily to conditions in Pegu and lower Burma.

Cesare Fedrici, the trading prospector from Venice, visited Pegu in 1569 and set down for posterity his impressions of the royal city after its conquest by the Toungoos. He describes it as being two cities, one old and one new. In the old city the marts stand where both foreign and native merchants do their trading and where they have a central warehouse made of brick.[242] The new city, which was just being completed in 1569, is described as the administrative center of the kingdom; the royal palace and the residences of the nobles are built therein. While the old city is spread out over a great area, the new metropolis is depicted as a city planner's dream:

It is a great Citie, very plaine and flat, and foure square, walled round about, and with Ditches that compasse the Walls about with water, in which Ditches are many Crocodiles. It hath no Drawbridges, yet it hath twenty Gates, five for every square on the Walls, there

---

239 *Ibid.*, pp. 157–59; Pires divides his account into just three parts: Arakan, Pegu, and Burma.

240 Cidade and Múrias (eds.), *op. cit.* (n. 39), III, 129. He nowhere mentions the name of Tabin-shwehti, whom he considers a rebel. On wars against Ayut'ia cf. above, p. 533.

241 Burnell and Tiele (eds.), *op. cit.* (n. 25), I, 97.

242 An eighteenth-century author, Sangermano, describing the cane and wood houses of the Burmese, remarks that it was then unlawful for the natives to use bricks. "Such few brick buildings as do exist," he asserts, "are used more as magazines than as dwelling-houses." See Jardine (ed.), *op. cit.* (n. 235), p. 162.

are many places made for Centinels to watch, made of Wood and covered or gilt with Gold, the Streets thereof are the fairest that I have seene, they are as straight as a line from one Gate to another, . . . and they are as broad as ten or twenty men may ride abreast in them: and these streets that be thwart are faire and large, these streets, both on the one side and the other, are planted at the doores of the Houses with Nut trees of India, which make a very commodious shadow, the House be made of wood, and covered with a kind of tiles in forme of Cups, very necessary for their use: the King's Palace is in the middle of the Citie, made in forme of a walled Castle, with ditches full of water round about it, the Lodgings within are made of wood all over gilded, with fine pinacles and very costly worke, covered with plates of gold.[243]

While Balbi's account follows this description in general, he places the royal palace and the residences of the nobles in the old city. Fitch, who obviously relies on Fedrici's description of Pegu, likewise puts the court establishments in the new city.[244] The travelers' descriptions of Pegu have particular importance, because it was systematically destroyed in 1600 by the Arakanese and the Siamese. The Jesuits have left some vivid word pictures of the misery which swept the delta in the wake of these invasions.[245] Again destroyed in the eighteenth century, modern Pegu still retains traces of the old walls and moats, and the remains of the great pagodas and images, which graced the city during its golden age.[246]

The travelers of the late sixteenth century likewise comment on the leading features of some of the other delta towns. "Cosmin" (Bassein) still appears to be the port of Pegu[247] most generally entered by those coming from Bengal. It takes ten days to sail through the waters of the delta from the bar at Cape Negrais to Pegu and three days from the bar to "Cosmin" (Bassein).[248] On both sides of the waterways the banks are lined "with many great Villages which they call Cities."[249] On these inland creeks many entire families live and earn their livings on boats. The territory around "Cosmin," according to Balbi, is heavily wooded and frequented by hordes of wild animals; the people of the town itself are not safe at night from attacks by tigers.[250] For fear of the tigers their houses are built on stilts and are entered from the ground by long ladders. Still the town is attractive and the surrounding countryside produces an abundant supply of fruit.[251] At Dalla there are large stables and training grounds for the royal elephants, since they catch many of the huge creatures in this part of the delta.[252] "Dagon" (Rangoon), the main port of Pegu, is compared to

---

[243] Translation from Purchas (ed.), *op. cit.* (n. 16), X, 120–21.

[244] *Ibid.*, p. 157.

[245] Letters of Pimenta and Boves as reprinted in *ibid.*, pp. 211, 216.

[246] See John Murray (pub.), *A Handbook for Travellers in India and Pakistan, Burma and Ceylon* (London, 1949), pp. 691–92.

[247] Purchas (ed.), *op. cit.* (n. 16), X, 129–30.

[248] *Ibid.*, p. 185.

[249] *Ibid.*, p. 130.

[250] *Ibid.*, p. 152.

[251] Fitch in *ibid.*, p. 185.

[252] Balbi in *ibid.*, p. 153; Fitch in *ibid.*, p. 186.

Venice in some detail by Balbi;[253] its great staircases, tiger statues, temples and monasteries, open squares, huge bell, crowded marketplaces and a pagoda almost as high as the campanile of St. Mark all remind the lonely Venetian of similar sights in his native city. At Syriam, a smaller port where the tidal waves (*Maccareo*) make the harbor dangerous, ships are to be seen from Mecca, Malacca, and Sumatra. Here, Balbi reports,[254] stand ruined walls and bulwarks which were destroyed in 1567 when Pegu invaded the city and subjected it to vassalage. The point of debarkation for the boats which ply the network of creeks from Bassein eastward is apparently at "Meccao" (unidentified).[255] Here the merchants load their wares into carts and wagons and get themselves into "delings" (hammocks)[256] for the overland trek to Pegu.

Pires and Fedrici both give excellent accounts of trading conditions in Pegu, though one is describing the situation while the country was still under its Mon rulers and the other relates the practices followed under the Toungoo dynasty. In the early sixteenth century each of the three major ports is administered by a "toledam" (governor), the chief of these being the governor of "Dagon" (Rangoon).[257] Import duties amount to 12 per cent, but if any extraordinary difficulty arises a present to the "toledam" evidently helps to clear it up.[258] The currency of Pegu is coins of copper, tin, and lead as well as small white cowries.[259] Gold has the same value in Pegu as it has in Malacca, and a great deal of silver is shipped from Pegu to Bengal because it is worth somewhat more there. Each year one ship from Gujarat sails to the ports of Martaban and Rangoon to exchange opium and cloth for the lac, precious stones, and silver available in Pegu. It should be remembered that when Pires wrote, the Portuguese had not yet established regular trading relations with Pegu, and so he must have received most of his information from the merchants doing business at Malacca.

Fedrici[260] advises his readers that the best commodities to sell in Pegu are the colorful textiles and yarns of St. Thomas (or Mylapore), the finer cloths of Bengal, opium from Cambay, and pepper from Sumatra. The larger vessels in his time apparently dock at "Cosmin" (Bassein) and the smaller ones at Martaban. Once the cargo is unloaded, the royal officials take responsibility for conveying it to the custom house in Pegu. The merchants receive permits from

[253] *Ibid.*, pp. 153–54. Strangely enough, neither Fedrici nor Fitch has anything to say about "Dagon."

[254] *Ibid.*, pp. 155–56.

[255] Sometimes written "Macao" or "Maccao"; see Yule and Burnell, *op. cit.* (n. 218), p. 402. On the 1692 map of Asia by Sanson, cartographer to King Louis XIV, a city named "Macaon" is shown on the coast on the southeast side of the Irrawaddy basin.

[256] Derivation of word not known; it is possibly Persian. See *ibid.*, pp. 234–35.

[257] Pires in Cortesão (trans. and ed.), *op. cit.* (n. 46), I, 97–98.

[258] *Ibid.*, p. 99.

[259] Actually Pires (*ibid.*, p. 100) says that cowries were accepted only at Martaban and Arakan and that about 15,000 equaled one *viss* (the standard weight) in value. Contrast this to the flat statement by D. G. E. Hall that cowrie shells "were never in use in Burma" (in Philips [ed.], *op. cit.* [n. 139], p. 115).

[260] Purchas (ed.), *op. cit.* (n. 16), X, 127–28.

the port authorities to proceed by themselves to Pegu. The customs inspection is very rigorous, and the officials watch especially for those who try to smuggle diamonds, pearls, and fine textiles into the country. Once he and his wares have cleared the customs, the foreign trader ordinarily rents a house on a six months' lease to which he takes his merchandise. Sales are made through eight royal brokers called "tareghe" [261] who receive a commission of 2 per cent for their services. The broker assigned to a given merchant possesses exclusive rights of sale and gets his percentage whether or not he personally makes the sale. All goods are sold at the market price and the broker guarantees payment to the merchant if he, rather than the merchant, actually makes the sale. Private transactions are apparently possible; on a sale made directly by the merchant the broker still gets his fee and he is relieved of responsibility for guaranteeing payment. It is rare that merchandise is not paid for because the creditor has the right to imprison the debtor. Should payment still not be forthcoming, the creditor then has the right to sell the wives, children, and slaves of the individual in default.

The only monies officially accepted in Pegu are copper and lead coins called "ganza." [262] The king does not mint them and every person has the right to make his own. Consequently, the foreign merchant is warned to be cautious about those which have too much lead in them to be acceptable. The wary merchant will see to it that the coins are weighed at each transaction by a public assayer to determine their worth in terms of "byze" (*viss*). The assayer guarantees the value of the money which he has weighed by placing it into a sack to which he attaches his seal. For this service the merchant has to pay a regular monthly fee. While the heaviness of the money makes large transactions awkward, there is no question about its acceptability as payment for valuable purchases of gold, silver, rubies, lac, and rice.[263] Gold and silver may not be used as mediums of exchange.

Those who go to Pegu with the specific intention of buying jewels should plan to stay a full year in order to buy most advantageously during the off-seasons for trade. A plentiful supply of rubies and other jewels is marketed through brokers who administer the royal monopoly of the precious stones. The foreign merchant, even those who have no professional knowledge of gems, need not hesitate to approach one of these jewel brokers. They are so determined to protect their reputations and the lucrative jewel trade of Pegu that they will go out of their way to treat prospective buyers fairly. The buyer

[261] Probably derived from the Telugu word, *taraga* (broker). See Yule and Burnell, *op. cit.* (n. 218), p. 685. Cf. the *Cohong* at Canton. The brokerage practices described here remained in force long after the British occupation of Burma in the nineteenth century. See Hall, *op. cit.* (n. 18), p. 18.

[262] Malay, *Gangsa* meaning "bell-metal." See Yule and Burnell, *op. cit.* (n. 218), p. 278. Pires (in Cortesão [trans. and ed.], *op. cit.* [n. 46], I 99) remarks that the "Ganza" of Martaban are the most widely circulated coins.

[263] Fedrici in Purchas (ed.), *op. cit.* (n. 16), X, 131–33; cf. the statement in Harvey, *op. cit.* (n. 191), p. 122: "There was no coinage, but goods were sometimes weighed against *ganza*, an alloy of lead and brass which passed as currency either in odd lumps or in bars of specified weight stamped by merchants of repute but usually false."

may take the rubies on approval for several days and have them appraised by disinterested parties. Still, when it comes to concluding a bargain, it is better for the buyer "to have knowledge in jewels, by reason that it may ease the price." [264] In settling on a price, the broker and the merchant do their bargaining by touching hands under a cloth. The object in this method of bargaining is to keep the onlookers from knowing what is being asked and bid, and what price is finally agreed upon.

The kings of Pegu, whether Wareru or Toungoo, excite the interest and admiration of the European travelers. Varthema, who visited there around 1505, concludes that Binnyaran II, the Wareru king, though rich, powerful, and generous, does not enjoy "as great a reputation as the King of Calicut." [265] In Varthema's eyes he looks and acts like an oriental potentate for he wears rubies on his toes, gold bracelets on his arms and legs, and has a startling propensity for giving lavish gifts. A war was in progress between Pegu and Ava when Varthema was there, but Binnyaran still took time to give an audience to the Italian merchant, and to accept his strange gift of branches of coral. Pires reports that the king is always in residence in the city of Pegu and that he possesses large numbers of elephants. The king's chief adviser is called the "cobrai," who is "the captain and governor of the kingdom." [266] Subordinate to the "cobrai" are, in order of prestige, the "toledams" (governors) of Rangoon, Martaban, and "Cosmin." Barbosa testifies that Binnyaran is known as "the King of the White Elephant." [267] Castanheda observes that when the king and his sons travel about the city they are carried in splendid litters and followed by a vast multitude on foot. When the king and his court attend a boat festival, they watch the gay processions and races from a building in the middle of the river where the judging is done and the prizes awarded. Binnyaran is devoted to the hunt, especially for elephants, and reputedly is seldom at war with his neighbors. The chief lord of Pegu, presumably Pires' "cobrai," acts as godfather to the crown prince, and the chief lord's wife performs as his nurse. The purpose of this arrangement is to keep the chief lord from trying to usurp the throne when the prince becomes king. While the king is constantly surrounded by nobles, he is particularly inclined to trust eunuchs from Bengal, who, consequently, often rise to high positions of power and influence. [268]

Barros, as discussed earlier, [269] describes the overthrow of the Wareru dynasty of Pegu by the political machinations and military activities of Tabinshwehti, the ruler of Toungoo, and the establishment in 1539 of Tabinshwehti's capital at Pegu. It must therefore be remembered that the Europeans who write about the "kings of Pegu" on the basis of visits or reports made in the latter half of

---

[264] Fedrici in Purchas (ed.), *op. cit.* (n. 16), X, 135.
[265] Temple (ed.), *op. cit.* (n. 5), pp. 81–3.
[266] Cortesão (trans. and ed.), *op. cit.* (n. 46), I, 101.
[267] Dames (ed.), *op. cit.* (n. 77), II, 154–55.
[268] Azevedo (ed.), *op. cit.* (n. 79), III, 19–20. On eunuchs in Bengal see above, p. 416. Castanheda also observes that foreigners are not permitted to ride in litters without royal permission.
[269] Cf. above, p. 543.

the century are actually referring to rulers of the Toungoo dynasty. Fedrici visited Pegu on three different occasions between 1566 and 1578 in the time of Bayin Naung (reigned 1551–81), brother-in-law and successor of Tabinshwehti. Aside from describing the placement of the king's palace in the new city,[270] Fedrici reports that within the royal enclosure four rare white elephants are kept. The foreign merchants are apparently required to pay a fee to help maintain the elephants, and, whether they cared to or not, the king commands that they view the elephants in their stalls at a designated visiting time. The king holds these white elephants in such high esteem that he would risk his whole kingdom to acquire any which might be held by another monarch.[271] Bayin Naung allegedly possesses four thousand mature elephants who are trained for battle. Not far from the city itself he has a hunting palace which is located in a great forest. Fedrici then describes at some length how the huntsmen use female elephants to lure the wild bull elephants into the palace enclosure. Once the captive elephants are tamed, they are trained to fight and to carry "on their backes a Castle of wood" with four armed soldiers in it.[272]

Bayin Naung has no naval establishment but his land force and wealth are so great that he "farre exceds the power of the great Turks. . . ."[273] He is reported to have twenty-six crowned kings as his vassals,[274] and an army of 1,500,000 men at his command.[275] It is possible for this huge army to live off the land because the soldiers will eat anything from which they are able to get nutrition. The army is divided into corps of elephant and horse cavalry, as well as infantry units of riflemen and pikemen. Except for rifles and ordnance, the armor and weapons are inferior. The riflemen are good marksmen, because they are required to practice shooting every day. Nor does the king want for wealth. He has numerous warehouses full of gold and silver and this treasure is constantly being augmented. He also possesses a monopoly of the rubies and other precious stones.[276] Near to the royal palace is a large court enclosing four gilded houses each of which contains numerous statues of fabulous value. When the wealthy potentate travels in procession through the city, he rides in a high, gilded coach covered by a canopy and pulled by sixteen horses. He has one principal wife and three hundred concubines by whom he reportedly has ninety children.[277]

[270] Cf. above, p. 543.

[271] Without doubt a reference to the war which Bayin Naung fought against Ayut'ia in 1563–64, allegedly over white elephants. See Harvey, *op. cit.* (n. 191), pp. 167–68. This was essentially a ceremonial gesture, like the solemn throwing down of the gauntlet in Europe, rather than the reason for war. See Hall, *op. cit.* (n. 30), p. 214.

[272] Fedrici in Purchas (ed.), *op. cit.* (n. 16), X, 121–24. [273] *Ibid.*, p. 125.

[274] Actually he governed only Pegu and the Talaing country himself. Vassal kings ruled at Toungoo, Prome, Ava, and Chiengmai. The "twenty-six crowned heads" probably refer to the *sawbwas*, or the Shan chieftains. Guzman (*op. cit.* [n. 44], I, 171–73) comments on Bayin Naung's conquests and lists twelve kingdoms which fell victim to him.

[275] This is a conceivable number because all Burmese as slaves of the ruler were liable to military service whenever needed. See Jardine (ed.), *op. cit.* (n. 235), p. 97.

[276] For confirmation see Sangermano in Jardine (ed.), *op. cit.* (n. 235), p. 91.

[277] Fedrici in Purchas (ed.), *op. cit.* (n. 16), X, 125–26.

In a great hall Bayin Naung holds court every day in the presence of his lords to hear the supplications of his subjects.[278] The king sits on a high seat, his lords at a lower level, and the supplicants on the ground forty paces from the king. All supplicants, no matter what their rank or status, are equally entitled to a royal audience. It is required, however, that they appear in court with their petitions written out on a palm leaf. They are also expected to bring a present, the value of which should correspond to the importance of the matter in question. The royal secretaries take the written petitions before the king and read them to him each in turn. If the king favors a petition, the supplicant is asked to turn his present over to the secretary. If the king disallows a petition, the supplicant is commanded to leave the royal presence and take his gift with him.[279]

Balbi and Fitch were both in Pegu in the middle of the 1580's during Nanda Bayin's reign (1581–99). Though both copied from Fedrici some of their general comments about conditions in Pegu, they have statements to make about its ruler which are independent and different. Nonetheless, Fitch's dependence upon Fedrici ensnares him into giving a misleading account of the Pegu which he actually visited. For, the reign of Nanda Bayin, in contrast to that of his father, was not one of glory and splendor but rather of defeat and decline. Balbi's account agrees far more with the other sources on this reign. Of particular interest is the Venetian's audience with Nanda Bayin in 1583. Balbi, with his "nagirano" (interpreter), entered the courtyard to the sound of trumpets, knelt, bowed, and kissed the earth three times in front of the king and his "semini" (lords)[280] and displayed some valuable emeralds which he had brought to Pegu for the king's inspection. Evidently pleased with the emeralds, the king asked Balbi's name, nationality, how long ago he had left his native country, and where he had gotten the emeralds. Upon learning that both Balbi and the emeralds had come from Venice, he asked about its location and king. When told that Venice was a republic and had no king, the Burmese ruler was so astounded and amused that he laughed until he became speechless. After recovering himself, Nanda Bayin inquired about the strength and military capabilities of Venice. Balbi assured him that Philip II, the most powerful ruler in Christendom, was an ally of Venice, and that his native city feared nobody and sought friendship with all. In addition to issuing an order to his "Terreca" (treasury) to pay for the emeralds, the king gave him some presents and commanded that the "decacini" (customs) should not make Balbi pay duty.[281]

From Balbi's account it can be gathered that the military might of Nanda Bayin seems less impressive than his father's. In contrast to the four thousand

---

[278] This is a reference to the tribunal called the *Hlut-daw*, the high court and council of the Burmese monarchy. See Jardine (ed.), *op. cit.* (n. 235), p. 81n.

[279] *Ibid.*, pp. 126–27.

[280] From *smim*, the Talaing word for lord. Harvey, *op. cit.* (n. 191), p. 178.

[281] Purchas (ed.), *op. cit.* (n. 16), X, 157–59.

elephants reportedly owned by his father, Nanda Bayin is said to have just eight hundred battle elephants. Though he has much artillery available, he lacks gunners who can handle it properly. Furthermore, in 1583, he was having deep trouble with the ruler of Ava who refused at the time of his coronation to pay homage or recognize his suzerainty. Trade relations between Ava and Pegu were also halted as tension between the two states mounted. Suspecting that some of his own lords were conspiring with the king of Ava against him, Nanda Bayin issued an *ola* (a palm-leaf mandate) commanding that the alleged plotters and their families should be burned in a great public execution. Balbi describes with horror this mass execution of four thousand men, women, and children. Then the king quickly got together an army of three hundred thousand persons and threw up an encampment outside of the city. After surviving an attack of the smallpox, Nanda Bayin moved against Ava. When their forces met, the two rulers engaged in personal combat and the king of Pegu after a bitter struggle finally killed his opponent.[282] Upon the death of its king, the army of Ava was defeated, the city razed, and its inhabitants forced to flee in all directions. Hardly had Nanda Bayin returned to Pegu when the king of Ayut'ia raised the standard of revolt by letting him know that he would no longer be a vassal.[283] Even in Pegu itself, fires suspiciously broke out which destroyed many houses. While the king sought out his enemies ruthlessly, the crown prince prevailed upon him to moderate his wrath. From his vivid depiction of these troubles, it can readily be seen that all was far from serene in Burma when Balbi was there (1583–86).[284]

To Arakan,[285] the only Burmese state to resist Pegu effectively throughout the century, scattered references appear frequently in the European sources. Conti disembarked at Arakan in the early fifteenth century and made his way overland to Ava. João de Silveira is the first Portuguese known to have gone into Arakan, and he arrived there in 1518. Subsequently, other Portuguese halted periodically along its coast to conduct trade, but not much business was carried on there since Chittagōng and Pegu were much greater marts. Portuguese often attacked the coastal towns of Arakan in reprisal to the raids which Arakanese pirates periodically made upon their ships going to the Ganges delta. European freebooters likewise descended upon its isolated, scattered, and lightly defended ports to pillage them. In the latter half of the sixteenth century the Arakanese and the Portuguese at Chittagōng established a working alliance which enabled both of them to defy the Mughuls of Bengal and the Toungoos of Pegu. This co-operation enabled Arakan to tighten its control over Chittagōng, which it had claimed as a vassal state since 1459, and to expand southeastward

---

[282] Apparently he was not actually killed on the spot, but died shortly thereafter while trying to rally his followers. See Harvey, *op. cit.* (n. 191), p. 180.

[283] Cf. above, pp. 535–36.

[284] Purchas (ed.), *op. cit.* (n. 16), X, 159–64. For a few additional remarks see the letter of Friar Peter of Lisbon (December 28, 1589) written from Cochin to Lisbon about his experiences in Pegu during 1586–87 (Hakluyt, *op. cit.* [n. 114], VI, 385–87).

[285] Portuguese variation, probably through Malay, of *Rakhaing*, the name used by the Arakanese.

against Pegu. It was the king of Arakan, Minyasagyi (reigned 1593–1612), who co-operated with Felipe de Brito in occupying, burning, and depopulating Pegu in 1599–1600.[286]

Barbosa has some interesting information about Arakan during the reign of Minyaza (1501–23), one of the kings of the Myohaung dynasty.[287] He reports that there are twelve cities of consequence in the kingdom, each of which is ruled over by a governor. Every year twelve newly born girls, "daughters of the noblest and fairest women that can be found," are selected by the governors of each of the twelve cities to be brought up at the royal expense in a local palace maintained by the king. These girls are reared in luxury and taught to dance and sing. Each year twelve of those who have become twelve years of age are sent to the king at Myohaung. Here each is clothed in a white robe inscribed with her name. On the day of the girls' interview with the king they sit in the sun from early in the morning to noon until they get so warm that their white robes are wet with perspiration. They are then brought into a hall where the king is seated with the leading lords of the realm. Their wet robes are removed and given to the king who smells them each in turn. A robe which has an unsatisfactory scent is handed over to a lord of the realm along with the maiden whose name is written on it. The king keeps for himself those robes and girls whose scent meets with his approval. Thus, each year the king selects by smell those from a group of twelve maidens who will be added to his harem.[288] This king is, of course, wealthy and a devotee of pleasure.

Far more prosaic are the accounts given in Castanheda and Barros about the visits of João de Silveira to Arakan in 1517–18.[289] On his way to Chittagōng from Ceylon, Silveira made a brief stopover in the estuary of Arakan, thirty-five leagues (140 miles) south of Chittagōng. At this time Arakan was in vassalage to Bengal and so the governor ("lascar") of Chittagōng was a Bengali rather than a dependent of the king of Arakan. Because his reception in Chittagōng was far from friendly, Silveira blockaded the port. But finally discouraged, he returned to the delta of the "river of Arakan" and conducted negotiations there. The king, whose capital was at Myohaung about fifteen leagues (60 miles) upriver[290] from the estuary, sent an emissary to Silveira with friendly greetings, a ruby ring, and an invitation to visit the capital. Though the royal messenger tried to reassure Silveira that he would be received amicably, his experience at

---

[286] Harvey, *op. cit.* (n. 191), pp. 137–41; 183.

[287] Dames (ed.), *op. cit.* (n. 77), II, 151–52.

[288] That palace women were selected by smell does not appear in the other sources. It may well be one of those apocryphal stories told by sailors about little known places. The repetition of the mystical number "twelve" also seems to strengthen the case for its being a tall tale. For analogous examples see John W. Spellman, "The Symbolic Significance of the Number Twelve in Ancient India," *Journal of Asian Studies*, XXII (1962), 79–88.

[289] Azevedo (ed.), *op. cit.* (n. 79), II, 445–47; Cidade and Múrias (eds.), *op. cit.* (n. 39), III, 71–72.

[290] Barros in Cidade and Múrias (eds.), *op. cit.*, p. 71; actually the modern town of Myohaung is fifty miles up the Kaladan and Lemro rivers, and it is serviced by the port of Akyab. The fact that the capital was so far upriver probably accounts for Barbosa's assertion that Arakan had no port.

Chittagōng apparently made him suspicious of treachery. After proceeding upriver a few miles, the Portuguese captain decided to abandon the project and turned his ships around and set sail for Ceylon. For a long time thereafter, the Portuguese officially expressed the feeling that the Arakanese are false and perfidious, and that they should have little to do with them.

Fedrici,[291] who writes about Arakan from what he heard in Chittagōng, reports that in 1569 an Arakanese messenger was sent to the Portuguese captain in Chittagōng proffering friendship and inviting him to visit the capital of King Minsetya (reigned 1564–71). It is in this period that the Portuguese begin to combine forces with the seagoing Arakanese against Pegu and Bengal. Fedrici affirms that the ruler of Pegu is determined to subject Arakan to vassalage, but that he has no naval force with which to do it. The Arakanese, who are able to equip for war as many as two hundred vessels, clearly can defend themselves against an attack by sea. A land attack by Pegu is made precarious by the rugged terrain of the Arakan Yoma and by the sluices and moats protecting the city of Myohaung. Fitch, who traveled in eastern Bengal reports that the "Mogen" (Mugs)[292] of "Recon" (Arakan) are constantly at war with "Tippara" (Tippera) and that Chittagōng is frequently under the control of Arakan.[293] At this period (1580's) it is most likely true, as it was not when the Portuguese first arrived there, that Chittagōng was governed by a brother or clansman of the king of Arakan.[294]

The people of Burma are generally characterized as being tawny, stocky, and good-looking. The women are lighter in color than the men and possess beautiful figures. In shape, manners, and features both sexes resemble the Chinese; in color they are lighter than the Bengalis and darker than the Chinese. Among their qualities most frequently referred to are industriousness, honesty, peacefulness, and timidity in war. Those Peguans whom Pires saw in Malacca wear white cloths around their loins. The men gather the hair on the tops of their heads and tie it into place with a white piece of cloth. Their teeth are black from chewing betel. The women of Pegu wear their hair following the Chinese fashion in a roll on the top of the head held together with golden pins. Linschoten includes pictures of Peguans in his work.[295]

Many of the European authors (Castanheda is a notable exception) comment censoriously on Peguan customs. Although they are judged to be civilized in most ways, a number of the Europeans recoil in horror from their willingness

[291] Purchas (ed.), *op. cit.* (n. 16), X, 138.

[292] A name commonly used by foreigners to refer to the natives of Arakan, particularly those who live on the borders of Bengal and in Chittagōng. See Yule and Burnell, *op. cit.* (n. 218), pp. 455–56.

[293] Purchas (ed.), *op. cit.* (n. 16), X, 183.

[294] Harvey, *op. cit.* (n. 191), p. 141.

[295] Based largely on the descriptions by Castanheda (in Azevedo [ed.], *op. cit.* [n. 79], III, 16), Pires (in Cortesão [trans. and ed.], *op. cit.* [n. 46], I, 102–03), and Linschoten (in Burnell and Tiele [eds.], *op. cit.* [n. 25], I, 101). For a characterization written almost three hundred years later by Sangermano see Jardine (ed.), *op. cit.* (n. 191), p. 157. Sangermano's description of physical features and dress agrees generally with the above, but his estimate of Burmese character is far lower.

to eat anything, including scorpions, serpents, and grass.[296] The men of Pegu, according to their wealth and social position, are reported by many of the sixteenth-century writers to insert little round bells into their sexual organ in the flesh of the foreskin. These bells, which are described as being the size of acorns or small plums, are made of gold, silver, or lead and the more expensive golden ones are said to have delightful "treble, contralto, and tenor tones." The men of Pegu, Pires reports, are very popular with the ladies of Malacca, "the reason for this must be their sweet harmony." [297] The bells are reportedly the invention of an early Burmese queen who wanted to enlarge the male sexual organ for the greater gratification of women and to break the Burmese men of their addiction to sodomy.[298] Barros, who cautiously admits that he is writing on the basis of what he has heard about local lore, links the introduction of these strange sexual practices in an unclear manner to a traditional story still current in the East, which alleges that the people of Pegu are descended from the marriage of a woman with a dog. This purportedly dates back to a time when a Chinese junk was shipwrecked on the coast and the sole survivors were a Chinese woman and a dog.[299] Skeptical of this story himself, Barros gives an alternative explanation which is equally fanciful, though based on European traditions, to the effect that the Burmese are the descendants of expatriates from the Judea of King Solomon who fled eastward in search of the mythical kingdom of Ophir.[300] The only part of the native tradition which accords with modern

[296] See especially Fedrici in Purchas, *op. cit.* (n. 16), X, 125; Sangermano also writes (Jardine [ed.], *op. cit.* [n. 235], p. 159): "Every herb and the leaves of every tree, provided they are not positively venemous, are used in these [common curry] dishes; and the very richest kind is that which contains the flesh of some animal that has died."

[297] Cortesão (trans. and ed.), *op. cit.* (n. 46), I, 103.

[298] This report, so far as I can determine, first appears in Conti (Major, *op. cit.* [n. 31], Pt. IV, p. 11); Barbosa (in Dames [ed.], *op. cit.* [n. 77], II, 154) and Pires (in Cortesão [trans. and ed.], *op. cit.* [n. 46], I, 102) likewise write at some length about it. Pigafetta (in Robertson [ed.], *op. cit.* [n. 136], II, 169) dwells on it at even greater length but refers it to Java. Oviedo (D. José Amador de los Rios [ed.], *Historia general y natural de las Indias, islas y tierra-firme de mar oceano por . . . Gonzalo Fernandez de Oviedo de Valdes* [Madrid, 1852] Bk. XX, chap. xxxv, p. 105) writing on the basis of information given him by Urdaneta, refers it to Celebes. Barros (Cidade and Múrias [eds.], *op. cit.* [n. 39], III, 130) probably on the basis of Barbosa's and Pires' reports, likewise mentions it. Linschoten (Burnell and Tiele [eds.], *op. cit.* [n. 25], I, 99–100) tells the same story and reports that he brought one of the bells home as a souvenir for his collector-friend, Dr. Paludanus. Fitch, who traveled both in Burma and Siam, reports that this practice prevails among the men in both places (Purchas [ed.], *op. cit.* [n. 16], X, 196–97). Camoëns and Garcia de Resende, the Portuguese poets, allude to this custom in their famous works. Until about 1700 the European writers continue to comment on the prevalence of this custom in southeast Asia. Thereafter nothing is said about it, and no trace of the practice seems to remain today. There seems to be hardly any doubt that it once existed, but has now died out. Also see H. Yule, *A Narrative of the Mission . . . to the Court of Ava in 1855* (London, 1858), p. 208 n.

[299] Camoëns in the *Lusiads* (X, 122) writes in Burton's translation:

> "Arracan-realm behold, behold the seat
> of Pegu peoples by a monster-brood;
> monsters that gendered meeting most unmeet
> of whelp and woman in the lonely wood."

Professor C. C. Berg tells of having heard the same story himself in the twentieth century.

[300] Cidade and Múrias (eds.), *op. cit.* (n. 39), III, 130.

scholarly theory is the remote association of the early Burmese people with China.

The women of Burma reputedly go about in almost complete nudity to entice the men and to keep them away from homosexuals.[301] Some of the Burmese sew together the sexual organ of their female children and it remains that way until they are married.[302] Men of the upper classes often invite a friend or even a stranger to initiate their new wives into sexual activity. Merchants and other strangers who come to Pegu are given great hospitality. According to local custom, any visitor is said to have the right to choose one from a number of possible women to share his residence for the entire period of his stay in Pegu. He must, however, make a contract with her parents to pay for her, and must not see other women during the contract period. Once he leaves, the girl returns to her home and no stigma is attached to her name. She may thereafter marry without trouble into the best families in the land. Should the same merchant return and ask for her again, she is obliged to return to him and her husband is required to acquiesce. Since no shame is involved in this relationship for any of the parties concerned, she may without difficulty return to her husband after the merchant has departed.[303]

Even the urbane Barros (not to mention Maffei) is a bit shocked by the stories which come to his ears about the customs of Pegu. But he is willing to incorporate these "nefarious abuses" into the *Décadas* as an example of what can happen in the absence of Christian belief. In his words, these people have "always been heathens and therefore under the influence of the devil."[304] At the same time, the Portuguese official within Barros cannot help showing satisfaction that Pegu and the rest of continental southeast Asia have been so little infected by the virus of Islam. He is conscious that in religion (including temples, priests, and idols thereunder) the Peguan and the Siamese practices resemble each other.

In December, 1554, Pinto wrote from Malacca to the fathers of Portugal that the city of Pegu is the Rome of its area.[305] At the center of the city there is a huge temple (*varella*) covered with gold to which people make pilgrimages.[306] These heathens worship idols of various sizes, descriptions, and composition. Some are made of precious metals and "ganza"; some are of marvelous height and stand erect, while others are elaborately decorated but not so tall. Certain idols are designed to represent the supreme deity, while others are statues of saints. In every habitation of the kingdom there are local idols and pagodas, and then there are those which are as famous in Asia as the pyramids of Egypt are in Europe. At Martaban there is a fabulous reclining idol which lies in the

[301] Linschoten in Burnell and Tiele (eds.), *op. cit.* (n. 25), I, 100.

[302] Both Fedrici and Linschoten report this (*ibid.*, p. 100, n. 1) and apparently there is no doubt that this and similar practices were followed in a number of Eastern countries.

[303] *Ibid.*, pp. 98–99.

[304] Cidade and Múrias (eds.), *op. cit.* (n. 39), III, 130; also Maffei, *op. cit.* (n. 98), p. 288.

[305] Fernão Mendes Pinto to Fathers of Portugal (Malacca, December 5, 1554) in Wicki (ed.), *op. cit.* (n. 80), III, 140–55.

[306] Castanheda in Azevedo (ed.), *op. cit.* (n. 79), III, 17.

midst of forty-eight stone pillows and is called the "god of sleep."[307] At Pegu there is a gilded idol with a huge paunch who is the god of pregnant women and he is called "Quiai Colompon" (*Quiai* is the Mon word meaning "holy") which means, according to Pinto, the god of 104 gods. Near a town of which Castanheda does not know the name, there stands an important temple on a river bank close to the sea. This unnamed temple is served by fish who, it is said, never leave its vicinity. These fish are so tame, though they are of the size and appearance of sharks, that they will surface and open their mouths to be fed by any person who splashes his hand in the water and calls out a certain name.[308] Mariners who round Cape Negrais all look for a gilded pagoda which shines in the sun and can be seen for a long distance.[309] In "Degu" (Rangoon) a pagoda stands which is so tall that it can be seen from a large part of the kingdom and people from all over the land make pilgrimages to it on regular feast days.[310] Without question this is a reference to the majestic Shwe Dagon Pagoda about which Fitch admiringly writes: "It is the fairest place, as I suppose, that is in the world."[311] The travelers also estimate that Pegu would have plenty of gold for commerce, if so much of it were not used in gilding its innumerable pagodas, temples, and idols.

In the vicinity of the pagodas are places of worship dedicated to idols and set aside for prayer. Nearby monasteries, usually built as pious works by the original founders, are constructed of gilded wood. Other buildings serve as repositories for religious statues, one of them housing more than 120,000 images.[312] Some religious houses are reserved for women who spend their time in praying for the deceased donors of the monastic establishments. Priests, called "rolis,"[313] live cloistered lives in large monasteries which house three or four hundred men. Many of the religious establishments have large and small bells, some of the bells being larger than those at Santiago de Compostela in Galicia.[314] Some of the monasteries live on incomes left to them by their

[307] Letter from Malacca (1554) in Wicki (ed.), *op. cit.* (n. 80), III, 147–48. Pinto gives detail on a number of gods and holy places.

[308] Azevedo (ed.), *op. cit.* (n. 79), III, 20.

[309] Balbi in Purchas (ed.), *op. cit.* (n. 16), X, 150; this is the beautiful Hmawdin Pagoda which still stands as a landmark.

[310] Castanheda in Azevedo (ed.), *op. cit.* (n. 79), III, 17.

[311] Purchas (ed.), *op. cit.* (n. 16), X, 193; for a description of it see Murray (pub.), *op. cit.* (n. 246), pp. 648–87. It has remained unchanged in size, height, and shape since 1564.

[312] Castanheda in Azevedo (ed.), *op. cit.* (n. 79), III, 18. Pinto (in Wicki [ed.], *op. cit.* [n. 80], III, 148) mentions a shrine of 110,000 images.

[313] Castanheda in Azevedo (ed.), *op. cit.* (n. 79), p. 17. Often written "raulim" by other Portuguese authors. It is derived from the Pali and Burmese term, *rahan*, meaning "holy men." See Dalgado, *op. cit.* (n. 53), II, 251. The earliest reference to the "raulim" in a Jesuit letter is in one which was sent to Coimbra from Cochin in 1548 or 1549. The author received his information from a Portuguese who had twice visited Pegu. See Wicki (ed.), *op. cit.* (n. 80), I, 260. At this date there were also four students from Pegu in the College at Goa from whom the Jesuit writer also obtained information.

[314] Castanheda in Azevedo (ed.), *op. cit.* (n. 79), III, 17; Balbi (in Purchas [ed.], *op. cit.* [n. 16], X, 155) tells of a mammoth bell at Rangoon which had an inscription on it that nobody, not even the Peguans, could decipher. Such a bell with a Talaing inscription on it was possibly cast at the end of the thirteenth century. See Anon., "Talaing Inscription in a Bell Cast by Anauppet-lun Mrin," *Journal of the Burma Research Society*, XVIII (1928), 21.

founders; others are poor and their monks are forced to live from alms. The monks shave their heads and trim their beards by plucking hairs out of them. The *tallipoies* (mendicant priests)[315] are said by Fitch to be of lower rank than the "rolis."[316] Their dress consists of a brown cloth next to the body and an outer garment of yellow, both of which hang down one shoulder and are bound about them with a broad girdle. Around their necks suspended on a string they carry a piece of leather which they use to sit on. They wear no shoes or head covering, but carry a sombrero to protect themselves from the sun and rain.[317]

To prepare for the priesthood, youths attend school until they are twenty years of age or more. Once their education is complete, they are taken before a "roli" who examines them many times and determines if they are serious about renouncing their friends, the company of women, and are ready to assume the garb of a "tallipoie." The "roli" being satisfied, the novice broadcasts his intention of renouncing the world by donning rich apparel and riding through the streets on a horse accompanied by pipers and drummers.[318] A few days later, he puts on the yellow garment of the "tallipoie" and is carried through the streets in a litter procession to a tiny abode along the highway outside the city. There he takes up his begging vessel to go out and find his food. He is not permitted to ask for anything, but must live entirely upon what the people voluntarily hand out to him. Each time the new moon rises the people send rice and other provisions to the *kiack* (holy place) where the *tallipoies* assemble to have a feast.[319] They fast for thirty days each year.[320] The only public services which they hold are sermons at which they preach against all abuses. Many people throng to hear them. Before entering the temple, the people wash their feet. Once inside, they raise their hands up to their heads as a salute first to the priest or priests and then to the sun. Thereafter they sit down with the others. The priest or priests are seated on their leather pads. These priests also assist in the ceremonies attending illness, marriage, and death.

The priests of Burma also participate in political ceremonies. Though Barros seems to be the first to mention the following episode, the fullest description of it is in Maffei's work.[321] When, in 1519, Antonio Corrêa concluded at

---

[315] A word of obscure origin, but it seems to be a Burmese appellation for the priests of Talaing (the Mon people of lower Burma). See Dalgado, *op. cit.* (n. 53), II, 341–43.

[316] Purchas (ed.), *op. cit.* (n. 16), X, 193.

[317] By sombrero, Fitch (*ibid.*) is probably referring to the palm-leaf fan which the priests are obliged to carry when out-of-doors. For a more detailed and comprehensible description by Sangermano see Jardine (ed.), *op. cit.* (n. 235), p. 114.

[318] Fitch in Purchas (ed.), *op. cit.* (n. 16), X, 193; almost the same description is given by Sangermano in Jardine (ed.), *op. cit.* (n. 235), p. 121.

[319] Fitch in Purchas (ed.), *op. cit.* (n. 16), X, 194. Actually they have festivals at the time of the full moon and fifteen days thereafter. See Jardine (ed.), *op. cit.* (n. 191), p. 118. Pinto (in Silva Rego [ed.], *op. cit.* [n. 179], V, 368) mentions a festival called "talanos" which is held for the seriously ill. *Kiack* is the Talaing word which means the Buddha's place of residence. See R. H., "Talaing Place-Names in Burmese," *Journal of the Burma Research Society*, XX (1930), 23.

[320] Castanheda in Azevedo (ed.), *op. cit.* (n. 79), III, 18; Sangermano makes it a fast of three months (Jardine [ed.], *op. cit.* [n. 235], p. 118).

[321] *Op. cit.* (n. 98), I, 280–81.

Martaban a commercial treaty with Pegu, the final ceremony was held in a large temple and attended by the dignitaries and priests of both Portugal and Pegu. The viceroy of Martaban, called the satrap or "samibelgan"[322] by Maffei, was accompanied to the meeting by one of the high "rolis" and a vast assemblage of the townspeople. As a prelude to the ceremonies of oath-taking, the "samibelgan" read aloud in his own language the terms of the treaty which were written on a golden plaque in both Portuguese and "Peguan." Thereafter one of the Portuguese did likewise. Then the "roli" intoned some texts from their writings, and burned some pieces of saffron-colored paper (a color which they consider holy) along with some odoriferous leaves. He then took the hands of the "samibelgan," placed them on the ashes, and asked the viceroy questions which led him to swear that his king would live up to the conditions of the treaty with Portugal. This part of the ceremony was conducted with great solemnity as the crowd observed a respectful silence.

Corrêa and the other Portuguese in attendance had quite a different attitude, the majority of them believing, when it came their turn, that a Christian could not validly swear to uphold obligations made to pagans. As part of what the Portuguese thought of as a farce, the chaplain of Corrêa's vessel, attired in his surplice, brought to the ceremony, instead of the Bible ordinarily used for swearing an oath, a beautifully bound book of songs and moral platitudes. Corrêa in mockery opened the book at random and his hand accidentally fell on these words from the Holy Scriptures: "Vanitas vanitatum et omnia vanitas." This chance encounter with the word of God forced him to regard the ceremony with respect and to recall that Heaven requires that oaths made to infidels and pagans shall be religiously kept. And so Corrêa, feeling bound to act in good faith, swore his oath on the book as if it were the Bible itself. While Maffei certainly is using this story to point out to his European audience the wondrous workings of the Christian God, it is particularly interesting as an example of how the Portuguese sometimes thought about their obligations to pagan peoples and of how the church itself officially viewed such undertakings.

The first European to gain any insight into the doctrines of the Buddhists of Burma was the Franciscan friar, Pierre Bonifer, a Frenchman and a doctor of the University of Paris.[323] While in India, Bonifer had probably been told, even as the Jesuits had earlier heard in Coimbra, that "if a father . . . were to go there [to Pegu] then all the people would become Christians."[324] Along with

---

[322] An approximation of the Burmese title equivalent to viceroy: *shin-bai-yin-hkan-min*. See Dalgado, *op. cit.* (n. 53), II, 278. Barros (in Cidade and Múrias [eds.], *op. cit.* [n. 39], III, 131) gives this title in a somewhat clearer transliteration: "samibelagão." Cf. the title for governor ("toledam") given by Pires (above, p. 547).

[323] For a brief account of his mission see A. Meersman, O. F. M., "The Franciscans in the Ancient Burmese Kingdoms of Ava and Pegu, 1557–1818," *Archivum franciscanum historicum*, XXXI (1938), 358; greater detail on both the mission and Buddhist doctrine as he understood it may be found in Maffei, *op. cit.* (n. 98), II, 286–89.

[324] From a letter dated Cochin (late 1547 or early 1548), probably written by Brother Adão Francisco, which relays some elementary detail on Burmese Buddhism based on what Brother Adão was told by a man in India who had twice visited Pegu. See Wicki (ed.), *op. cit.* (n. 80), I, 260.

his companion, Friar Pedro Paschasius, Bonifer sailed from Mylapore to Pegu, probably in the fall of 1565.[325] Bonifer remained at Bassein for a time studying the Mon language, reading native books on the Buddhist faith, and tending to the religious needs of the Portuguese colony. Unfortunately for his evangelizing hopes, Bonifer arrived in Pegu when King Bayin Naung was encouraging a fervent Buddhist revival. This king's vigor in battle was matched only by his great enthusiasm to be a model Buddhist ruler and he did all within his power to be so regarded throughout the Buddhist world. He built pagodas wherever his campaigns took him, distributed widely many copies of Pali texts, fed monks, and encouraged the collection and study of the *dammathat* (code of civil law).[326] He sent presents to the celebrated Tooth of Buddha shrine in Ceylon, and, when the tooth was confiscated by the Portuguese, he dispatched emissaries to Goa in 1560 in the vain hope of ransoming it.[327] He forbade the Muslims and Shan people within his dominions to kill sacrificial animals. And Father Bonifer, who disputed with some of the Buddhist priests of Pegu, was railed at as an impostor and a trouble-maker. Finally, on the advice of his Portuguese friends who had heard threats made against him, Bonifer left Bassein in fear of his life.

On the basis of the letters which Bonifer wrote to Europe, Maffei in 1588 was able to publish a summary of what he understood the beliefs of these Buddhists to be and to give a list of some of their religious terms. The best educated of the Burmese priests are said by the Jesuit scholar to hold the idea that there have been an infinite number of worlds which succeed one another throughout eternity.[328] Each of these worlds possesses its own set of gods from the vast pantheon which the Burmese postulate. They believe that this present world must have had five gods, four of whom have long since departed and the fifth of whom died almost three thousand years ago.[329] This means that at present they are without a god; within an indefinite number of years, they believe, another god will appear whose death will be followed by a universal conflagration from which a new world will emerge with its own new and particular

---

[325] While Maffei and Meersman (above, n. 323) place him in Pegu from 1557 to 1560, the basic extant letter on which we rely for information on his mission is dated from "Cosmin" (Bassein) on February 18, 1556. Fróis (in Wicki [ed.], *op. cit.* [n. 80], III, 364) writes from Malacca on December 15, 1555, that he left "just now from Santo Thome." He must have been there for a period before writing his letter, because it shows a degree of knowledge about Buddhism and the Mon language which probably would not have been acquired too readily in India. For the text of his letter, see *ibid.*, 817-20. Bonifer includes the first list of Buddhist terms in the Mon language to reach Europe, as far as is now known.

[326] Hall, *op. cit.* (n. 30), p. 216. The kings of Burma were traditionally looked upon as patrons and guardians of its Buddhist faith. Politically, the kings ordinarily cultivated good relations with the monks for they were "the real spokesmen of the people and the monasteries were the popular assemblies...." See Niharranyan Ray, *An Introduction to the Study of Theravāda Buddhism in Burma* (Calcutta, 1946), p. 212.

[327] See above, p. 344.

[328] For confirmation see Sangermano in Jardine (ed.), *op. cit.* (n. 235), p. 9.

[329] According to information obtained by Sangermano (*ibid.*, p. 102) in 1763 from a celebrated Burmese priest and tutor of the king, just four gods have appeared in the present world and have achieved a state of Nirvana, the last of whom was Godama who died 2,306 years before 1763.

gods.[330] They believe that their gods have been created by certain men who exist in different guises and who possess earthly and ethereal qualities. They assign dead souls to three different locales: the place of torment is called *Naxac* (Hell),[331] the center of delight which resembles the paradise of the Muslims is called "Scuum" (Heaven),[332] and another place named *Nizan* (*Nirvana*),[333] the meaning of which is deprivation, death, and destruction of both the body and the soul. In the first two places the souls are detained until they are called into some new world and this process continues until they finally end up in *Nizan*, a state of complete annihilation. "These are," writes Maffei, "the elements of the Peguan doctrines about which they possess many large and complete books."[334] Though his outline of Burmese belief is clearly not based upon serious study of these books, Maffei is able, from Bonifer's letter, to give vaguely some of the basic tenets of traditional Burmese cosmography and religion.

The people of Pegu, thanks to their priests, are well educated and candidates for conversion. They have among them a learned elite who study another language (Pali) which is for them what Latin is for the scholars of Europe.[335] The language of Pegu (Talaing) differs from those spoken by the neighboring Siamese, "Bramás" (Burmese), and Arakanese. In Pegu it is held that the Siamese language is derived from Talaing.[336] Pegu possesses an ancient literature and its scribes write both on paper with ink and on palm leaf with stylus.[337] All supplications to the king are presented in writing and read to him by one of his secretaries. Traditional law exists, even though justice is usually meted out by fiat of the monarch. Murder is ordinarily punished by having the perpetrator of the crime pay a sum to the aggrieved family, the size of which is determined by the victim's rank or status.[338] On one occasion in 1567, when Fedrici was in Martaban, the Portuguese there murdered five royal messengers who were on their way to the battlefront with personal supplies for the king. Under these extraordinary circumstances the king ordered that the Portuguese should be

[330] On their beliefs about the destruction and reproduction of the world see *ibid.*, chap. v.

[331] *Naxac* is the Mon word for hell; cf. the Sanskrit word, *Naraka*, which means an infernal place. See Wicki (ed.), *op. cit.* (n. 80), III, 818, n. 5.

[332] "Scuum" is read as "Sevo" by Wicki in *ibid.* It is equivalent to the Mon word for heaven, *Swaw*, and the Sanskrit word, *Svarga*.

[333] *Nirvána* in Mon = *Nizan*, and in Sanskrit = *Nibbân*.

[334] Maffei, *op. cit.* (n. 98), II, 288. Evidently, Bonifer brought a collection of books from Pegu back to Goa. See Fróis' letter to Portugal from Goa (December 6, 1560), in Wicki (ed.), *op. cit.* (n. 80), IV, 778. Peguan youths in the college at Goa might conceivably have read and translated these books for the Jesuits.

[335] Castanheda in Azevedo (ed.), *op. cit.* (n. 79), III, 18.

[336] Barros in Cidade and Múrias (eds.), *op. cit.* (n. 39), III, 130; for confirmation see Sangermano in Jardine (ed.), *op. cit.* (n. 235), p. 42.

[337] Castanheda in Azevedo (ed.), *op. cit.* (n. 79), III, 18, says paper and ink; Fedrici in Purchas (ed.), *op. cit.* (n. 16), X, 127, talks of supplications written on palm leaves with a stylus. Actually both were used. Their paper was made of macerated bamboo and colored black; it is called *praibach*. See Sangermano in Jardine, *op. cit.* (n. 235), p. 180.

[338] Castanheda in Azevedo (ed.), *op. cit.* (n. 79), III, 18; also Fedrici in Purchas (ed.), *op. cit.* (n. 16), X, 118.

imprisoned until his return. But the Portuguese captain refused to deliver the accused men to the authorities, and took advantage of the absence of the men of the city to parade his troops through the streets every day. "I thought it a strange thing," writes Fedrici, "to see the Portugals use such insolency in another mans Citie." [339]

The European writers on Burma may be divided into two groups: Varthema and the Portuguese who deal with Burma before the final establishment of the Toungoo dynasty at Pegu in 1539, and the non-Portuguese (Maffei, Fedrici, Balbi, Linschoten, and Fitch) who comment on conditions under the Toungoo rulers. Barros is a particularly valuable source on the fall of the Wareru rulers and the foundations of a united state under the Toungoos. While the earlier commentators are not very specific about the activities of the Mon kings, those who write about the Toungoo rulers give rich detail on their wars and building programs. Pires and Fitch are particularly useful on the conditions for trade and business in south Burma. All of the authors, except Castanheda, are shocked by the low level of sexual morality prevailing in Burma. Without exception they are almost all overcome by the number and splendor of Burma's pagodas, temples, and statues—a concern for architecture which is reminiscent of the European wonderment about the buildings and sculptures of India. Castanheda, Fitch, and Maffei exhibit considerable knowledge about the importance of the Buddhist monks in Burma, and try to understand something about their training, alms-gathering, and rites. Like modern observers, these early commentators are struck by the vast expenditures of the Burmese Buddhists on ceremonials, food for the monks, and the building of monuments. [340] Maffei is the only writer to attempt to discourse on their doctrinal beliefs and to give sample religious terms in the Mon language. All of the Europeans write from experiences or reports based on information gathered in the delta area of the Irrawaddy or along the coast of Arakan. None of them seems to have penetrated to the interior, and what they have to say about cities such as Ava is based entirely upon what they heard elsewhere. One of the most valuable features of these writings for historians of Burma is the large number of place names, commercial terms, and administrative titles which they contain.

5

INDOCHINA

Throughout recorded history, Indochina, as its name indicates, was the place where the Hindu and Chinese cultures met, clashed and sometimes fused. Long before Marco Polo visited the peninsula in 1288, Champa, the predominant

---

[339] Purchas (ed.), *op. cit.* (n. 16), X, 119.

[340] Cf. Manning Nash, "Burmese Buddhism in Everyday Life," *American Anthropologist*, LXV (1963), 285–95.

"Hinduized" state of the south, was being challenged by the expansion of the "Sinicized" Annamese state of the north. The Venetian traveler left a few comments about Champa, and, possibly, a good deal more about the Cochin-china area where the Annamese were then dominant.[341] When Odoric of Pordenone traveled in these regions, Champa was undergoing a temporary respite from the onslaughts of its northern neighbors. The friar roamed southern Indochina during the reign of Chê A-nan (1318–42), the founder of the twelfth dynasty in Cham history. He reports that the country was then prosperous, enjoyed rich fishing grounds off its coast, and that the ruler himself had no fewer than two hundred children by his various wives. Neither Polo nor Odoric mentions Cambodia, the great Hinduized state of the Khmers with its capital at Angkor, which was already beginning to decline and which was then being invaded by Hinayana Buddhism from neighboring Siam.

Between the time of Odoric's report and the arrival of the Portuguese in the East, nothing more was heard in Europe about the struggles going on in this remote peninsula where several contending states were meeting, clashing, retreating, advancing, and dying. In 1431 the rulers of Cambodia, under relentless attack from Siam, deserted the city of Angkor and retreated to a capital further to the east which would not be so exposed to attack from Ayut'ia. In 1471 all of Champa south to Cape Varella was annexed by the Annamese, and what remained was a tiny, truncated state which continued to bear the same name.[342] The decline of Champa and Cambodia was paralleled in time by the southward movement of the Annamese from Tongking towards the Mekong delta and by the rise of Ayut'ia, to the west of Cambodia, as a great and menacing seat of power. The three Laotian states on the upper Mekong River continued to lead semi-independent existences while nominally and sometimes actually in vassalage to Siam or Burma. In this confused state of affairs, it is hardly to be wondered at that the first Portuguese to comment on Indochina were not always entirely clear or in agreement on such elementary matters as the exact placement or relative strength of the shifting component parts of the peninsula.

News of Indochina began to trickle back into Portugal shortly after the conquest of Malacca. Albuquerque's emissaries to Ayut'ia returned with information on Cambodia, nominally a vassal of Siam. In 1513 King Manuel, in a letter to Pope Leo X which was published in Rome, let the rest of Europe know that Cambodia was one of the most powerful and strategically located states of the distant East.[343] Pires, who gathered his information in Malacca, gives substantial

---

[341] For a summary of the argument that Polo's "Greater Java" was really Cochin-China see A. J. H. Charignon, "La grande Java de Marco Polo en Cochinchine," *Bulletin de la Societé des études indochinoises* (Saigon), New Series, Vol. IV (1929), No. 4, pp. 345–47. As used in the sixteenth-century and earlier accounts, Cochin-China corresponds to the territory now called Tonkin and northern Annam. The probability is that this name is derived from an Arabic designation. See L. Aurousseau, "Sur le nom de Cochinchine," *Bulletin de l'École française d'Extrême-Orient* (Hanoi), XXIV (1924), 551–79.

[342] E. Aymonier, "The History of Tchampa (The Cyamba of Marco Polo, Now Annam or Cochin China)," *Imperial and Asiatic Quarterly Review*, New Series, VI (1893), 375–76.

[343] Groslier, *op. cit.* (n. 23), p. 142.

data on Cambodia, Champa, and Cochin–China, but his work was not published until its appearance in 1550 in Ramusio's first volume. The remainder of the Portuguese secular writers (Barbosa, Pinto, Castanheda, and Barros) attempt nothing but general descriptions of Indochina. The most detailed and accurate accounts published in the sixteenth century come from missionary informants. Gaspar da Cruz, the pioneer Dominican missionary in southeast Asia, spent about a year in Cambodia during 1555–56 in a fruitless effort to establish a mission there. In hope of finding a more cordial reception, he went to Canton in 1556 and spent a few months on the coast of South China. He returned to Portugal and shortly thereafter published his *Tractado . . . (1569)* [344] in which he discusses his experiences in Cambodia. The Spanish Augustinian, Mendoza,[345] includes an account of the Indochinese states near the end of his famous book on China in a section summarising the Far Eastern experiences of Friar Martin Ignatius de Loyola.

The materials in Pires, Cruz, and Mendoza are the best European sources published in the sixteenth century, and they can be supplemented by odd fragments of data in the Portuguese chroniclers and the Jesuit letterbooks and histories. In the beginning years of the seventeenth century, as a result of the Spanish effort to obtain a foothold in Cambodia (1593–1603),[346] several more informative books and documents appeared in Spain in quick succession. However, they will not be considered here since they were not published in the sixteenth century.[347] The European sources, while admittedly meager, are nevertheless important because the native annals on the period before 1600 are sparse, non-existent, unreliable, or written so long after the event as to be suspect. Here, as in many other parts of southeast Asia, the early history has to be reconstructed in large part from foreign sources.[348]

The earliest geographical descriptions of the Indochinese peninsula, particularly in its relationships to neighboring territories, appear in Barros and in Pinto's letter of 1554 from Malacca. The Portuguese chronicler, who places this region, in his eighth division of the East, at the southeasternmost projection of

[344] C. R. Boxer (ed.), *South China in the Sixteenth Century* (London, 1953), p. lix. For further discussion see below, pp. 747–48.

[345] For details see below, pp. 644–46.

[346] For details see Lawrence P. Briggs, "Spanish Intervention in Cambodia," *T'oung pao*, XXXIX (1950), 132–60.

[347] An unpublished description of Cambodia and Angkor by Diogo do Couto was discovered by C. R. Boxer in 1954. Apparently the continuator of Barros hoped to insert it into the text of the sixth *Década*, but was prevented from doing so by overly zealous censorship. Prepared in its present form around 1611, it has finally been published and edited by Groslier in *op. cit.* (n. 23), pp. 68–74. The first printed references to the ruins of Angkor were included in Ribadeneyra, *op. cit.* (n. 23), pp. 173, 187. He reports that some who have seen the magnificent ruins believe that they were constructed by Alexander the Great or the Romans, a conventional explanation advanced by Europeans of this period to account for a number of Oriental architectural masterpieces.

[348] The Cambodian documentation for the sixteenth century has either been destroyed or has completely disappeared (Groslier, *op. cit.* [n. 23], p. 164); on the Annamese sources see P. J. Honey, "Modern Vietnamese Historiography," in Hall (ed.), *op. cit.* (n. 8), p. 94. Also see Antoine Cabaton, "Quelques documents espagnols et portugais sur l'Indochine aux XVIe et XVIIe siècles," *Journal asiatique*, Series X, Vol. XII (1908), pp. 255–60.

the continent, concentrates his attention upon the basin and delta of the Mekong River. After naming Cambodia, Champa, and Cochin–China as the three greatest states of the peninsula, Barros observes that least is known about Cochin–China because its coast is very stormy and rough and its people not much involved in maritime activities.[349] Xavier, on his way to Japan in 1549, observes that Cochin–China borders on China, and tells about the storms and turbulent seas which almost brought disaster to his ship off its rugged coast.[350] Camoëns dramatizes the difficulties of navigating around Indochina in the story which he tells of his shipwreck at the Mekong delta in 1560 and of how he saved the manuscript of the *Lusiads*. Pinto, who writes from what he heard in Ayut'ia in about 1548–49, reports that Portuguese who had earlier visited in Cambodia learned that the king and all his people would quickly become Christians if only missionaries could be sent. He equates Champa in size with Portugal and notices that at the mouth of the bay of Cochin–China stands the fortified island of Hainan, the "first" outpost of China and subject to the jurisdiction of the governors of Canton.[351]

The maps of the peninsula prepared during the sixteenth century do not go beyond these generalities in their representation of Indochina. The first rough sketch of its coastline appears on the planisphere of 1527 prepared by Diogo Ribeiro. The map in the 1554 edition of Ramusio's first volume[352] appears, from its depiction of the Mekong delta, to be based on Barros, or perhaps both the cartographer and the chronicler used a common source unknown to us. No marked improvement of the cartography of the peninsula again takes place until the publication of Ortelius' atlas in 1595. The sixteenth-century maps give relatively little detail on particular places within the Indochinese states.[353]

From his vantage point in Malacca, Pires was able to obtain from his merchant informants a rough idea of each of the peninsula's leading states as they looked around 1515. Cambodia, which he locates on the seacoast between Siam and Champa, is a country with a deep hinterland through which run many navigable rivers. It is rich in foodstuffs and produces substantial quantities of good rice, meat, and fish as well as "wines of its own kind."[354] Though it has little gold to export, Cambodia sells abroad its lac, ivory, dried fish, and rice. It imports Bengali textiles, spices, mercury, liquid storax, and red beads.[355] The ruler of Cambodia is a valiant heathen who fights with his neighbors and bows his head to none of them. His people are warlike and possess many horses and trained elephants. Their ships, which mainly trade at Lugor in Siam, often form into

349 Cidade and Múrias (eds.), *op. cit.* (n. 39), I, 363–64.

350 Letter of November 5, 1549, from Kagoshima in Schurhammer and Wicki (eds.), *op. cit.* (n. 93), II, 180–81.

351 Eglauer (trans.), *op. cit.* (n. 181), I, 254.

352 Following fol. 34.

353 For further discussion see Groslier, *op. cit.* (n. 23), pp. 146–50.

354 Pires in Cortesão (trans. and ed.), *op. cit.* (n. 46), I, 112. For emendations of Cortesão's translation based on a comparison with the Ramusio version see Groslier, *op. cit.* (n. 23), pp. 143–44.

355 For confirmation of this list of imports see the material from the Chinese sources as analyzed in P. Pelliot, *Mémoires sur les coutumes du Cambodge de Tcheou Ta-kouan* (Paris, 1951), p. 27.

pirate squadrons to prey upon friend and foe alike. At the death of a king the lords burn themselves as do the king's wives and other widowed women. The likelihood that concremation was practiced in Cambodia is very slight. Pires must have heard about it in relation to Champa where concremation certainly was the custom and where Odoric of Pordenone had already observed it in the fourteenth century.[356]

To the east of Cambodia, particularly towards the interior, lies the country of Champa.[357] In Pires' estimate, it is a land power with no large ports, no great river marts, and no Muslim merchants.[358] Its economy is based on agriculture rather than trade, and it is rich in all kinds of foodstuffs. The chief product sold abroad is highest quality calambac (aloe-wood)[359] of which Champa has whole forests. Most of its trade is with Siam rather than Malacca. Its exports consist primarily of calambac, dried salt fish, rice, local textiles, some pepper, and gold.[360] The commodities imported are generally the same as those in demand in Cambodia, especially Indian textiles and spices. Gold, silver, and Chinese "cash" (low value coins made of an alloy of copper and lead with a square hole in the center) are the ordinary mediums of exchange. Champa's ruler is a rich heathen prince who rules over many subjects and is often at war with the king of Cochin-China.

Between Champa and China, Pires locates the wealthy and powerful Anna-mese kingdom of Cochin-China. Its territory extends deep into the interior and is traversed by large navigable rivers. But most of the population resides along its coastal fringe rather than up its river valleys. It is an entirely heathen country, hostile to the Moors, and closely attached by trade and political ties to China. The king of Cochin-China is related to the Ming rulers by marriage and is in vassalage to Peking. He keeps a permanent ambassador at the Chinese court, and, even though generally bellicose, he never is at war with China.[361] Like that of its smaller and poorer neighbor, Champa, the power of Cochin-China is geared to the land and not to the sea. Its numerous ships and war junks are primarily used to carry and protect the merchandise bought and sold at Canton. Cochin-China imports sulfur and saltpeter, constituents of the gunpowder used in Cochin-China to manufacture fireworks and munitions. The other items imported are

[356] Groslier, *op. cit.* (n. 23), p. 144.

[357] Barbosa in Dames (ed.), *op. cit.* (n. 77), II, 208, incorrectly makes it an island.

[358] Cortesão (trans. and ed.), *op. cit.* (n. 46), I, 112–14.

[359] Barbosa (in Dames [ed.], *op. cit.* [n. 77], II, 209–10) confirms Pires' statement that the best of the aromatic aloe-wood originates in Champa. Also see Orta's comments in C. Markham (trans.), *Colloquies on the Simples and Drugs of India* (London, 1913), p. 263.

[360] Pires (Cortesão [trans. and ed.], *op. cit.* [n. 46], I, 113) makes a puzzling statement which seems to mean that crude gold comes into Champa from the mines of Menangkabow in Sumatra and that it is sold in some other form to buyers in Cochin-China.

[361] The Yung-lo emperor of China had begun sending maritime expeditions southward early in the fifteenth century with the object of incorporating China's southern neighbors into the Ming system of tribute and trade. The second Le dynasty of Annam forced the Ming government of China to withdraw its armies from the peninsula in 1428. After the setback, Peking was content to recognize the Le rulers as the actual governors of northern Indochina and to require nothing from them except formal vassalage. See Hall, *op. cit.* (n. 30), p. 174.

precious stones, small quantities of opium and pepper, and liquid storax. For sale abroad Cochin-China itself produces pottery and porcelain, superb taffeta, high quality silk, and a limited quantity of seed pearls. Only on rare occasions do the merchants of Cochin-China come to Malacca; on these occasions they exchange gold, silver, and the products of China for sulfur and other items.[362]

Father Gaspar da Cruz, who was possibly acting on the information which Pinto reported back to Europe about Cambodia's readiness for conversion and its king's request for missionaries,[363] left Malacca in 1555 with high hopes of establishing a mission there. While the Dominican proved to be a good observer of the natural features of Indochina, he rapidly became disillusioned about Christianizing the country. Though he necessarily had to communicate through a "third party," or interpreter, he was himself a serious student of the religions then dominant within Cambodia. While his account of religion in Cambodia (published in his *Tractado* . . . [1569]) is brief, it brings out clearly his ability to discern and correctly evaluate the strength of the hated faiths which stood in the way of his own efforts to spread the gospel. When he finally left Cambodia in despair, he admits that he had made but one convert; ironically, this man was dead before Cruz's departure.[364] His discouraging experience probably helps to explain why it was so long before other Christian missionaries tried their hand at evangelizing in Cambodia.

In discussing the geographical boundaries of China, Cruz incorporates into his delineation a number of valuable observations on the states of Indochina. His comments on Cochin-China are essentially in harmony with those made by the informants of Pires forty years earlier, but he emphasizes even more strongly the close ties between the Annamese and the Chinese. In dress, policy, government, and language the two peoples exhibit striking similarities. The Annamese write in characters as they do in China, but "while they can understand each other in writing, they cannot understand each other's speech."[365] Cochin-China is heavily populated, fertile, and self-sufficient. Even though no trading is done abroad, its people enjoy a high standard of living. About Champa, Cruz has practically nothing to say.

It is surprising, however, how much Cruz reports about Laos and the Laotians.[366] He is prompted to digress from his major task of describing China's boundaries when recalling that the Laotian kingdom (Luang Prabang) was overrun by the Burmese in 1556, while he was in Lovek, the capital of Cambodia.[367] Merchants from Laos, he reports, came down the Mekong annually to trade at Lovek, even though the return journey upstream usually

[362] Pires in Cortesão (trans. and ed.), *op. cit.* (n. 46), I, 114–15.
[363] Above, p. 563 and Cruz's own statement in Boxer (ed.), *op. cit.* (n. 344), p. 59. Cf. also Fróis to Portuguese Fathers (Malacca, December 15, 1555) in Wicki (ed.), *op. cit.* (n. 80), III, 364.
[364] Boxer (ed.), *op. cit.* (n. 344), p. 63.
[365] *Ibid.*, p. 73.
[366] *Ibid.*, pp. 76–78. He refers to them also as "Siões mãos" or Siamese Mons.
[367] On Bayin Naung's northern campaign of 1556 see Harvey, *op. cit.* (n. 191), pp. 165–66.

took them about three months. With the Burmese occupation of their territory, the Laotian contingent already in Cambodia in 1556 made no effort to leave at the regular time and so Cruz had the opportunity to observe them and inquire about their homeland. He found out that high mountains separate Laos from China and that border raids in both directions are common. The Chinese maintain a permanent border garrison in Kwangsi province which tries without success to halt the Laotian raids. In normal times the Laotian merchants travel to Ayut'ia, Pegu, and Cambodia with musk and gold to exchange for cotton textiles and other everyday items.[368] The Laotians are not very brown in color, the men dress in cotton loincloths, and the women are covered from the breasts to the knee. They are idolaters like the Burmese, Siamese, and Cambodians, and their priests "wear yellow clothes girt about as the rest of the people, with certain folds and seams in which they hold their superstitious charms."[369]

It is the Mekong which links Laos with Cambodia. This large, deep river, reported to originate in China, passes through great stretches of uncultivated, unpeopled, and densely forested mountains. Cruz himself took a journey on the river and tells of seeing in the hinterland of Cambodia great numbers of wild elephants, buffaloes, deer (*meru*), and rhinoceroses. He describes the rhinoceroses in some detail and reports eating "its great lump of flesh that falls from the nape"[370] and hangs down on its chest. Along with rhinoceros meat he sampled the wild citrus fruits and grapes growing in the riverine wilderness. The Mekong, in its passage through the peopled and cultivated parts of Cambodia, "causeth a wonder . . . worthy of reciting."[371] He locates with exactitude the four arms of the river at "Chudermuch" (Phnom Pénh)[372] and correctly reports that the Cambodians refer to the main course of the river as the "Sistor" (Srei Sistor), and to the river which runs by the capital as the "Arm of Lovek," or what is now called the Tonle Sap. He clearly explains the phenomenon of the annual reversal in the flow of the Tonle Sap and the great floods which this produces in Lovek and nearby places.[373] But, when he tries to account for "the cause of this miracle," he comes forth with an utterly fantastic explanation according to which the influx of the spring tides in the delta is supposed to push back the rivers.[374]

Aware from his arrival that evangelizing in Cambodia was hopeless, the Dominican with the help of his interpreter questioned the priests about the religions already dominant in the capital. He learned in this manner that the

---

[368] Barros (above, p. 526) remarks that silver comes to Ayut'ia from the Laotians.

[369] Cruz in Boxer (ed.), *op. cit.* (n. 344), p. 77.

[370] *Ibid.*, p. 78.

[371] *Ibid.*

[372] From Khmer, *Chademuk* or *Chordemuko*, which means "four arms," and was the old name for Phnom Pénh. *Ibid.*, p. 78, n. 1.

[373] The annual floods of the Mekong begin in May and reach their peak in October. *Ibid.*, p. 79, n. 1.

[374] Groslier, *op. cit.* (n. 23), p. 151.

ruler, Ang Chan I (d. 1566),[375] and his principal advisers and favorites are all
Brahmans. This being true, he concludes that the task of Christianizing them is
next to impossible because Brahmans ". . . are the most difficult people to
convert. . . ."[376] From the court priests, Cruz learned that they believe in one
god called "Probar Missur" (Préas Baram Eysaur),[377] who created the heavens
and the earth. This god was granted permission to bring about creation by
"Pralocussar" (Préas Lok Eysaur)[378] who in turn received his authority from
"Praissur" (Préas Eysaur).[379] In addition to these three gods the Cambodian
Brahmans also worship "Praput prasar Metri" (Préas Put Préas Séar Metrei),[380]
a Buddhist deity. The existence of this particular Buddhist cult in sixteenth-
century Cambodia is strange, inasmuch as it is usually associated with the
Mahayana form of the faith, the influence of which is generally supposed to
have been supplanted by this time through the spread of Hinayanist Buddhism
into Indochina.[381] It is nonetheless clear from Cruz's account that Brahmanistic
and Buddhistic beliefs existed side by side as late as 1556 in the court religion of
Cambodia and that Ang Chan was deeply devoted to their tenets and resented
the Dominican's attacks upon them.

Cruz also found the priests and monks of popular Buddhism to be formidable
enemies. Through his disputations with them, he learned some of their doctrines.
The Cambodian Buddhists believe in the existence of twenty-seven heavens,[382]
divided into three sets, to certain of which every living being, including the flea
and the louse, is admitted because each has a soul. To the lowest of these heavens
go ordinary beings who are not priests, and they find therein meat, drink, and
fair women. Above the first set of heavens are a series of superior heavens to
which they assign priestly hermits who spend eternity in the enjoyment of
refreshing breezes. The most elevated set is the one whose gods have "round
bodies like balls,"[383] and those who are admitted to this final glory are blessed
by being given similar godlike figures! As a whole his description of the
Buddhist paradises conforms relatively well with the facts, even if some of

[375] The chronology for the Cambodian kings of this period is still undetermined.

[376] Cruz in Boxer (ed.), *op. cit.* (n. 344), p. 60. Cf. also the difficulties posed by the Brahmans in
India (above, pp. 253, 441–42). Cruz brings out clearly here and in what follows that the traditional
Hindu rites of the Khmers were still being followed at the court of Ang Chan. See Groslier, *op. cit.*
(n. 23), p. 157.

[377] This is one of the titles of Shiva (Boxer [ed.], *op. cit.* [n. 344], p. 60, n. 2). Groslier (*op. cit.* [n. 23],
p. 158) proposes a different possibility in reading this name. In an effort to show that Cruz was
trying to relay a rough conception of the *Tri-mūrti*, he suggests that the Dominican is here referring
to *Paraméçvara*, a name which often is used to denote Brahma.

[378] Title of a Bodisatta in Cambodia (Boxer [ed.], *op. cit.* [n. 344], p. 60, n. 3). Groslier (*op. cit.*
[n. 23], p. 158) agrees with this identification and also points out that traditionally it is used as another
name for both Shiva and Vishnu.

[379] Another Cambodian title for Shiva (Boxer [ed.], *op. cit.* [n. 23], p. 60, n. 4).

[380] Title of the future Buddha (*ibid.*, p. 60, n. 5). Groslier (*op. cit.* [n. 23], p. 158, n. 2), who bases his
reading on a number of later inscriptions, prefers *Srei Ar* to *Séar*.

[381] Groslier, *op. cit.* (n. 23), p. 158.

[382] Just twenty-six in the schematic plan normally accepted. Possibly Cruz confused the "heavens"
with their twenty-seven celestial mansions. See Boxer (ed.), *op. cit.* (n. 344), p. 61, n. 1.

[383] *Ibid.*, p. 61.

his explanations are vague and incomplete.[384] Just as the Buddhists believe in a multiplicity of heavens, so do they postulate a series of thirteen hells to which souls are condemned according to the degree of their sinfulness.[385] Cruz also lists the ranks of the Buddhist ecclesiastical hierarchy: the "Massancraches" (Maha Sangréach)[386] are the supreme priests and they sit above the king; the "Nacsendeches" (Neak Sámdach),[387] who are comparable to bishops, are the equals of the king; the "Mitres" (Methéa?)[388] are on the level of the ordinary priest and have a status inferior to the king's; the two lowest ranks are called the "Chapuzes" (Chao ku ses)[389] and the "Sazes" (Sâkhi ses).[390] Priests of all ranks are numerous and highly venerated. Cruz estimates that one-third of the male population belongs to the Buddhist clergy.[391]

Except for the clergy, the people of Cambodia are the slaves of the king. Ang Chan I is depicted as being the absolute master of his realm. He came to power after putting down a great rebellion against his brother and predecessor.[392] Cruz insists that the ruler is well informed on every movement made by his subjects. Everyone alike has free access to the king and one vies with the other to keep him in touch with what is happening within the kingdom. Nothing escapes him and nothing can be done without his approval. He is the sole proprietor of the land, and when a householder dies the property which is left reverts to the crown; the man's family, after hiding whatever it can, must begin anew.[393] In a country where the king is so undeniably absolute and so unswervingly hostile to the Christian mission, Cruz passionately concludes that conversions simply cannot be hoped for, especially if it is recalled how deeply the majority of the people respect and revere the Buddhist priests.

Mendoza's remarks (made in 1585)[394] on Cambodia and its neighbors need to be read in the light of the efforts already in motion (1583–1600) by the Franciscan missionaries and the Iberian adventurers to acquire a permanent foothold in Indochina. The Augustinian historian clearly possessed up-to-date

---

[384] See the analysis in Groslier, *op. cit.* (n. 23), p. 159. He notes that the Cambodians believe in three categories of heavens: the first group of six is reserved for mortals still unfree from desire; the second group of sixteen is for priests who have not yet cut all their ties with earthly desires; the third group of four is for those who have vanquished all desire.

[385] These *norok* are more properly purgatories. Boxer (ed.), *op. cit.* (n. 344), p. 62, n. 1; Groslier, *op. cit.* (n. 23), p. 159, n. 1.

[386] Title of the high priest of Cambodia. Boxer (ed.), *op. cit.* (n. 344), p. 62, n. 2.

[387] *Ibid.*, p. 62, n. 3.

[388] *Ibid.*, p. 62, n. 4. Groslier (*op. cit.* [n. 23], p. 159, n. 4) believes that this derivation is questionable.

[389] Buddhist novices (Groslier, *op. cit.* [n. 23], p. 159, n. 4). The derivation from *chipor*, a monk's robe, included in Boxer (ed.), *op. cit.* (n. 344), p. 62, n. 5, seems somewhat less likely. The suggestion for this derivation was given to Groslier by Georges Coedès.

[390] Also Buddhist novices (Groslier, *op. cit.* [n. 23], p. 159, n. 4).

[391] Boxer (ed.), *op. cit.* (n. 344), p. 61.

[392] A vague reference to the way in which Ang Chan gained the throne from a usurper who had ousted his brother in 1512. See *ibid.*, p. 63, n. 1.

[393] Essentially this general description of the king's position harmonizes with what is known from other sources. On the special problem of inheritance practices see Groslier, *op. cit.* (n. 23), p. 155.

[394] George T. Staunton (ed.), *The History of the Great and Mighty Kingdom of China* ... ("Hakluyt Society Publications," Old Series, Vol. XV [London, 1854]), II, 311–15.

information on the arrival of Diogo Veloso in Lovek and the renewal of missionary enterprise there around 1583. Evidently he derived it in the main from a letter
which Friar Sylvestre d'Azevedo, the Portuguese Franciscan, sent to Malacca.
This document with its request for more missionaries and greater support for
the Christian enterprise in Cambodia was addressed to Friar Martin Ignatius
de Loyola, the Spanish Franciscan.[395] Loyola had circumnavigated the world
and had then written down his experiences when he returned to Europe in
1584. Mendoza learned from Loyola's account about the various parts of the
Portuguese East, though he treats them in sketchy fashion. His accounts of
Cochin-China and Champa, for example, show no advance over the earlier
descriptions, most of his information merely confirming in generalities what
Pires and Cruz had already spelled out with greater precision. The major
difference is that Mendoza, who was writing at the height of Europe's enthusiasm for the Far Eastern missions, is convinced that the people of Cochin-
China and Champa are ripe for conversion. His account was therefore probably
designed as an appeal to Philip II and Pope Gregory XIII to dispatch more
missionaries to Indochina for its quick conversion—possibly as a prelude to
military invasion of, or certainly as a prelude to the missionary penetration of
China proper.

Mendoza reports that Friar Sylvestre d'Azevedo is learning Cambodian and
preaching in that language. He also lets the world know that Azevedo has been
vainly appealing to Malacca for more missionaries. It is because of his frustration
over Malacca's reluctant attitude to support him that Azevedo writes directly
to Loyola asking for his intervention in Spain on behalf of the mission in
Cambodia. The emissaries who brought the letter to Loyola in Malacca informed the Franciscan orally that Azevedo is second only in importance to
King Sâtha (reigned 1576-96) himself and that the ruler refers to him as "pae"
(father).[396] This "new Joseph in Egypt" is permitted to sit in the king's presence
and has obtained permission from the crown for missionaries to proselytize in
his kingdom. It is also reported that Sâtha has permitted them to erect crosses
throughout his kingdom. As confirmation of the king's devotion to the cross,
Loyola was shown two large wooden crosses embellished with silver and gold
which had been made in Cambodia and sent by the king himself to Malacca.[397]
In Mendoza's complacent view, Cambodia is a great, heavily populated and
fertile country which is simply waiting to become Christian.[398] Naïve as

---

[395] On Veloso's and Azevedo's careers see above, pp. 309-12.

[396] Cambodian *pâ* = father. See Groslier, *op. cit.* (n. 23), p. 31.

[397] At an earlier time the king, according to reports, wrote a letter to Malacca requesting aid and
with it sent the two crosses as a token of his good will towards Christianity. One of the crosses was
put up in front of the Dominican convent at Malacca and the other in front of the church at Cochin.
See *ibid.*, p. 31, n. 4.

[398] In passing, Mendoza (Staunton [ed.], *op. cit.* [n. 394], II, 311-12) mentions the elephants and
rhinoceroses of the country and notes that Philip II was given a present of a rhinoceros which was
then (*ca.* 1585) on public display in Madrid. Those who saw it were impressed with its thick, tough
hide. Some of the more curious speculate about its being the unicorn, but Mendoza is not in agreement because those who have seen the "true unicorn" deny that it is the rhinoceros.

Mendoza undoubtedly was about Indochina, his optimism can best be understood by recalling that he wrote at a time when a wave of mission enthusiasm swept Europe, when the Japanese envoys were there,[399] and when close co-operation between Spain and Portugal for the conquest and conversion of the overseas world seemed more than an idle daydream.

What sixteenth-century Europe actually knew about Indochina was based upon the oral and written reports of daring merchants, itinerant soldiers, and devout missionaries. The data which Pires compiled for trading purposes around 1515 reflected the essential self-sufficiency of each of the Indochinese states, their direct trading connections with Siam to the west and China to the east, and their independence of the mart of Malacca. From Pinto and Cruz, we know that Portuguese merchants had been trading in Cambodia for some years before 1555 and that they had probably become involved in the commerce of Ayut'ia and Lovek as they sought to buy more cheaply the prized musk of Laos and the excellent aloe-wood of Champa by getting closer to the source. Ordinarily, they did not proceed to the eastern side of the peninsula because of the extremely difficult terrain, the bad sailing conditions, and the dearth of valuable trading items. Most of what Indochina had to offer to international commerce was evidently available in the Cambodian cities at satisfactory prices. Because they halted in their travels at Cambodia, we have available much more data on Cambodia than on either Champa or Cochin-China. Because of Lovek's connection on the upper Mekong with Laos, we know through the European merchants and missionaries a relatively large amount about the Laotian kingdom and its people.

The Europeans believed that the key to the entire peninsula lay in the control of the Mekong delta. Even when the Portuguese chroniclers have nothing else to say about Indochina, they comment on the relationship of the Cambodian cities to the international centers of trade at Malacca or Canton. Cochin-China, closely tied to Peking and under its benevolent suzerainty, they see as essentially a continental state; like China itself, it is not inclined to welcome maritime traders. Champa had the reputation of being a declining state forced to fight land wars for self-preservation and given to pirating ships which dared to sail within sight of the peninsula's southeastern shore. The control of Cambodia was considered an essential first step to commercial, religious, and military expansion in Indochina. The co-operation, late in the century, of merchant-adventurer and missionary (epitomized by Veloso and Azevedo) was based on a growing conviction among the men in the field that a continental foothold was essential to the commercial and religious penetration of China. Neither the Portuguese of Malacca nor the administrators of Philip II were willing to give official backing to the private enterprises of the Europeans in Cambodia. Under these adverse conditions, their projects were bound to be ephemeral and ultimately collapse.

[399] See below, pp. 691–701.

Still, if it had not been for the grandiose aspirations of private individuals, our sources for the history of the sixteenth century in Indochina would be sadly impoverished. From the merchants we know something about the exports and imports of each state, the major centers of trade, and the direction of its flow. From all comers we have fragments of information on political personalities, institutions, and intrastate relationships, which are very helpful, for example, in determining the chronology of the Cambodian kings. From the missionaries we have specific data on the prevailing religious beliefs, institutions, and hierarchies which may provide valuable documentation for more generalized studies on Hinduism and Buddhism in southeast Asia. While not all of the extant material was published in Europe before 1600, most of it was in print by 1585, the date when Mendoza's work first appeared. What is more, by the late years of the century Cambodia began to be more than a name in Iberia as demands flowed into Madrid requesting money, arms, and missionaries for the Manila-centered interventionist movement. It was also becoming patently clear in the capital about the time of Philip II's death (1598) that the Iberian pioneers in Asia, if not halted, might involve the country in distant and expensive adventures which it could ill afford and from which it stood to gain little. Still, the hotbloods in the colonies kept alive into the next century the conquistadorial spirit and continued to lobby in Madrid for a united Iberian expansionist movement into continental eastern Asia.

6

SUMATRA, BORNEO, AND JAVA

Albuquerque's capture of Malacca in 1511 inaugurated a period of rapid Portuguese expansion into the southern and eastern parts of the insular world. Exploration ships were quickly sent out from the Portuguese base to establish direct relations with the Spice Islands. Trade and diplomatic missions like those sent to the continental states of Siam and Burma were likewise dispatched in short order to Pedir and Pasei in Sumatra. The Sumatran kings of Kampar and Indragiri, traditional vassals of Malacca, quickly sent emissaries to Albuquerque offering their submission to Portugal. The refugee sultan of Malacca himself helped to spread word of the Portuguese conquest to distant China by sending an emissary there to request support from his suzerain. Gujarati and Javanese traders, who had opposed Albuquerque, let it be known in other parts that the new power in southest Asia was a religious, commercial, and political threat to entrenched interests. Individual Portuguese, like Duarte Coelho[400] who participated in the capture of Malacca, soon sought out trade, adventure and military employment throughout the whole Portuguese empire from India to

[400] For a brief summary of his swashbuckling career see Macgregor, *loc. cit.* (n. 24), pp. 36–37.

China. Of the various nearby islands, Sumatra, because of its strategic location across the strait, the vassalage of its Malay states to Malacca, and its Malay cultural base, very quickly began to interest the Portuguese.

The history of Sumatra is closely related to the histories of both Java and Borneo. Today these three great islands (except for north Borneo), in addition to smaller island groups, form the base of the new state of Indonesia. The geography, flora and fauna, ethnography, and languages of these islands are marked by diversity; but their peoples possess common attributes of community organization, customary law, animistic beliefs, and history which, it is hoped, will provide a solid foundation on which to build unity and statehood.[401] The Indonesian islands throughout their histories have had in common a series of foreign contacts and invasions which has left them with similar accretions from outside civilizations. Even in the pre-Christian era, merchants and priests from south India and emissaries from Han China appear to have touched upon southern Sumatra, western Java, and eastern Borneo. But while foreign annals contain odd bits of data about intercourse with the peoples of Indonesia, the oldest native inscriptions which have so far come to light (in eastern Borneo) are dated from the fifth century A.D., and they confirm the fact that Hindu culture and religion were already influential in the archipelago.

From this time until about A.D. 700, the Chinese annals and the writings of Buddhist pilgrims identify and comment upon the principalities and towns in the islands and upon the spread of Buddhism in them. The Buddhist temples and sculptures of Java indicate that in the eighth and ninth centuries two great centers of Hindu-Indonesian culture already existed, one at Palembang in south Sumatra and another in central Java. In the tenth century the renowned Buddhist kingdom of Shrivijay flourished on Sumatra, and, according to the evidence of inscriptions, the center of power in Java shifted to the east at about this same time. In the beginning of the eleventh century the kingdom in east Java was swept by turbulence, while, according to Chinese records, the Sumatran kingdom prospered and continued to dominate the international trade passing through the straits. Subsequently, the Sumatran state under pressure from south Indian rulers began to decline while a temporary revival of political authority occurred in east Java. In the twelfth century, Muslim traders, particularly from India, began to appear in increasing numbers as they sought to obtain spices at the source. By the end of the thirteenth century the Buddhist state of Majapahit had become the center of political power in Java. Javanese accounts record the ensuing efforts of the Majapahit rulers to establish imperial sway over the rest of Indonesia and to stand off the growing power of Islam.

The gradual waning of Majapahit power after 1389 allowed the religion of Islam to spread more rapidly than before into the areas of Indonesia to which merchants came. It is at this point also that the Malay Peninsula and Malacca

---

[401] For a summary statement see Bernard H. M. Vlekke, *Nusantara, a History of Indonesia* (rev. ed.; Chicago, 1960), pp. 13–15; for a similar statement on social affinities in terms of historiography see C. Hooykaas, "A Critical Stage in the Study of Indonesia's Past," in Hall (ed.), *op. cit.* (n. 8), p. 317.

gradually became the new focus of economic and political activity in southeast Asia. In the fifteenth century, with the support of the early Ming rulers of China, Malacca rose to preponderance, and its rulers, their fortunes being tied to commerce, soon became devotees of Islam which they helped to introduce by the sword into other places on the peninsula and northern Sumatra. Elsewhere in insular southeast Asia conversion to the teachings of the Prophet slowly came to be a prerequisite for political and commercial success in the fifteenth century. By 1500 four coastal towns in northern Java were ruled by followers of Islam as were the most important islands in the Moluccas. The Portuguese arrived in southeast Asia when the region was just beginning to be transformed by the impact of quickened commercial relations and a new and aggressive religion.[402] Indeed, it was probably the arrival of the Portuguese in the area which stimulated the Muslims to extend rapidly their political and military activities east of Malacca in order to protect their commercial outposts against the attacks expected from the Europeans.

When Marco Polo visited Perlak on the northern tip of Sumatra in 1292, he noticed that Muslim merchants were already there and that the little port had accepted Islam as its faith. It was probably from this place that the teachings of the Prophet first began to spread to the rest of Sumatra and to the other port cities of southeast Asia increasingly being frequented by Gujarati merchants.[403] The fifteenth-century Europeans who went to the East were likewise impressed by the power and prestige which the followers of Islam enjoyed in the marts of Asia, and Conti found it necessary to embrace Islam himself in order to travel freely about. Santo Stefano first mentioned Sumatra in his book published in 1497,[404] but it was not until Varthema's *Itinerary* appeared (1510) that Europe began to receive a few details of this great island. Before mid-century only slight additions were made to the slowly emerging picture of Sumatra—by the narratives of Crignon about the French voyage of 1529 and by the anonymous Venetian who contributed information to the *Viaggi fatti alla Tana* (1543) on the basis of his experiences in India a decade before.

The Ramusio volumes which began to appear in 1550 included these earlier published accounts, and made available for the first time the materials in Barbosa and in the letters of Empoli. In the great Portuguese histories the best account of Sumatra appears in Barros; but Castanheda, whose description is similar to Barbosa's, also has independent contributions to make. Only a few incidental references appear in the *Commentarios* of Albuquerque, but Lemos gives valuable firsthand information on affairs in Acheh (Sumatra) around 1579. Maffei, in his references to Sumatra, repeats much of what had already been said by the Portuguese chroniclers, though he adds a few additional details on the difficulties between Pasei and the Portuguese. While Fedrici, Balbi, and Fitch report

---

[402] This summary of pre-European history is based on Vlekke, *op. cit.* (n. 401), chaps. i–iii.

[403] *Ibid.*, pp. 66–67.

[404] The sole item of interest is his remark to the effect that the chief of the port which he visited was a Moor, "but speaking a different language [probably Malay]." See Major (ed.), *op. cit.* (n. 31), Pt. VI, p. 7.

what they heard in Malacca about Sumatra, it is Linschoten who gives the fullest information published in the late sixteenth century. Further details are also added by the early Dutch voyagers to Sumatra, and by Guzman's account of the difficulties which stood in the way of missionizing on the island. Of all those who report on Sumatra, the only firsthand accounts published in the sixteenth century are those of Varthema (there possibly *ca.* 1506), Empoli (1515), Crignon (1529), Castanheda (possibly, 1528–38), Lemos (1579), and the reports on the early Dutch voyages (1597–99).

Most of the sixteenth-century writers agree that Sumatra was known in the West to the cartographers of antiquity, but they differ on the names under which it is to be identified. Barros contends that it was a part of the "Quersoneso" (Chersonese), while Castanheda helps to perpetuate the idea that it was really "Taprobana."[405] Though Barros believes it to be the southern part of the Ptolemaic peninsula of gold (Golden Chersonese), he clearly understands that Sumatra is an island separated by a narrow strait from the "land of Malacca." He also speculates that originally Sumatra was part of the continent, an idea which Camoëns also took up.[406]

Sumatra, avers Barros, is 220 leagues (880 miles) in length and from 60 to 70 leagues (240 to 280 miles) in width; Barbosa and Castanheda give it a circumference of 700 leagues (2,800 miles).[407] Its southern and northern extremities which command the entrances to the Straits of Malacca are further from the continent than its central portion which lies directly across the strait from the tip of the peninsula. Because of the island's peculiar geographical configuration, shipwrecks are common along the west coast. The equator passes through the island which extends to six degrees south latitude. The southern part which is encompassed by several smaller islands is divided by a very narrow strait (the Sunda Strait) from the great island of Java. This end of Sumatra is not so heavily peopled as is the northern section where most of the traders congregate.

Along the eastern coast of the island huge marshes and numerous river deltas generally dominate the landscape. The interior is mountainous and in the heavily forested mountains stands a lake from which many of the rivers originate.[408] Since it is on the equator, Sumatra has a hot, humid climate which

[405] For Barros' description of Sumatra see Cidade and Múrias (eds.), *op. cit.* (n. 39), III, 231–37; for Castanheda's see Azevedo (ed.), *op. cit.* (n. 79), I, 456–57. Varthema (in Temple [ed.], *op. cit.* [n. 5], p. 84) and Linschoten (in Burnell and Tiele [eds.], *op. cit.* [n. 25], I, 107), chronologically on either side of Castanheda, likewise identify it with Taprobane. Barros, who clearly identified Taprobane with Ceylon (above, p. 342) and the Golden Chersonese with the Malay peninsula (above, p. 506), categorically places Sumatra as the southern part of the "Aurea Quersoneso" (Cidade and Múrias [eds.], *op. cit.* [n. 39], II, 250) and he is followed in this by Maffei, *op. cit.* (n. 98), I, 167.

[406] For recent arguments to the same effect see Vlekke, *op. cit.* (n. 401), pp. 8–9. Also see Linschoten in Burnell and Tiele (eds.), *op. cit.* (n. 25), I, 108.

[407] Sumatra's length is actually 1,100 miles, its extreme breadth is 250 miles, and its area is 164,198 square miles. The circuit of the island is about 2,300 miles. See A. Cortesão (ed.), *op. cit.* (n. 46), I, 165, n. 1.

[408] On the lakes of Sumatra as sources of its rivers see William Marsden, *The History of Sumatra . . .* (2d ed.; London, 1784), p. 9.

helps to produce a luxuriant vegetation. Tropical diseases run rampant and foreigners are particularly susceptible to them. The island produces gold, iron, tin, brimstone (sulfur), copper, and naphtha, a rock oil which flows from a fountain in the kingdom of Pasei.[409] In the center of this kingdom there rises a volcanic mountain like Etna in Sicily which constantly burns. It is called "Balahião" by the natives of Pasei.[410] While sulfur is produced by the volcanoes, gold is mined and dug from the river bottoms of the interior in the kingdom of Menangkabow.[411] Trees and plants which are numerous and of many varieties produce the fruits that are used for food and ornamentation. They are also the sources of white sandalwood, benzoin (an incense), aloe-wood and camphor like that produced in Borneo and better than that from China. The spices which grow in Sumatra are common pepper, long pepper, ginger, and cinnamon. Large quantities of silk are produced for export to India. Insects and wild animals are so numerous that they cannot be named. Fish abound in the rivers and in some places, such as in the river of "Siaça" (in the kingdom of Siak),[412] the natives take only the roe for food. As a rule the Sumatrans live on a diet of millet, rice, seeds, and wild fruits.

The population is made up mainly of native heathens and foreign Muslims who originally came to the island for trade. In about 1370 (i.e., 150 years before the governorship of Diogo Lopes de Sequeira [1518–21])[413] Moors from Persia, Arabia, Gujarat, Hindustan, and Bengal began to trade and settle the coastal regions and gradually to extend their political control over them. The natives, unable to resist the encroachments of the Muslim traders, retreated into the mountains of the interior. Throughout the island, stand many well-populated but simple cities largely composed of thatched houses.[414] Across the strait from Malacca towards the interior live the most warlike people in the world; they are called "Batas" (Bataks) and they eat human flesh, particularly the flesh of prisoners taken in battle.[415] The "Sotumas,"[416] who live further south, are more civilized. Though both the natives and the Muslims have their own languages, they nearly all speak the Malay tongue of Malacca and follow certain Malay customs.[417]

All the natives are small, well-proportioned and brown-skinned with dark, flowing hair. That they do not resemble the Javanese, their nearest neighbors,

---

[409] See *ibid.*, p. 23, who describes this as an "earth oil used chiefly against the destructive ravages of the white ants. . . ."

[410] On central Sumatra there are still five active volcanoes. See Crawford, *op. cit.* (n. 34), p. 415.

[411] Castanheda in Azevedo (ed.), *op. cit.* (n. 79), I, 456. For confirmation see Marsden, *op. cit.* (n. 408), pp. 133–34.

[412] Crawfurd (*op. cit.* [n. 34], p. 379) calls it the finest river in Sumatra.

[413] Somewhat too late. We know from Marco Polo that they were in Perlak in 1292. See above, p. 573.

[414] Castanheda in Azevedo (ed.), *op. cit.* (n. 79), I, 456.

[415] For confirmation of their cannibalism, see Crawford, *op. cit.* (n. 34), p. 42, and for a horrifying description see Marsden, *op. cit.* (n. 408), pp. 298–300.

[416] Unidentified.

[417] See Barros in Cidade and Múrias (eds.), *op. cit.* (n. 39), III, 233; and Castanheda in Azevedo (ed.), *op. cit.* (n. 79), I, 456. Cf. Marsden, *op. cit.* (n. 408), pp. 159–66.

gives rise to the generalization that great, natural variations may occur within very short distances.[418] This difference is all the more remarkable in that the people of Sumatra are referred to under the general name of "Jaus."[419] Even in Sumatra people admit that the Javans were once masters of the island, and that in earlier times the Chinese had control of the trade between the island and India. Such striking differences in facial features appears to substantiate for Barros his belief that the Javans are not native to the country in which they live but are originally a people who came there from China. This assumption is reinforced, he believes, by the fact that the Javans resemble the Chinese in appearance, politeness, and mechanical ingenuity. Until the coming of the Portuguese, the Sumatrans, like the Javans, fought with arrows and other primitive weapons. They were quick to learn, however, how to manufacture firearms, brass and iron cannons, and new types of war vessels.

Thirty kingdoms, according to Barros, existed along the coasts of Sumatra when the Portuguese first arrived in India.[420] Some of these numerous "kingdoms" were little more than cities. Their number was sharply reduced in time as the larger and more powerful states expanded and annexed their neighbors. In the interior, which is thought to be very extensive, many lords and princes reign about whom the Portuguese have no information. Pedir,[421] which was a famous city-state even before the founding of Malacca, is reputed to be a center of the pepper trade as great as Malabar.[422] In earlier times ships from all over the area congregated at Pedir because it dominated the traffic in the strait. But with the founding of Malacca, and especially after the arrival of the Portuguese in the East, Pedir began to decline and its place was gradually taken by Pasei. The neighboring state of Acheh was then but a minor state; in the late sixteenth century it became the greatest of them all. Barros tells us that in their positions relative to each other, the status of these Sumatran states is constantly changing, a condition which gives the Portuguese ample opportunity to play one off against the other.[423]

Varthema, who possibly visited Pedir around 1505, describes it as a well-organized mercantile center; on one street alone he found five hundred money changers. In its harbor, he reports, are built huge junks "which carry three masts, and have a prow before and behind, with two rudders before and two

---

[418] Barros in Cidade and Múrias (eds.), *op. cit.* (n. 39), III, 233.

[419] The Muslim traders applied the term "Jawi" to all the natives of the archipelago, especially the Malays. See Crawfurd, *op. cit.* (n. 34), p. 419.

[420] Cidade and Múrias (eds.), *op. cit.* (n. 39), III, 233–34. Many of these names correspond closely to the nineteen "kingdoms" and eleven "lands" set down by Pires. This similarity in the two lists led Cortesão ([ed.], *op. cit.* [n. 46], I, 135–36, n. 1) to suggest that "Barros used Pires' work, directly or at second-hand." Most of the writers list no more than seven states, and content themselves with remarking that Sumatra contains many other kingdoms as well.

[421] The name of a Malay state in eastern Sumatra no longer in existence. Its territory apparently extended from Diamond Point to Acheh. For further details see Crawfurd, *op. cit.* (n. 34), pp. 330–31, and Cortesão (ed.), *op. cit.* (n. 46), I, 139–40.

[422] Castanheda in Azevedo (ed.), *op. cit.* (n. 79), I, 456.

[423] Barros in Cidade and Múrias (eds.), *op. cit.* (n. 39), III, 234.

behind."[424] Aside from pepper, Pedir produces silk, benzoin, aloe-wood, and fireworks. The people of the city sleep in good beds and are extremely agile swimmers. Pedir's houses are low, walled domiciles constructed of stone and many of them are covered with the shells of great sea turtles. Varthema was also impressed with the art objects, probably from elsewhere, which he saw for sale in the markets of Pedir.[425]

The king of Pedir, according to Barros, married two of his nieces to his slaves, the lords of Daia and Acheh, shortly after the Portuguese conquered Malacca.[426] This event gives the chronicler an opportunity to digress on the institution of slavery as it exists in the East. He claims that free persons are put into slavery through being captured in war, as punishment for civil offenses, sale by others, and sale by the slave himself. Parents often sell their children for very low prices, Barros himself admitting that he had in his own house at the time when he wrote a Gujarati slave who had been sold by his mother for a pittance. Even persons of noble lineage ofttimes sell themselves into bondage in order to raise money for their own use. Slaves of noble background are in constant demand by the great lords who pay steep prices for them, treat them honorably, and use them as military retainers. Noble slaves are sometimes married to women of the owner's family, invested with large estates, and named heirs of the owner's properties. Barros was clearly intrigued with what were for Europeans novel variations on the institution of slavery; he seems to have understood that bondage in the Oriental sense is not necessarily permanent, that redemption is always possible, and that the slave is far more than a mere chattel, for he has the right to marry free persons and to own and bequeath property.[427]

On his way to Malacca in 1511, Albuquerque brought his fleet into the port of Pedir. There the conqueror met Portuguese merchants who informed him about the harsh conditions in the Malay port for Christians bent on trade. He then sailed eastward from Pedir to Pasei, "the principal port of the island of Sumatra,"[428] to demand that its ruler hand over a Moorish renegade from Malacca who had tried to murder certain Portuguese. The king of Pasei, named "Geinal,"[429] in his reply vowed that the Moor had left his territory but that he would try to find the culprit. In the belief that he was being deceived,

---

[424] Temple (ed.), *op. cit.* (n. 5), p. 86.

[425] *Ibid.*; Varthema has often been charged with repeating tales told to him by others rather than having actually described what he saw (providing that he was ever east of India at all). From our viewpoint, his characterization is nonetheless important, even if false, for his book was widely circulated. See above, p. 165. The only native type of exquisite art which he might have seen is the fine filigree work of the coastal goldsmiths. See Marsden, *op. cit.* (n. 408), pp. 141–42.

[426] Cidade and Múrias (eds.), *op. cit.* (n. 39), III, 409.

[427] Cf. Crawfurd, *op. cit.* (n. 34), pp. 404–5. And for confirmation of this practice at Pedir in the eighteenth century see Marsden, *op. cit.* (n. 408), p. 333. See Bruno Lasker, *Human Bondage in Southeast Asia* (Chapel Hill, N. C., 1950), pp. 26–36.

[428] Birch (ed.), *op. cit.* (n. 10), III, 59.

[429] See Barros (in Cidade and Múrias [eds.], *op. cit.* [n. 39], III, 235) for this name; Castanheda (in Azevedo [ed.], *op. cit.* [n. 79], II, 131) calls him "Coltazina" or Sultan Zina. Professor C. C. Berg suggests that his name was possibly Qain-al Abidin.

Albuquerque broke off communications and sailed out of the port of Pasei. While marauding in the straits against ships engaged in the Malacca trade, Albuquerque subsequently attacked and captured a Javan junk which had "Geinal" aboard. The captive king told Albuquerque that he was on his way to Java to seek help against a rebellious nobleman who had unseated him. The Portuguese conqueror, in his desire to establish cordial relations with people of influence in the spice trade, treated "Geinal" kindly and promised that he would help to restore him to power after conquering Malacca. The king agreed that upon being reinstated he would acknowledge the suzerainty of Portugal and pay tribute.[430] It was in this manner that the Portuguese tried to replace the Moors as king-makers in Sumatra.

Once Malacca had been captured, Portuguese influence on the east coast of Sumatra mounted correspondingly.[431] But, since their fortunes in southeast Asia rose and fell, the Portuguese were unable at any time to coerce the princes of Sumatra into permanent submission. Over the course of the century, Acheh gradually rose as a major center of resistance to Portuguese efforts to concentrate the spice trade at Malacca. The rulers of Acheh, in alliance at times with other insular princes, repeatedly besieged Malacca itself. When Linschoten wrote he was able to say that the Portuguese do not reside in Sumatra, do very little business there, and are constantly threatening, but not acting, to conquer the recalcitrant islanders.[432] He might have added that the Christian missionaries were likewise unable to penetrate Sumatra effectively.

The Portuguese chroniclers, who become interested in Pasei through the story of Albuquerque's agreement to help restore "Geinal," recount that succession in this state is by assassination.[433] Divine ordinance, according to Barros, is believed to be the source of the custom whereby the people depose one ruler and establish in his place another of their choice. Each new ruler is told the day, the hour, or the week of his death. At the appointed time the people of the city pour out into the streets and raise a great cry. In their delirium they attack and kill the king and his advisers. On one occasion three different kings were crowned in a single day. Similar stories are told about succession practices in Bengal, and it appears that this mode of ceremonial killing was inaugurated in Pasei by the Bengali groups so influential there.[434] About the other major states of the island, the Portuguese say little not directly related to their commercial and military roles. An exception is the remark of Albuquerque to the effect that the Hindus of Menangkabow are especially proficient in the manufacture of

---

[430] *Ibid.*, pp. 64–65.

[431] "Geinal" soon broke off connections with the Portuguese, though he finally recovered his kingdom. In 1521 he was killed by the Portuguese in alliance with the ruler of Aru and a rival prince replaced him. Thereafter Pasei seems to have lost its importance as a trading center, even though the Portuguese established a fortress and a factory there in 1522.

[432] Burnell and Tiele (eds.), *op. cit.* (n. 25), I, 108–9. Also see the work of Lemos, written around 1580, which is a plea for the Portuguese to take advantage of disruptions in Acheh and conquer it.

[433] Cf. Barbosa in Dames (ed.), *op. cit.* (n. 77), II, 189.

[434] See Pires in Cortesão (ed.), *op. cit.* (n. 46), I, 143; cf. above, p. 415.

arms[435] and greatly revere "a certain golden headdress which, as they relate, Alexander [the Great] left there with them when he conquered that country."[436]

When Albuquerque dispatched three reconnaissance ships under the command of António de Abreu to the Moluccas in 1511, they followed the route most commonly used by the spice ships trading between the islands and Malacca. Normally, after passing through the straits, the trading vessels followed the western coast of Borneo southward, crossed the Java sea, and then sailed along Java's northern coast to the southern strand of Celebes and from there on to the Spice Islands themselves. As a consequence, Borneo, especially its northern and eastern coasts, were not ordinarily touched upon by the fleets sailing to and from the Moluccas. Occasional fleets tried sailing around Borneo as an alternative route, but it did not become common practice until the end of the century. De Abreu, who followed the regular route, had the first opportunity given a Portuguese to get by direct experience some sense of the number and size of the islands in the archipelago. There were reports aplenty at Malacca of the eastern islands from the Asian and Muslim traders there, but the Portuguese now had a chance to see for themselves how vast and complex the archipelago really was. And they lost very little time after 1511 in finding out about the ports and peoples involved in the eastern end of the spice trade. Just a decade after the Portuguese arrived in the Moluccas, the tiny fleet which Spain had sent out under Magellan appeared on the scene. The Portuguese, possibly because of the policy of secrecy, have very little to say about either Borneo or Java, and the missionary accounts are also very slight on these two islands. The Spanish, whose knowledge of the archipelago was much more limited than that of the Portuguese, were on the contrary much freer in relaying to the rest of the Christian world whatever they knew.

Borneo was not visited by a Portuguese expedition until 1526. While Varthema may have touched upon the southwest coast of Borneo in about 1506, his desultory description of it published in 1510 includes little beyond mere mentions of the clothing worn by the inhabitants, their pagan beliefs, and the export of camphor.[437] Much the best of the early sources are the accounts by Maximilian of Transylvania and Pigafetta of the visit made in 1521, by the survivors of Magellan's expedition, to the kingdom of Brunei in northern Borneo. This was five years before Dom Jorge de Menzes, the Portuguese governor of the Moluccas, touched there on his way to Ternate. Thereafter the Portuguese began to take a more serious interest in Borneo. In 1548, two years before

---

[435] Cf. Linschoten in Burnell and Tiele (eds.), *op. cit.* (n. 25), I, 110; also Crawfurd, *op. cit.* (n. 34) p. 274.

[436] Birch (ed.), *op. cit.* (n. 10), III, 162; this is possibly a vague reference to the belief that the kings of Menangkabow were descended from Iskander, the Alexander the Great of Asian mythology. Menangkabow was not converted to Islam until the middle of the sixteenth century. Stories of the exploits of Alexander were carried into southeast Asia at an early date by Muslim merchants. For a history of the Alexander romance in Malay literature see P. J. van Leeuwen, *De Maleische Alexander-roman* (Utrecht, 1937).

[437] Temple (ed.), *op. cit.* (n. 5), pp. 89–90.

Ramusio published the accounts of Borneo by Barbosa, Pires, Maximilian, and Pigafetta, Oviedo issued Book XX of his *Historia general y natural de las Indias* in which he gives one of the lengthiest descriptions of Borneo to see print in the sixteenth century. Oviedo bases his description on Maximilian and Pigafetta, and on reports which he apparently received from persons like Urdaneta who had participated in the Loaisa expedition of 1526.[438] Gómara, the Spanish contemporary of Castanheda and Barros, first published his popular *Historia general de las Indias* at Saragossa in 1552. Like Oviedo's earlier work, Gómara's *Historia* includes a substantial section on Brunei's king and the customs of his people.[439]

Though Portuguese merchants traded regularly in Borneo beginning in 1530, very few of their reports seem to have gotten into print during the sixteenth century. Castanheda, like the Spanish historians, first refers to Borneo in his discussion of the Magellan enterprise,[440] and subsequent allusions to it are made in connection with his recital of the Portuguese projects in the Moluccas.[441] Barros fails to add materially to the information presented by the earlier authors, at least in those volumes of the *Décadas* printed during the sixteenth century. The Jesuit letterbooks and historians are likewise almost completely silent about Borneo. Even Linschoten, who specialized in finding out about areas where the Portuguese were least active, has almost nothing specific to add. Oliver van Noort, the Dutch navigator, landed at Brunei in 1598, but regular trade between the Hollanders and the islanders did not commence until 1606. Thus, neither the Portuguese nor the Dutch sources are of great value for the study of Borneo in the sixteenth century. The Spanish materials, both before and after the establishment of the Spanish at Manila, are better than any others available in Europe before 1600.

The European sources, meager as they are, have importance for the history of Borneo because there are almost no native annals or monuments of so early a date which tell of the island's past. The Javan, Muslim, and Chinese sources provide bits of data on pre-sixteenth century history, but it has been seriously alleged that "the true history" of the northern kingdom of Brunei begins with Pigafetta's account of the visit there of the companions of Magellan.[442] But Pigafetta was not even the first European to comment on Borneo. Odoric of Pordenone, in the fourteenth century, visited parts of coastal Borneo and relayed a few items of interest about them to Europe; he tells us, for instance, that a flour called sago flour is there manufactured from the pith of the sago palm, and it makes, he asserts, "the best *pasta* in the world." Varthema, Barbosa, Pires, and Maximilian all wrote their accounts of Borneo before Pigafetta set down his, though the works of Varthema and Maximilian were the

[438] Above, p. 117.
[439] Swecker, *op. cit.* (n. 11), p. 20.
[440] Azevedo (ed.), *op. cit.* (n. 79), III, 163–64.
[441] The only substantial description comes in connection with the visit there in 1530 of Gonçalo Pereira on his way from Malacca to Ternate (*ibid.*, IV, 227).
[442] Crawfurd, *op. cit.* (n. 34), p. 70.

only ones of the three to precede Pigafetta into print. Thus, it seems, highly dubious, even on the basis of the European sources alone, that Brunei's "true history" begins with Pigafetta. It is, however, accurate to say that modern students of Brunei's early history derive more data from the European sources than from any other foreign or native corpus of materials.

Most of the sixteenth-century cartographical representations of Borneo, and particularly of its east coast, are somewhat fanciful and vague.[443] Pires, usually so well informed, is the only one of the writers to make the mistake of talking about Borneo as a group of islands. The others are agreed in treating it as a single, large island situated roughly in the open sea northwest of the Moluccas and astride the equator. In general, they all have a tendency, however, to place it too far north and closer to China than it really is, possibly because both China and Borneo were sources of camphor. But Oviedo is somewhat more precise. He locates Borneo and the neighboring island of Halmahera (Gilolo) in the general vicinity of the Moluccas.[444] Most of the specific materials in the European accounts relate to Brunei, but Castanheda lists five great seaports that he says were known to the Portuguese.[445] In his transcriptions they are called "Moduro" (Marudu?),[446] "Cerává" (Sarawak?),[447] "Laue" (Lawai),[448] "Tanjapura" (Tanjungpura),[449] and "Borneo" (Brunei) "from which the island derives its name." The most active of these ports as international trading centers are Brunei, Lawai, and Tanjungpura, but rich merchants reside in all of them and carry on a brisk trade with China, the "Laqueas"(Liu-ch'ius), Siam, Malacca, Sumatra, and other neighboring islands.[450]

While Borneo is declared to be a rich island, the Portuguese made no attempt in the sixteenth century to invade and conquer it. Unlike Malacca, it is a place which is "well furnished with victuals,"[451] including thereunder meat, fish, rice, sago, and a wine called "tampoi" (Malay, *tâmpang*) which Castanheda esteems

[443] *Ibid.* The first extant map to show Borneo with its complete coastline and in a relatively correct form is an anonymous chart of *ca.* 1535 owned now by Boies Penrose. See Cortesão and Teixeira da Mota, *op. cit.* (n. 2), I, 123–24. It was not, however, until the production of Berthelot's map of 1635 that Europe had a fairly accurate cartographical representation of Borneo. See Cortesão (ed.), *op. cit.* (n. 46), I, 132, n. 1. For a modern map of Borneo which includes the place names which appeared on sixteenth-century maps see figure II in J. O. M. Broek, *Place Names in 16th and 17th Century Borneo* (Minneapolis, n. d.). This valuable little treatise, in mimeographed form, was prepared under the auspices of the Department of Geography, University of Minnesota. Unfortunately, the author seems not to be aware of Castanheda's list of town names.

[444] De los Rios (ed.), *op. cit.* (n. 298), II, 16–18. For a summary of Oviedo's discussion of Borneo see Swecker, *op. cit.* (n. 11), pp. 192–93.

[445] Azevedo (ed.), *op. cit.* (n. 79), IV, 227.

[446] Marudu is the name of a large bay on the north coast. See Broek, *op. cit.* (n. 443), Fig. II. A town named Marudi is situated on the modern map to the southwest of Brunei.

[447] Sarawak is on the west coast. See *ibid.*

[448] Not on modern maps, but charts of the sixteenth to the eighteenth centuries place it on the southwestern coast under this name, and with slight variations (e.g., "Laoe") in spelling. See Cortesão (ed.), *op. cit.* (n. 46), I, 224, n. 1. It may very well be that Lawai was a great port in the delta of the Kapuas River. For details on this identification see Broek, *op. cit.* (n. 443), pp. 12–15.

[449] On the problem of locating this region or town see *ibid.*, pp. 15–20.

[450] Castanheda in Azevedo (ed.), *op. cit.* (n. 79), IV, 227.

[451] Barbosa in Dames (ed.), *op. cit.* (n. 77), II, 206.

more highly than "any of the other counterfeit wines"[452] of the East. The "true camphor" produced in Borneo is valued like gold in India and brings a much higher price than the camphor of China. It is the best of the edible camphors and is used in India as a medicine and as an additive to betel. The Persians try to pawn off imitations of Borneo camphor on their customers because of its great value.[453] Borneo is also renowned for its diamonds which are found along the west coast in the vicinity of Tanjungpura and are finer stones than those of India.[454] In their annual voyages to Malacca, the merchants of Borneo also bring with them gold of low assay value, wax, honey, and aromatic woods.[455] They pay no formal duties at Malacca, but are required to give the port officials a fixed present.[456] In their purchases the Borneo merchants concentrate on Cambay and Bengal textiles, copper, mercury, cinnabar, Indian drugs, and beads of all descriptions. Apparently, the merchants were able, in turn, to trade the brightly colored cloths, beads, and trinkets to the primitive Dayaks in return for their stores of gold.[457]

The coastal peoples of Borneo are deemed to be peaceful, honest, good-looking, and civilized. Most of the merchants are Muslims who dress in Malay style and use the Malay language. The early writers stress that the majority of the people are heathen, and Barbosa, possibly on the basis of reports from Malacca,[458] asserts that the king is also a heathen.[459] Pires, who wrote at about the same time, contends that most of the people are heathen and that the king of Brunei had but recently become a Moor.[460] Pigafetta, who was received by the ruler of Brunei in 1521, describes him as a corpulent Moor of forty who goes under the name of Rājā "Siripada" (Sripadh).[461] Modern scholars, primarily on Pires' authority, agree that Islam was accepted by the ruler of Brunei in about 1500. They also believe that Borneo became one of the main centers of Muslim commercial and religious activity after Malacca fell to the Portuguese.[462]

The town of Brunei, the administrative capital of north Borneo, is best

---

[452] Azevedo (ed.), *op. cit.* (n. 77), IV, 227; "tampoi," which was widely exported to other places, is a very sweet liquor made from the fruit called *tâmpang* (Dalgado, *op. cit.* [n. 53], II, 348). Pigafetta and his companions were served arrack when they visited Brunei.

[453] For references to camphor and its uses see Barbosa in Dames (ed.), *op. cit.* (n. 77), II, 207; Castanheda in Azevedo (ed.), *op. cit.* (n. 79), IV, 227; and Orta's lengthy colloquy in Markham (trans.), *op. cit.* (n. 359), pp. 86–98. For other early references to the camphor of Borneo see Yule and Burnell, *op. cit.* (n. 218), pp. 116–17. Professor Berg points out that camphor was probably not used as an additive to betel. The confusion arises, he believes, over the fact that the Javanese word *kapura* means either lime or camphor. Lime is still used in making a quid of betel.

[454] Castanheda in Azevedo (ed.), *op. cit.* (n. 79), IV, 227.

[455] Pires in Cortesão (ed.), *op. cit.* (n. 46), I, 132.

[456] *Ibid.*   [457] *Ibid.*, p. 133.

[458] For example, António de Brito, the first governor of Malacca, reported to Lisbon that the king of Brunei was a heathen. Modern scholars believe, however, that the coastal towns had accepted Islam before the arrival of the Portuguese in the East (Hall, *op. cit.* [n. 30], p. 184).

[459] Dames (ed.), *op. cit.* (n. 77), II, 207.

[460] Cortesão (ed.), *op. cit.* (n. 46), I, 132.

[461] Robertson (ed.), *op. cit.* (n. 136), II, 35. *Sripadh* means "His Majesty."

[462] Hall, *op. cit.* (n. 30), and see map on p. 178 depicting the spread of Islam, and p. 199.

described by Pigafetta on the basis of his two-day stay there. He places the city some distance up the Brunei River and recounts how he and his seven companions were taken from their ship up to the city in light canoes called *praus*. Except for the houses of the rājā and some of his chiefs, the entire city is built over the water. Its habitations are constructed of wood which rest on high pilings. The city's everyday business is transacted by women who travel around in boats at high tide. He estimates the population at twenty-five thousand hearths (or about one hundred thousand people),[463] a figure which later writers consider to be grossly exaggerated.[464] On disembarking from the *praus*, Pigafetta's group rode to the royal palace on the backs of gaily bedecked elephants. The palace itself is said to be protected by a brick rampart on which fifty-six brass and six iron cannons are mounted. In the residence where the Europeans were housed, they slept on cotton mattresses covered with silk sheets, ate a vast selection of meats with golden spoons from porcelain dishes, and had their sleeping quarters lighted by torches of white wax which burned constantly.[465]

The reception of the Europeans on their visit to the royal palace is one of several such ceremonies recorded by the Western writers on Asia. Mounted on elephants, the visitors rode through the streets between rows of armed guards and moved directly into the royal enclosure. They were received in a great hall by a company of nobles and invited to be seated on a carpet. At the opposite end of the reception room, they saw an elevated hall separated from the main court by windows and silk hangings. When the curtains were pulled aside, the visitors could see the ruler and his young son sitting at a table and surrounded by women servants. They were not allowed to communicate with the sultan directly, but could do so only through his representatives, who, in their turn, talked to their ruler through a speaking tube in the wall. After being cordially received and sumptuously feted, the Europeans learned from the courtiers that the ruler never ventures out unless he goes hunting and that all of his acts are recorded by ten scribes called "xiritoles"[466] who write on very thin bark.[467] This rājā, like the rulers of Malacca, runs the international trade in his port cities through an administrator called in their language a "xabandar" (Persian, *shāh-bândar*, or "king of the port").[468] The rājā's authority must have extended to the southernmost reaches of the island (though probably not to the interior), for Pigafetta reports that Brunei's forces sacked Lawai in 1521 for seeking to shift its allegiance to a ruler in Java.[469]

[463] Robertson (ed.), *op. cit.* (n. 136), II, 34. Oviedo gives the figure of 20,000 small houses in De los Rios (ed.), *op. cit.* (n. 298), II, 17. On this occasion Oviedo is following Maximilian's *De Moluccis.* . . . The English translation is in C. H. Coote (ed.), *Johann Schöner* (London, 1888), p. 136.

[464] Crawfurd, *op. cit.* (n. 34), pp. 70–77, is particularly prone to discount Pigafetta's accuracy, and he notes that in the mid-nineteenth century Brunei's population was estimated at a mere 12,000.

[465] Robertson (ed.), *op. cit.* (n. 136), II, 31–33.

[466] Juru-tulis or "secretaries."

[467] Robertson (ed.), *op. cit.* (n. 136), II, 35.

[468] Castanheda in Azevedo (ed.), *op. cit.* (n. 79), IV, 227.

[469] Robertson (ed.), *op. cit.* (n. 136), II, 37.

The common people, aside from those belonging to the mercantile community are said to have a language of their own.[470] Maximilian of Transylvania and Oviedo are unique among the writers in the comments which they make on the beliefs and attitudes of the primitive islanders.[471] As pagans, these people worship the sun as the lord of the day and the moon as the mistress of the night, and believe them to be the parents of the stars. In their everyday activities they are charitable and just, and have a great love for peace and leisure and a hearty distaste for war. Rulers who become involved in hostilities are strongly disliked and are forced to take the most dangerous position on the battlefield. A king who guards the peace is as revered as a god. It is not to be assumed that these people want peace at any price. If they suffer an unprovoked attack, they will submit to the inevitable and fight. But, as soon as the wrong has been righted, they make haste to sue for peace. They consider it an honor to be the first to request peace, an infamy to be the last, and a crime to refuse it. In personal relations, robberies and murders are completely unknown among them.[472]

This characterization of the peace-loving and honorable primitives of Borneo which originates with Maximilian contrasts sharply with the lurid stories of war and cannibalism in the accounts of post-sixteenth century writers who lived among the Dayaks and other tribes of the island for substantial periods of time.[473] It is likely that the letterwriter and chronicler were being misled on this matter by their informants; Oviedo himself expressed doubt about one story, also included by Maximilian, which told of a pearl as large as a goose egg decorating the crown of the king of Borneo. When Oviedo checked out this tale with Juan Sebastián del Cano, he was informed that it was a joke. Oviedo also was skeptical about certain rumors which were relayed to him about the natives of a south sea island who had ears so large that they could envelope the entire body with one of them. While he discards this story with the pungent remark that "the Spaniards were looking for spiceries and not fables,"[474] he seems to have accepted somewhat innocently a spurious description of "noble savages" similar to other descriptions which were being circulated in his day and long thereafter. None of the other sixteenth-century accounts of Borneo supports this characterization; in fact, they contain only scattered and incidental references to the natives of the island.

The Spanish in the Philippines were for a short time involved in the affairs of Borneo. Not long after their occupation of Manila, the Spaniards were to learn by experience that life in Borneo was not idyllic and that it could be real

---

[470] Barbosa in Dames (ed.), *op. cit.* (n. 77), II, 207. Most of the Dayak tribes, one of them being the Kayans, have their own languages. None of them has invented a script of its own. Crawfurd, *op. cit.* (n. 34), pp. 127–28.

[471] See the English translation of his *De Moluccis . . .* , in C. H. Coote (ed.), *op. cit.* (n. 463), pp. 134–37. Oviedo's account is almost a direct translation of this.

[472] For a summary see Swecker, *op. cit.* (n. 11), pp. 192–93.

[473] For a series of characterizations by nineteenth-century European visitors to the tribes of Borneo see Crawfurd, *op. cit.* (n. 34), pp. 128–32.

[474] As quoted in Swecker, *op. cit.* (n. 11), p. 193.

and earnest. In 1578, Sirela (also known as Maleka), a deposed ruler of Brunei, arrived in Manila to ask help against his domestic enemies. Francisco de Sande,[475] the Spanish governor, responded to this request by outfitting and leading an expeditionary force against Brunei with the design of reducing it to vassalage and of opening it to Christian missionaries. After a short fight, the Spaniards succeeded in restoring Sirela and extracting guarantees from him of vassalage and friendly relations. Soon after their departure, the ruler of Brunei again was in trouble and in 1581 was forced to request aid once more from his Manila supporters. On this occasion, Captain Gabriel de Rivera was sent out at the head of a task force and he succeeded in putting Sirela back into power. After the accomplishment of his mission, Rivera explored the coast of Borneo before returning to Manila. Rivera was shortly thereafter sent as an emissary to Spain, but the Spanish made no further efforts in the sixteenth century to effect closer relations with Brunei or any other parts of Borneo.[476] Their attention was diverted after the union with Portugal (1581) to the possibility of richer conquests in China, Japan, and Indochina. In fact, when Mendoza talks about the eastern archipelago he mentions Borneo only once and characterizes it as one of the places where the hated Moors have made a deep impression.[477] It was not until around 1600 that a Portuguese factory and a Catholic mission were finally established at the town of Brunei.

The people of Java were far better known to the Portuguese than was Java itself. When Albuquerque arrived in Malacca, a numerous colony of influential Javan merchants were resident there and many Javans had fought in the army which the Portuguese defeated. Still, the news of Albuquerque's conquest of the entrepôt at the straits prompted one of the rulers of Java to dispatch an emissary to Malacca with gifts and the offer to supply the Portuguese government with all of the supplies and foodstuffs necessary for the maintenance of the city. This particular Javan ruler, who was often at odds with the Malays because of their harsh treatment of his subjects, initially welcomed the change in government and even volunteered to supply men to help the Portuguese hunt down the hapless Malay sultan.[478] Albuquerque sent the emissary home with the gift of one of the elephants he had captured at Malacca. The Portuguese conqueror himself was so impressed with the ability of the Javans as carpenters and shipbuilders that he sent sixty of them with their families back to Cochin.[479] Barbosa, who apparently quizzed the companions of Albuquerque at length when they returned to India, comments on the Javan ships with four masts "which differ much from the fashion of ours, being built of very thick timber,

[475] For the objectives of his mission see the documents in E. H. Blair and J. A. Robertson (eds.), *The Philippine Islands (1493–1803)* (Cleveland, 1903), IV, 148–55; for a letter of 1573 from King Sebastian of Portugal to the ruler of Borneo which was confiscated by the Spanish, see *ibid.*, pp. 173–74.

[476] Zaide, *op. cit.* (n. 208), p. 273.

[477] Staunton (ed.), *op. cit.* (n. 394), II, 261.

[478] Albuquerque in Birch (ed.), *op. cit.* (n. 10), III, 163.

[479] On boat construction along the northern coast of Java see Crawfurd, *op. cit.* (n. 34), p. 176.

so that when they are old a new planking can be laid over the former, and so they remain very strong."[480] Thus, from the very beginning of their enterprise in southeast Asia, the Portuguese realized that the Javans, like the much-admired Chinese, were excellent craftsmen and tough commercial competitors. It is perhaps these attributes among others which leads Barros to believe that there is more than a slight relationship between the Javans and the Chinese.[481]

De Abreu, on his way to the Moluccas in 1511, made a stopover at the port of Geresik in northeastern Java and presented its ruler with gifts from Albuquerque. But not all of the Javan princes viewed the Portuguese intrusion with so much equanimity. The Muslim state of Japara on Java's northern coast, one of the chief intermediate ports on the route between Malacca and the Spiceries, reacted quickly and violently to the Portuguese seizure of Malacca. Afraid that the Europeans would disrupt and destroy the free flow of trade in the waterways of the archipelago, Japara sent a fleet against Malacca in 1513. The Portuguese beat off the attack, but in the process they made a mortal enemy of the rising Muslim state which continued, in spite of this setback, to extend its jurisdiction over the northern coast of Java. Its ruler in a short time became the sultan of Demak. The island thereafter suffered a number of internal wars as several of the Muslim states combined forces against the declining Buddhist kingdom of Majapahit.

While the Portuguese were aware of the deep internal divisions in Java, they were unable with their limited resources to take advantage of them for their own ends. In 1522, Henrique Leme was sent to western Java to make an alliance with a Hindu prince. When the Portuguese returned five years later, they found that this town had also fallen into the hands of the Muslims. By 1535, most of the northern coast of Java had succumbed to Islam as Demak reached the zenith of its power. It was only at the extreme eastern edge of the island that the Hindus retained a remnant of control. Franciscans were sent to eastern Java around this time in an effort to convert its rulers, but this enterprise enjoyed no success. When Demak's supremacy faded around 1540, the leadership in northern Java was retaken by the Muslim state of Japara. It was the queen[482] of this kingdom who sparked the allied Muslim attacks on Malacca of 1550 and 1574. The rise of Pajang and Mataram, two interior states, paralleled the decline of the coastal sultanates in the last generation of the sixteenth century. While the Portuguese by their constant attacks certainly contributed to the downfall of the coastal states, the shift in the center of power to the Muslim states of the interior did nothing to bring the Europeans into closer touch with Java.[483]

It can be clearly seen from the foregoing that the Portuguese had but few opportunities after 1512 to learn about Java at first-hand. Consequently, the

---

[480] Dames (ed.), *op. cit.* (n. 77), II, 173–74.

[481] Cf. *ibid.*, pp. 191–92, n. 1; Cortesão (ed.), *op. cit.* (n. 46), I, 179. Also see above, p. 576.

[482] Professor Berg doubts that a woman ever ruled over Japara. He suggests that this is a reference to a mythical queen who represents a demonical force in Javanese traditional history.

[483] Hall, *op. cit.* (n. 30), p. 204.

published European sources on Java in no way reflect how much more importance this island intrinsically had in the life of the archipelago than other places,
like Sumatra, on which the Portuguese accounts are much fuller.[484] Illustrative
of Java's higher level of civilization is the fact that it was an economic fulcrum
in the archipelago and that the Javanese writings are fuller and more detailed
and inscriptions more numerous than those of any other part of Indonesia. But
it is also true that the Javan writers are not always reliable, "their notions of the
past being a product of imagination and entirely unchronological."[485] The
European sources, therefore, as inaccurate and piecemeal as they are in some
respects, have the virtue of being realistic and of dating events with a relatively
high degree of exactitude. The Portuguese, as limited as they were in their
ability to trade at the great ports of Java, were forced to seek out smaller and
less cosmopolitan places. Consequently, they mention places and events of local
significance which are omitted by the religious and court-minded scribes of
Java. Finally, the Portuguese in their preoccupation with economic affairs,
tend to bring into their accounts the common practices of the marketplace
and of everyday life rather than concentrating on the glories of princely
conquests.[486]

No certain reference to the name Java appears in European literature until
Marco Polo. Whether Polo himself ever visited what he calls "Greater Java"
is in doubt because his data, it is alleged, does not correspond with what is
generally known about the geography and products of the island we call Java
today. It has been argued at length and with some plausibility that his data
does not jibe with the facts because in talking about "Greater Java" he was
actually describing Cochin-China.[487] Odoric of Pordenone, however, seems
beyond doubt to have visited Java on his way to Canton in the early fourteenth
century. He writes that the island was then ruled by a great lord who lived in a
sumptuous palace and had seven lesser rulers as his vassals. Odoric also heard
about the Mongol expedition from China against Java. Over a century later
Conti, who may have gotten as far to the east as Sumbawa, inveighs against the
Javans for eating unclean animals, their habit of running amuck, and their
addiction to cockfighting as a chief form of amusement.[488]

The authors of the sixteenth century who comment at some length on Java,

---

[484] Pires, whose descriptions of Java and Sumatra on the basis of personal visits there were among
those parts of his work not procured and not published by Ramusio, also exhibits this bias. His
account of Java, however, is far better than any of those published in the sixteenth century. See
Cortesão (ed.), *op. cit.* (n. 46), I, 166–200. For an excellent study which compares Pires with
other leading sources on the last years of the Majapahit empire see H. J. de Graaf, "Pires' Suma
Oriental en het tijdperk van den godsdien-stovergang op Java," *Bijdragen tot de taal-, land- en volkenkunde*, CVIII (1952), 132–71.

[485] C. C. Berg, "Javanese Historiography—A Synopsis of Its Evolution," in Hall (ed.), *op. cit.*
(n. 8), p. 13. On Berg's historiographical ideas see J. G. de Casparis, "Historical Writing on Indonesia
(Early Period)," in *ibid.*, pp. 159–63.

[486] Vlekke, *op. cit.* (n. 401), pp. 92–93.

[487] Charignon, *loc. cit.* (n. 341), pp. 193–347.

[488] Major (ed.), *op. cit.* (n. 31), Pt. IV, p. 16.

its environs, and its people are the following: Varthema, Barbosa, Pigafetta, Oviedo, Barros, Castanheda, Albuquerque, Góis, and Linschoten. Of these writers, the only ones who may possibly have written from personal experience are Varthema and Castanheda. While Varthema may have landed on the northeastern corner of the island, the account of his fortnight's experience there is so dubious that Crawfurd brands it as being "false or worthless." [489] Castanheda's references are much more factual, but they are all of the type which could have been learned from informants. Castanheda actually seems to follow Barbosa closely, though he adds a few significant particulars not found elsewhere in the published materials. Even Barros, who is normally so thorough, has very little specific data on Java. But this is certainly not because it was unavailable in Europe. Pires' detailed description of Java, though it was not published until the twentieth century, must have been known to Barros. In fact, he may even have used it for his narrative on the history of Mĕlayu. That he does not use Pires as a source for Java and for data vital to the spice trade appears to be a further indication of the fact that this information was highly classified in the sixteenth century. Of the authors actually published in the sixteenth century, the most informative on Java are Barbosa, Oviedo, Castanheda, and Barros.

The chroniclers agree in placing Java immediately to the east of Sumatra from which it is separated by the Strait of Sunda, a channel no more than fifteen leagues (60 miles) in width. [490] The island stretches in an east-west direction and its northern coast is 170 leagues (680 miles) in length. [491] About the southern coast and the width of the island the chroniclers admit that they have no exact information. [492] But the natives tell the Portuguese that the southern coast has few good harbors and that the breadth of the island is approximately one-third of its length. [493] A chain of mountains bisects the island along its length and renders communication impossible between the peoples of the northern and southern coasts. Along the northern coast are the ports of "Tūba" (Tuban), "Panaruca" (Panarukan), "Cidayo" (Sidayu), and "Agacī" (Geresik), the last of

---

[489] *Op. cit.*, p. 165; for a less critical estimate see Temple (ed.), *op. cit.* (n. 5), p. lxxvi.

[490] Barros in Cidade and Múrias (eds.), *op. cit.* (n. 39), II, 400. This geographical description was written by the Portuguese Livy himself. In the fourth decade, not published until 1615 and therefore not of concern here, the continuator (Couto) introduces a complication by making Java two islands; Sunda is separated from the rest of the island by a river. See Swecker, *op. cit.* (n. 11), pp. 77–78. Pires (in Cortesão [ed.], *op. cit.* [n. 46], I, 168) says that it is only one island but that it is divided by a river, a possible source of Couto's mistake. Castanheda in Azevedo (ed.), *op. cit.* (n. 79), II, 158 agrees with Barros in making it one island, and he says that the strait is from 10 to 20 leagues wide. The Strait of Sunda appears in relatively correct form for the first time on an anonymous planisphere prepared *ca.* 1545. See Cortesão and Teixeira da Mota, *op. cit.* (n. 2), I, 155–57.

[491] Castanheda in Azevedo (ed.), *op. cit.* (n. 79), II, 158. This is overestimated by about 100 miles (Crawfurd, *op. cit.* [n. 34], p. 167). But Barros' mistake is greater; he gives 190 leagues (760 miles). See Cidade and Múrias (eds.), *op. cit.* (n. 39), II, 400.

[492] Even by Linschoten's time (*ca.* 1585), the Portuguese seem not to have known much more about Java's geography. See Burnell and Tiele (eds.), *op. cit.* (n. 25), I, 111–12.

[493] Crawfurd, *op. cit.* (n. 34), p. 167 indicates that there are just two moderately good harbors on the south. The breadth of the island varies from 48 to 117 miles.

which is the chief trading port of the island and the one at which De Abreu called on the first Portuguese voyage to the Moluccas.[494] Actually these were all ports on the northeastern coast opposite the island of Madura and free of all Muslim control. Pigafetta, on the basis of what his Javanese pilot told him, lists[495] the largest cities of Java as "Magepaher" (Majapahit), the capital, as well as Daha,[496] "Dama" (Demak), "Gagiamada" (unidentified), "Minutaranghen" (unidentified), "Cipara" (Japara),[497] the port of Demak, Tuban, and "Cressi" (Geresik). He also mentions the names of Surabaya, and of the islands of Bali and Madura as places closely associated with Java. Linschoten mentions "Sunda Calapa" (possibly Djakarta or Bantam) on the northwestern coast as the "principal haven in the Iland."[498]

Java is reputed to be the most bountiful island in the world in foodstuffs. Rice, meat, pepper, cinnamon, and ginger are abundant, cheap, and of good quality. Sunda (western Java) is universally mentioned as a great source of pepper, but unfortunately for the Portuguese it fell under Muslim control shortly after the conquest of Malacca. Linschoten gives to his Dutch readers a long list of the products of Java with their prices, as well as details on what imports are most desired by the islanders, and lets them know that the coins in use are "caixas" (cash) from China.[499] Java also produces some gold and copper. Oviedo generously concludes that everything in Java is as good as it is in Spain.[500]

In the interior of the country most of the people are heathen, while in the port cities the Moors predominate. Though the island is politically divided, the king of Java at the time of Malacca's fall was called "Pateudra" (Pate Udara),[501] one of the last rulers of the Majapahit dynasty. Though his Islamic vassals were in rebellion against him, the "heathen king" was still able to control them as of about 1515. "Pationus" (Pate Unus), Muslim lord of Japara, attacked Malacca in January, 1513, and after being repulsed, began to work towards acquiring the throne of Demak and extending his jurisdiction to Sunda.[502] Henrique Leme was sent in 1522 to a port of Sunda (possibly "Calapa") in

---

[494] List of ports published in Castanheda (in Azevedo [ed.], *op. cit.* [n. 79], II, 158). For identifications see Cortesão (ed.), *op. cit.* (n. 46), I, 189–92. Pires (*ibid.*, p. 193) calls Geresik "the jewel of Java in trading ports" and he discusses most of the ports along the entire northern coast.

[495] Robertson (ed.), *op. cit.* (n. 136), II, 167–68.

[496] A city famous in the Hindu period near modern Kediri in eastern Java. Also spelled "Daia" and "Daya" in the European works.

[497] See Cortesão (ed.), *op. cit.* (n. 46), I, 160, n. 1, and pp. 187–88.

[498] Burnell and Tiele (eds.), *op. cit.* (n. 25), I, 112. For identification see Cortesão (ed.), *op. cit.* (n. 46), I, 172, n. 1.

[499] Burnell and Tiele (eds.), *op. cit.* (n. 25), I, 113–14; for confirmation see Cortesão (ed.), *op. cit.* (n. 46), I, 181.

[500] De los Rios (ed.), *op. cit.* (n. 298), II, 105.

[501] Barbosa in Dames (ed.), *op. cit.* (n. 77), II, 190. For further identification of individual rulers see Cortesão (ed.), *op. cit.* (n. 46), I, 175–76.

[502] Castanheda in Azevedo (ed.), *op. cit.* (n. 79), II, 242, gives 1512 as the date. For the date given above see Cortesão (ed.), *op. cit.* (n. 46), I, 151–52, n. 3. For further detail on the extension of Pate Unus' power to Sunda see R. A. Kern, "Pati Unus en Sunda," *Bijdragen tot de Taal-, Land- en Volkenkunde*, CVIII (1952), 124–31.

western Java to conclude a treaty with the local ruler who was still free of Muslim control. A treaty of commerce was signed and a *padrão* (marker) was set up on a site where the Portuguese were authorized to build a fortress.[503] Within a few years, however, this part of Sunda became Muslim and the Portuguese were forced to call only at the ports of eastern Java. Oviedo, on the basis of information conveyed to him by Urdaneta about his visit of 1535 to Panarukan, relates that there were then four kingdoms in Java which were constantly involved in war with one another. But the heathen (Hindu) ruler of Panarukan, the Spaniard admits, is a great friend of the Portuguese.[504] Very little specific information on political conditions emerges from the other sources.[505]

The people of Java, their customs, and skills, are granted most space by the European authors. This is so because many Portuguese learned to know the Javans working at trades and in crafts at Malacca and in the ports of India. Barbosa, Castanheda, and Linschoten, all three of whom had long experience in India, are in essential agreement in their descriptions of Javan physical features, personality and character, skills, and beliefs.[506] The men are chestnut-colored, strong and heavy-set, with broad faces and fleshy cheeks, heavy eyebrows, almost beardless, and with pitch-black hair cropped close to their heads.[507] They wear no head covering and ordinarily go naked above the waist. Their women are lighter in color with excellent complexions, ugly features, beautiful bodies, and graceful carriages. The Europeans judge both sexes to be exceedingly proud, daring, and skillful; at the same time they are alleged to be deceitful, treacherous, clumsy, obstinate, bellicose, and ill-tempered.[508]

But of their industry and ability there is no question or criticism. Barros compares them to the Chinese and judges them to be "the most civilized people of these parts."[509] They are expert carpenters, shipwrights, and locksmiths. They specialize in making arms of all kinds: guns, iron-tipped spears, krises, scimitars, wooden shields which cover the entire body, blowpipes which shoot poisoned arrows, and huge bows. In hunting and riding they show great daring and agility. And their skills are not limited to the use of primitive arms. They are esteemed highly in India as gunners, bombardiers, and makers of gunpowder.[510] Their women are adept seamstresses and musicians. Since the

[503] Azevedo (ed.), *op. cit.* (n. 79), II, 242–43.

[504] De los Rios (ed.), *op. cit.* (n. 298), II, 105.

[505] It is not clear precisely how many independent states existed in sixteenth-century Java. In 1579 when Drake touched on Java, the island was reportedly governed by six rājās: "Donaw," "Rabacapala," "Bacabatra," "Tymbanton," "Patimara," and "Mawgbange." See *The Famous Voyage* in Hakluyt, *op. cit.* (n. 114), XI, 132. The three Javan states of the Muslim period were Bantam, Demak, and Mataram; it was not until the eighteenth century that Mataram was divided into three states.

[506] Barbosa in Dames (ed.), *op. cit.* (n. 77), II, 191–94; Castanheda in Azevedo (ed.), *op. cit.* (n. 79), II, 158–59; Linschoten in Burnell and Tiele (eds.), *op. cit.* (n. 25), I, 114.

[507] Cf., for a similar description, Crawford, *op. cit.* (n. 34), p. 173.

[508] Contrast *ibid.* where they are judged to be "peaceable, docile, sober, simple, and industrious."

[509] Cidade and Múrias (eds.), *op. cit.* (n. 39), II, 400.

[510] For confirmation of their ability in these crafts see Crawfurd, *op. cit.* (n. 34), pp. 176–78.

Portuguese actually saw so little of life in Java itself during the sixteenth century, it is not surprising that they omit comment on the great skill of the Javans in agriculture and irrigation.

The customs and beliefs of the Javans appear strange, superstitious, and repellent to the Europeans. For some unexplained reason the Javans will permit nothing to be over or upon their heads. It is the worst insult possible to put a hand on a Javan's head, and he who does so places his life in jeopardy. They even build their houses just one story high so that nobody can walk over them.[511] Varthema, who perhaps heard about the ceremonial cannibalism of the Bataks of Sumatra, alleges that in Java parents sell their children to be eaten.[512] He also notices that the Hinduized Javans, like many in India, will worship the first thing they happen to meet in the morning. Pigafetta reports on the prevalence of concremation and unusual sexual practices.[513] Castanheda, following Barbosa, comments on their addiction to wizardry, sorcery, and love-enchantments. They believe that if one of their swords is completed at a designated propitious moment it will magically guarantee its wearer against death by the sword and defeat in battle. Wherever they happen to live, whether in a foreign city like Malacca or in a native town like Panarukan, the Javans are inclined, more than any other people of the archipelago, to run amuck as a way of obtaining satisfaction for real or imagined injuries. In war, likewise, they care very little about death.[514]

The European sources, as scanty and contradictory as they sometimes are, give the reader a real sense of the size and importance of the three Indonesian islands and their place in the history and trade of the archipelago. Naturally most of what they have to convey relates to the coastal towns and states and especially to those with which they had the greatest familiarity through steady intercourse. This leads the European writers to overstress the importance of the coastal areas which they know most about and to underplay the significance of interior territories which were learned about only by indirect report. They are also poorly informed about certain untouched coastal areas, such as the southern coasts of Sumatra and Java and the eastern coast of Borneo. On interior political divisions they are best on Sumatra and Java, though they exhibit practically no knowledge of Java's internal topography, climate, agriculture, or, in its highest sense, culture.

It was because of their relatively intimate degree of familiarity with coastal places and seagoing peoples that the Portuguese writers stress the expansion

[511] For confirmation of this custom from an independent Chinese source see W. W. Rockhill, "Notes on the Relations and Trade of China," *T'oung pao*, XVI (1915), 240, n. 1.

[512] Temple (ed.), *op. cit.* (n. 5), p. lxxvi.

[513] Robertson (ed.), *op. cit.* (n. 136), II, 169; Crawford (*op. cit.* [n. 34], p. 166) notes that concremation was still being carried on in Bali in the mid-nineteenth century. On sexual practices see above, p. 553n.

[514] Castanheda in Azevedo (ed.), *op. cit.* (n. 79), IV, 144; for confirmation see Pires in Cortesão (ed.), *op. cit.* (n. 46), I, 176. For discussion see Crawfurd, *op. cit.* (n. 34), p. 12.

and strength of the hated Muslims throughout the entire region. Most of their informants were obviously of the mercantile and shipping classes, and they seriously recounted to the Portuguese their own myths about the past. The Portuguese faithfully recorded these popular stories as the basis for the oral history of the region, and apparently heard or knew little about the priestly tradition regarding the past. The Portuguese, because their informants were merchants, are likewise overly impressed by what they consider to be the importance of the Malay language and Malay customs as universal unifying forces.[515] They know many more details about Javan customs than of those of the other peoples because of the undoubted presence of large numbers of Javans in Malacca and India. This fact perhaps helps to explain why they are most critical of Javan habits and adulate the peoples of Borneo of whom they knew but little. It is also clear that information on Borneo was not classified in Lisbon to the degree that the reports on Java and Sumatra were. Evidence for this is that Pires' materials on Borneo, like his discussion of the Philippines, were made available to, and published by, Ramusio. Such a conclusion is reinforced by the way in which Pires organized the *Suma oriental*: he grouped Borneo with the countries to the East (China, Japan, and the Philippines), while including Sumatra and Java in the section on the eastern archipelago and the spice trade, the part of his work which was originally suppressed and remained generally unknown until the twentieth century.

7

THE SPICERIES

A glance at a map of modern Indonesia reveals a profusion of islands which lie scattered in the seas south of the Philippines, east of Borneo and Java, north of Australia, and west of New Guinea. Men throughout history have sought to group these islands into neat archipelagos to talk about them intelligibly. The eye and mind working in harmony have great difficulty, however, in combining these unordered spots into comprehensible and manageable patterns. The task is rendered even more complex when it is necessary to group the islands into unities which pay some deference to the focal points of the region as they existed in the sixteenth century. To avoid doing violence either to geography or history, we shall denominate as the Spiceries all of those islands which actually grew the cherished spices as well as those which were intimately related economically, geographically, politically, or strategically to the trade and to the producing islands. For example, the five spice islands (Ternate, Tidore, Motir, Makian, and Bachan), the original sources of the clove, had to depend in the sixteenth century for food upon the large, nearby island of

[515] Cf. the list of words collected by Drake's men in Hakluyt, *op. cit.* (n. 114), XI, 132–33.

Halmahera (also called Gilolo or Batochino do Moro).[516] In our definition this forms an interdependent economic complex which we will refer to as the Moluccas. Two other insular groups, likewise part of a geographical entity and held together by various types and degrees of interdependence, were Amboina (Seram, Buru, and Amboina) and Banda (Gunuape, Mira, and Banda), the latter group being the source of nutmeg and mace. Celebes, the larger islands of the Lesser Sunda archipelago (Bali, Sumbawa, Flores, and Timor), and New Guinea will be considered as another entity within the Spiceries because of their locations and their traditional associations with the Moluccas. It is imperative to remember, however, that these groupings, like many constructs of the mind, tend to give an impression of greater unity and interrelatedness than can always be supported as times and conditions change.

Almost every European who wrote about Asia had remarks to make about the Spiceries. Explorers, merchants, statesmen, missionaries, and chroniclers eagerly gathered and assessed every scrap of information about the spices and the conditions of trade at the sources. The most authoritative of the numerous accounts are those of Varthema, Barbosa, Maximilian of Transylvania, Pigafetta, Oviedo, Gaetano, Castanheda, Gómara, Barros, Galvão, Linschoten, the Jesuit letters and histories, and the commentators on the explorations of Drake, Cavendish, and Lancaster. These authors represent a number of European nationalities: Italian, Portuguese, Spanish, English, and central European. A sizable minority of them write from personal experience in the Spiceries: Varthema (possibly), Pigafetta, Galvão, Gaetano, Xavier and his Jesuit successors, and the Dutch and English explorers. Barbosa, Castanheda, and Linschoten have the benefit of experience in India and of direct participation in the spice trade. The Portuguese chroniclers (Castanheda and Barros) and their Spanish contemporaries (Oviedo and Gómara) naturally take opposing views on the question of the ownership of the Spiceries,[517] but their descriptions of the islands themselves are similar.

Varthema may have touched upon Banda, Buru in the Amboina group, and Ternate in the Moluccas in 1505.[518] Irrespective of whether or not he was actually on the islands, Varthema's description (published in 1510) of these three groups in the Spiceries was the first to be circulated in Europe. None of the earlier travelers of the Renaissance, with the possible exception of Conti,[519] even claims to have been east of Borneo. So it was from Varthema that Europe received its first impressions of the places where the valuable cloves and nutmegs grew. He correctly reports that the nutmeg tree grows in Banda and locates

---

[516] Halmahera actually parallels the five smaller islands and is close to them. The Portuguese writers of the sixteenth century, as a rule, do not consider it to be one of the Moluccas. In the mid-seventeenth century the Dutch ordained that the clove trees in the Moluccas should be destroyed and production of cloves confined to Amboina and nutmeg to the Banda islands. The origin of the name "Moluccas" is unknown. See Philips (ed.), *op. cit.* (n. 139), p. 111.

[517] See above, pp. 114–19.

[518] Temple (ed.), *op. cit.* (n. 5), p. lxxv.

[519] See above, p. 61.

clove production in "Monoch" (the Moluccas).[520] Roughly accurate are his descriptions of the clove tree and the way in which the cloves are harvested. Of the physical surroundings and the peoples of the Spiceries he gives a dark picture. They have no government, live in gloomy, low houses built of timber, and are very primitive in their way of life. They are pagans whose beliefs resemble those held by the lowest castes of Calicut. Little can be hoped for from these people because they are stupid and lazy. They expend no labor in cultivating the spices, but simply gather and market them at the appropriate seasons of the year. While certainly inaccurate on a number of points, particularly on the absence of government, Varthema's low opinion of the people is one that later and better informed writers share.[521]

The Portuguese voyages to the Spiceries began on a systematic basis immediately after the conquest of Malacca in 1511. António de Abreu, the first to reconnoiter the route, coasted along the northern side of the Lesser Sundas as far east as Flores and then turned north to the Amboinas and Bandas.[522] In the course of this voyage the Portuguese observed the small volcanic island of Gunuape[523] in the Bandas from the cone of which there falls "continually into the sea flakes or streams like unto fire. . . .[524] They anchored at the port of "Guli-Guli" (Kolli-Kolli) on the island of Seram and went ashore only to find that the people were cannibals.[525] On the return voyage the junk commanded by Francisco Serrão was wrecked in the Banda Sea and he along with a few companions made their way to Amboina and eventually to Ternate about 1513. Here Serrão remained for the rest of his life (d. 1521) as adviser to the Muslim ruler of Ternate and as an occasional, albeit somewhat unreliable, informant for the Europeans on insular affairs. De Abreu returned with two vessels to Malacca and, on the basis of his information, new fleets were immediately outfitted and dispatched to the Spiceries.[526] But nothing about these voyages appeared in published form in Europe until the Spanish began to write about the Spiceries in connection with Magellan's circumnavigation of the globe.[527]

[520] Temple (ed.), *op. cit.* (n. 5), p. 89.

[521] For example, Alfred Wallace, the great biologist, who visited the Spiceries in the mid-nineteenth century, refers to the Amboines as being "half-civilized, half-savage, lazy people" (*op. cit.* [n. 94], p. 230).

[522] See Humberto Leitão, *Os portugueses em Solor e Timor de 1515 a 1702* (Lisbon, 1948), pp. 25–52.

[523] *Gunung-api* is Malay for "fire mountain" (Crawfurd, *op. cit.* [n. 34], p. 33).

[524] Galvão in Vice-Admiral Bethune (ed.), *The Discoveries of the World from Their First Original unto the Year of Our Lord 1555 by Antonio Galvano, Governor of Ternate* ("Hakluyt Society Publications," Old Series, Vol. XXX [London, 1872]), p. 117.

[525] Visconde de Lagoa and Elaine Sanceau (eds.), *António Galvão. Tratado dos descobrimentos* (3d ed.; Porto, 1944), p. 171, n. 3.

[526] For a review of these sailings see Leitão, *op. cit.* (n. 522), pp. 53–55.

[527] Pigafetta (in Robertson [ed.], *op. cit.* [n. 136], II, 81, 83) notes that the Portuguese had discovered the Moluccas ten years before his arrival there in 1521 and had studiously kept this knowledge a secret from Spain. Magellan apparently introduced Charles I to Varthema's account of the Spiceries (see *ibid.*, II, 211). When he was in Malacca, Magellan himself had corresponded with Francisco Serrão and learned from him about affairs in the Spiceries. About the unreliable character of Serrão's information on the location of the Moluccas (twice as far to the East of Malacca as they actually are), see C. E. Nowell, *Magellan's Voyage around the World: Three Contemporary Accounts* (Evanston, Ill., 1962), pp. 15–19.

Maximilian reports in his letter on the Moluccas published in 1523 that Magellan and Cristóbal de Haro,[528] possibly on the basis of information garnered from Serrão, had pointed out to King Charles I that the Spiceries and China were within the Spanish demarcation, that the Portuguese were going there illicitly, and that it was possible to avoid the Portuguese blockade and to sail to the clove islands by a presumed southwestern route. Those survivors of Magellan's expedition who arrived at Tidore on November 8, 1521, stayed in the Moluccas for about one month and a half. In relating the story of the experiences of Magellan's men in the Moluccas, Pigafetta and Maximilian also brought before their European audiences independent but similar word portraits of the only islands in the world where the prized cloves then grew. Maximilian apparently received most of his data from Juan Sebastián del Cano, the commander of the "Victoria," and several other survivors.

All of the five clove-growing islands of the Moluccas are normally dominated by the ruler of the chief island of Ternate. Tidore and Bachan likewise have formal royal establishments (sultanates), but Motir and Makian have no kings and are ruled "by the people."[529] Eight months before Pigafetta's arrival at Tidore, Francisco Serrão, the captain of Ternate's armed forces, had been poisoned while on a trading mission to Tidore. Ten days later, his master and the ruler of Ternate, Rājā Abuleis, met a similar fate at the hands of his daughter, the wife of the king of Bachan. Nine principal sons of Rājā Abuleis were left to contend among themselves for the throne. When the Spanish fleet arrived at Tidore, its ruler, Sultan Manzor, appears to have replaced the ruler of Ternate, temporarily, as the overlord of the clove islands.[530]

Manzor is pictured as a handsome and dignified Moorish ruler of forty-five years of age. To receive the foreigners he was barefooted and clad in a delicate white shirt with gold-embroidered cuffs, a sarong, and a silken turban. He welcomed the Spanish expedition in a friendly manner and volunteered to place Tidore, and, if possible, Ternate in vassalage to the king of Spain. Manzor was evidently concerned that the Portuguese from Malacca might be preparing reprisals against him for his part in Serrão's murder and hoped that the protection

[528] Cf. above, pp. 115–16; and also Coote (ed.), *op. cit.* (n. 463), pp. 111–12.

[529] Pigafetta in Robertson (ed.), *op. cit.* (n. 136), II, 71. Cf. Varthema, above, p. 594. Pigafetta's description of his experiences in the Moluccas may also be found in G. B. Ramusio, *Delle navigatione ...* (Venice, 1550), I, 403r–407r.

[530] Barbosa (Dames [ed.], *op. cit.* [n. 77], II, 200–201), who wrote in about 1518, notes that on Ternate "dwells a Moorish King whom they call Soltan Binaracola ... [who] was formerly King of all five, but now the four have risen against him and are independent." Pires (in Cortesão [ed.], *op. cit.* [n. 46], I, 214) reports that only the king of Ternate is called Sultan, the rest are rājās. He also records that "Raja Almancor" (Manzor) of Tidore is at war with Ternate. In fact, this was almost the regular state of affairs in the archipelago, for the rivals headed up competing alliances. The rulers of Ternate and Tidore struggled against each other for supremacy in the archipelago with the aid respectively of the *Oulilima* (Five-Power Alliance) and the *Oulisiva* (Nine-Power Alliance). Each camp frequently had allies on the same island, and neighboring communities (*kampongs*) fought each other in their roles as members of these competing alliances. Consequently, local strife and warfare were almost endemic to the Moluccas and to those of their neighbors who became involved in their power struggle. See Wessels, *op. cit.* (n. 21), p. 29.

of Spain might help him to retain his control in the islands.[531] Whatever his motives actually were, Manzor treated the Spaniards exceedingly well and did his utmost to gather together a cargo of food, water, and cloves for them before they would have to catch the monsoon. Within three days after their arrival, he had a building thrown up for them to use as their warehouse on shore. He sent envoys for cloves to neighboring islands and permitted a few of the Europeans to accompany them. Rulers of the other islands were allowed to come to Tidore to inspect the new arrivals and their two battered vessels. The Europeans entertained their visitors by firing their artillery and by presenting them with knickknacks of European manufacture. From observing Manzor and the other Moorish rulers, Pigafetta learned that they have as many women as they desire, that they keep them in harems, and that every family within a ruler's jurisdiction is required to present one or two daughters to the royal harem.[532]

Among those who came to see the Spanish expedition were some merchants of Halmahera and one of its rulers. This large island, Pigafetta reports,[533] is inhabited by Moors who control the coast and heathens who live in its interior, a division of power which the Europeans found to be quite common throughout the East Indies. The Moors, who first came into the Moluccas about fifty years before the Spanish arrived at Tidore, quickly took over the coastal areas and control of the trading towns.[534] By Pigafetta's time, Halmahera had three kings—two Moors and a heathen prince named Rājā Papua.[535] The Moorish rulers keep large harems and father hundreds of children; the heathens are not inclined to have so many wives even though Papua possesses a rich store of gold. The ordinary heathens are likewise less "superstitious" than the Moors, though "they adore," like Hindus, "for all that day the first thing that they see in the morning when they go out of their houses."[536] Rājā Jessu, one of the Moorish rulers of Halmahera and an aged man, visited the Spanish at Tidore to see how they fired their guns. About Halmahera itself, Pigafetta learned that it is so large that it takes native crafts (*praus*) four months to circumnavigate it. It also produces certain thick reeds (of which the Europeans bought many) that grow on rocks and which are filled with fresh, clear water.[537] A few cloves

---

[531] See Manzor's speech as given in Maximilian's words in Coote (ed.), *op. cit.* (n. 463), p. 140.

[532] Robertson (ed.), *op. cit.* (n. 136), II, 75.

[533] *Ibid.*, pp. 75–76.

[534] *Ibid.*, p. 115. This is roughly confirmed by Pires (in Cortesão [ed.], *op. cit.* [n. 46], I, 213).

[535] This mention of Papua, the first in a European source, has frequently been interpreted as a reference to the Papuans of New Guinea, and the survivors of Magellan are incorrectly credited with having discovered that island. For comment in depth see Arthur Wichmann, *Entdeckungsgeschichte von Neu-Guinea (bis 1828)* (Leiden, 1909), I, 12–13.

[536] Robertson (ed.), *op. cit.* (n. 136), II, 77.

[537] The Jesuit, Fróis, writes in 1556 (Wicki [ed.], *op. cit.* [n. 80], III, 542): "The whole island [Ternate] has . . . thick canes with a pleasant water in them which the Portuguese drink." Probably bamboos filled with water from local rivers. Wallace, *op. cit.* (n. 94), p. 61, observed that the Dayaks of Borneo used ". . . thin, long-jointed bamboos for water vessels. They are clean, light, and easily carried and are in many ways superior to earthen vessels for the same purpose."

grow on Halmahera, but they are not as good or as valuable as those which come from the five smaller islands.[538]

While waiting for a cargo, the Europeans went ashore on Tidore and visited a few of the smaller, nearby islands. Pigafetta used his time ashore to study the local scene. He depicts each of the five clove-producing islands of the Moluccas as a mountainous island, all of which are within sight of Tidore except for Bachan to the south. Bachan is the largest of the five islands and its peak is higher and blunter than those of the other mountains. The clove tree will not live in the flatlands but prospers on the sides of these volcanic mountains. Cloves become perfect because of the mountain mists which regularly cover them. Each island possesses groves of its own trees which the people watch over but never cultivate. Harvests occur twice each year, at Christmas time and at the nativity of St. John the Baptist (June 23), and every fourth year a bumper crop is gathered. The cloves must be harvested when they are red and ripe or otherwise they become so large and hard that only their husk is of value. Until the merchants come to purchase them, the cloves are dried and stored in pits. A few nutmeg trees also grow in the Moluccas. Pigafetta describes both the clove and the nutmeg trees and their fruits. Crawfurd remarks that the Italian's "Account of the clove is a good popular one, even at the present day [1856]."[539] Pigafetta also used his time to compile, probably while in Tidore and possibly aboard ship as well, his vocabulary of Malay which he calls "the words of those Moro people"[540] of Tidore. Only forty-seven words of his total compilation of 450 actually appeared in the sixteenth-century versions of his work.[541] In Tidore, he notices, cloves are called "ghomode"; in Sarangani (the islands south of Mindanao), "bongalauan"; and in Malacca, "chianche."[542]

Besides cloves, the Moluccas grow ginger roots which are dried in lime for preservation. Honey is produced and stored in the trees by small bees.[543] In addition, the islands yield a wide variety of tropical fruits as well as sugar cane, rice, poultry, goats, and palm products. The islanders, who normally go uncovered except for a breach cloth, manufacture their own clothes from the bark of trees. They soak the bark in water, beat it with sticks, and pull and shape it to the desired size and form. The bark so processed looks "like a veil of raw silk" and gives the appearance of being woven.[544] Pigafetta also describes the various stages in the production of sago flour and bread, and notices that the natives while at sea live almost exclusively on it. Multicolored and white

---

[538] All of the European writers agree that Halmahera produced no great amount of cloves. Also see Crawfurd, *op. cit.* (n. 34), pp. 10–11.

[539] *Ibid.*, p. 103. Also see Orta in Markham (trans.), *op. cit.* (n. 359), pp. 213–21.

[540] Robertson (ed.), *op. cit.* (n. 136), II, 117.

[541] See Ramusio, *op. cit.* (n. 529), I, 408v.

[542] Robertson (ed.), *op. cit.* (n. 136), II, 91, 215, n. 502 (discussion of local names). Cf. Orta's names in Markham (trans.), *op. cit.* (n. 539), p. 215.

[543] Robertson (ed.), *op. cit.* (n. 136), II, 115. Wallace, *op. cit.* (n. 94), pp. 153–54, describes the huge honeycombs of wild bees which hang from the highest branches of the tallest trees in Timor.

[544] Robertson (ed.), *op. cit.* (n. 136), II, 89.

parrots flourish in the islands, but those which are reddish speak much more distinctly than the others. The islanders prize highly and tell many wonderful stories about thrushlike birds called "bolon divata" (*Burung-dewata* or Bird of the Gods).[545] These extraordinary creatures, now called Birds of Paradise, are said to originate in heaven, never to fly except when there is a wind, and to render invincible and secure anyone who wears their skins into battle.[546] Of the preserved plumages brought back to Europe in the "Victoria," two were given to Charles I and one was sent by Maximilian to his father, the Cardinal of Salzburg.[547]

The houses of Tidore are elevated like those of other tropical places, though they are not built as high above the ground, and they are enclosed within fences of bamboo. When a new house is thrown up, the natives light a ceremonial fire and hold many ritual feasts before going to live in it. To the roof of the new house they fasten samples of the island's products to keep its occupants from ever being in want.[548] One day the Spanish, who guarded the merchandise in the storehouse ashore, were warned officially that they should not go outdoors at night because of danger from certain sorcerers. These anointed terrors, who were possibly running amuck, give the appearance of being headless as they roam through the town. Should they meet another man, they touch his head and rub some of their ointment on it. The accosted individual soon falls ill and succumbs within three or four days.[549] The divers of the island have remarkable ability in staying underwater for long periods of time. When the "Trinidad" sprang a mysterious leak in its hull, special divers were sent for who had long hair. These men, who could stay underwater for as long as an hour, tried to locate the leak by putting their heads against the bottom of the hull so that their long hair might be sucked into the hole along with the water.

Because the leak in the "Trinidad" was so serious and impossible to discover in the water, it was decided that she should remain behind for repairs and then try to make her way back to Spain via the Pacific.[550] The "Victoria" therefore left Tidore alone on December 21, 1521, with two native pilots aboard to lead her through the maze of islands to the south and west. Pigafetta provides long

[545] *Ibid.*, p. 105; these birds are called "Mamuco Diata" (*Manuk-dewato*) by Maximilian (Coote [ed.], *op. cit.* [n. 463], p. 143). For discussion of these appellations see Crawfurd, *op. cit.* (n. 34), p. 54, A more detailed analysis of these two common Malay terms for the "bird of Paradise," and of their use in English literature, may be found in C. P. G. Scott, "The Malayan Words in English," *Journal of the American Oriental Society*, Vol. XVIII, Pt. I (1897), 76–80 (The first part of Scott's article in *ibid.* XVII [1896]).

[546] Pigafetta in Robertson (ed.), *op. cit.* (n. 136), II, 105; Maximilian in Coote (ed.), *op. cit.* (n. 463), p. 143. For other stories see Linschoten in Burnell and Tiele (eds.), *op. cit.* (n. 25), I, 118. Actually the birds were probably not native to the Moluccas at all; the skins of the preserved birds given to the Europeans were probably prepared in the Aru Islands or New Guinea. See Wallace, *op. cit.* (n. 94), pp. 419–24.

[547] Coote (ed.), *op. cit.* (n. 463), p. 143.

[548] Robertson (ed.), *op. cit.* (n. 136), II, 107.

[549] *Ibid.*, pp. 106–07.

[550] On her unsuccessful effort to return see Henry R. Wagner, *Spanish Voyages to the Northwest Coast of America in the Sixteenth Century* (San Francisco, 1929), p. 96.

lists of individual island names for each of the small archipelagos through which the "Victoria" threaded its way.[551] He noticed that some of these places were peopled by pygmies and others by cannibals. After halting at Baru in the Amboina group, the men on the "Victoria" sighted the Banda archipelago and noted that it consisted of twelve islands on six of which nutmeg and mace grow in abundance. Pigafetta names all twelve islands and locates them at around 6 degrees south latitude.[552]

Southwest of the Bandas they entered the Lesser Sundas where they were hit by a heavy storm and had to take refuge on the island of "Malva" (now known as Alor or Ombai Island).[553] The people of this island are savage cannibals who "wear their beards wrapped in leaves and thrust into small bamboo tubes—a ridiculous sight."[554] Here the Spanish expedition stayed for two weeks to make necessary repairs on the ship, and Pigafetta notices that the natives cultivate long pepper and black pepper. On January 25, 1521, they sailed south-southwest of "Malva" to the island of Timor. Pigafetta then went ashore to ask the chief of the town of "Amaban" (Amaben) on the northern coast to sell them fresh meat.[555] Unable to get supplies here, they captured the chief of the neighboring village of "Balibo" (Silabão) and held him for ransom. While negotiating for provisions, Pigafetta learned that white sandalwood is grown on Timor and nowhere else,[556] and that traders come from as far away as Luzon to purchase sandalwood and wax. On the southern side of Timor live four heathen kings who have their residences at "Oibich" (Vaibico?), "Lichsana" (Lecam?), "Suai" (Suzi?) and "Cabanaza" (Camanassa).[557] Of these principalities "Oibich" is the most powerful and at "Cabanaza" the gold is found with which they pay for their purchases. While on Timor, Pigafetta also learned the names of eleven other islands in the Lesser Sundas from Flores westward to Bali.

The ships of the Loaisa (1525) and Saavedra (1527) expeditions across the Pacific got as far as Halmahera and Tidore. Urdaneta and his companions in the sole vessel remaining from the Loaisa expedition arrived on the east coast of Halmahera on October 29, 1526. From these survivors, who returned to Spain around 1536, Oviedo learned in detail about the difficulties which they experienced in the Spiceries at the hands of the Portuguese and their allies of Ternate.[558] Fortunately for them, they landed at "Campaho," a town which was in the hands

---

[551] For an effort to identify these many obscure names see *ibid.*, pp. 221–23.

[552] *Ibid.*, p. 153. They are actually at somewhat less than 5 degrees south latitude.

[553] See Cortesão (ed.), *op. cit.* (n. 46), I, 202 n. Alor is located between Flores and Timor in the Lesser Sunda chain.

[554] Robertson (ed.), *op. cit.* (n. 136), II, 157.

[555] For a map of Timor with early place names see Leitão, *op. cit.* (n. 522), facing p. 164.

[556] Actually it grows on a number of islands in the Malay archipelago, but Timor was certainly the most important source of supply. See Crawfurd, *op. cit.* (n. 34), p. 375, and Wallace, *op. cit.* (n. 94), p. 153.

[557] Robertson (ed.), *op. cit.* (n. 136), II, 163; for efforts to identify place names see map in Leitão, *op. cit.* (n. 522), facing p. 164.

[558] De los Rios (ed.), *op. cit.* (n. 298), pp. 65–100.

of "Quichil Bubacar,"[559] a vassal of the aged Sultan "Adulraenjami"[560] of Halmahera. "Adulraenjami" was himself an ally of "Rajamir" (Rājā Emir) of Tidore and an enemy of the Portuguese. From a slave who had been in the hands of the Portuguese for a time, the Spanish quickly learned that the Portuguese had taken reprisals against Tidore for the hospitality, aid, and vassalage which it had offered Magellan's companions. Urdaneta and five of his associates, including the interpreter Gonçalo de Vigo, were sent in *praus* to announce officially to "Adulraenjami" and "Rajamir" the arrival of this second ship from Spain. While they were given a cordial reception, it was not until the beginning of 1527 that the Spanish managed to get to Tidore through the Portuguese blockade and to join there with the survivors of the Magellan voyage. The Portuguese lost no time in attacking the new arrivals who were aided for a time by the governor of Makian ("Quichelhumar" or Kĕchil Umar), an enemy of Ternate and the Portuguese. The Portuguese finally destroyed the city of Makian while continuing to besiege Tidore. In February, 1528, Saavedra arrived at Tidore to reinforce the beleaguered Spanish. Though several efforts were made to find a route back across the Pacific, they all met with disaster.[561] The conclusion of the Saragossa arrangements in Europe in 1529 soon brought an end to the Spanish resistance in the Spiceries. Urdaneta and others took refuge for a time in the numerous islands of the Spiceries, but finally, after giving themselves up to the Portuguese, they began in 1534 and 1535 the long voyage back to Europe via Portuguese India.

At the conclusion of his discussion of the Iberian war fought in the Moluccas, Oviedo devotes a chapter to a description of the Spiceries.[562] While he surveys most of the important islands, his account is particularly valuable for the light which it throws upon the political and social organization of the little known islands of Halmahera and Celebes, and certain islets near Celebes in which Urdaneta spent time in 1532 and 1533 as a refugee from the Portuguese.[563] Like the Jesuits at a later date, Oviedo brings out clearly the association, political and economic, existing between Halmahera, northern Celebes, and the Moluccas.[564] Oviedo describes Gilolo as being but one of the states on the island known to the natives as "Aliora" (Halmahera).[565] The principal city of Gilolo (modern spelling is Djailolo) is eight leagues (32 miles) northeast of Tidore, though Halmahera at one point is no farther than two leagues (8 miles) east of Tidore. The people are far from primitive, many of them being Muslims as well

---

[559] "Quichil" is from the Malay *kĕchil*, meaning small, and it is used as a title equivalent to Spanish "Don." Bubacar or Abu-Bahr was this governor's proper name. See *ibid.*, p. 65.

[560] *Ibid.*, p. 70. Berg suggests "Adulraenjami" should be written Abd-Rahman i.

[561] The most detailed study of this expedition is Ione S. Wright, *Voyages of Alvaro de Saavedra Céron, 1527–1529* (Coral Gables, Fla., 1951).

[562] De los Rios (ed.), *op. cit.* (n. 298), pp. 100–105.

[563] *Ibid.*, pp. 102–3. He comments most particularly on two islands called "Bangay" and "Tobucu." Banggai lies off a peninsula of the same name on the east coast of central Celebes.

[564] Below, pp. 614–15.

[565] Means "mainland" in one of the native tongues to contrast its large size with the tiny islands surrounding it. See Crawfurd, *op. cit.* (n. 34), p. 10.

as heathens. Parts of Halmahera are under the control of Tidore and Ternate, and they use in those places the weights and measures common to the entire area. Crimes are punished by fines, exile, or death according to the magnitude of the offense. Of medium stature like the Spanish, the people of Halmahera are slim, agile, and well proportioned. They wear cotton and silk vestments, and like Moors everywhere take as many wives as they desire. The fathers of their brides receive money for their daughters. Gold is highly prized, though they do not have deposits of it themselves but receive it from the merchants from Celebes who trade there each year.[566] The people of Halmahera also place high value on silver, colored textiles of silk and cotton from India and Portugal, and porcelains from China. At their fiestas and before going into battle they play musical instruments which sound like bells. They also have many drums to whose rhythm they chant as they row, even when at sea for long periods of time. They prize brass articles highly and give good prices for the commodities of Flanders (knives, daggers, scissors), trinkets of ivory and coral, and glass beads. The people of Celebes likewise esteem these same items, but are particularly anxious to have iron with which to make their arms and their axes for woodcutting. Though most of the people in Celebes are heathen, there are a few Moors in that island. All the people, Moors and heathens, tattoo themselves with pictures of living creatures to help raise their courage for battle, and many of them wear their hair coiled at the nape of the neck. Throughout the islands the medium of exchange is Chinese copper cash. Oviedo was presented with four pieces of cash by Martin de Islares, and he includes a picture of one of them in his book. He also reproduces a picture of a house in Gilolo, possibly drawn by or at the instruction of Islares and Urdaneta.[567]

Given the reports of the Spanish voyages to the Spiceries and the debates in Europe over ownership of the Spiceries, it was not long before maps were being drawn in Lisbon and Seville which included data on these islands. Francisco Rodrigues, a pilot on De Abreu's expedition to the Spiceries, is the first (*ca.* 1513) to depict in a beautifully executed chart the islands of Sumbawa, Gunung Api, Timor, Amboina, and Seram; and he also vaguely delineates the archipelago of the Moluccas.[568] Jorge Reinel, who ran away from Portugal to Seville in 1519 when Magellan's expedition was being prepared, may have placed the Moluccas on the chart which became the standard (*padrón*) map of the East used by the Spanish explorers.[569] With the return of the "Victoria" and the rise in tempers over the ownership of the Moluccas, the contest continued

---

[566] Gold is procured by washings in the northern part of Celebes. In the nineteenth century, Celebes exported more gold than any of the other islands of the Indonesian archipelago with the exception of Borneo. *Ibid.*, p. 88.

[567] De los Ríos (ed.), *op. cit.* (n. 298), Appendix, Plate I, figs. 1 and 2.

[568] See Cortesão (ed.), *op. cit.* (n. 46), I, 200; II, 523.

[569] Cortesão and Teixeira da Mota, *op. cit.* (n. 2), I, 19–20. This is based on the depiction of the Moluccas incorporated on the chart prepared about 1517 and attributed to Pedro Reinel. See *ibid.*, pp. 33–34; G. Caraci, the Italian student of historical cartography, credits Nuno Garcia de Toreno, first master of the charts at Seville, with preparing the charts for Magellan's voyage. See *ibid.*, pp. 87–89.

between Spain and Portugal to lure the leading cartographers of the day into their camps. Lopo Homem, who prepared a chart of the known world in 1523 and acted, in 1524, as an expert for the Portuguese delegation at the Badajoz-Elvas conference, had apparently offered to furnish the Spanish with materials for a price.[570] In Pigafetta's book (first published in France *ca.* 1525) were included a few drawings of islands in the eastern archipelago. The Portuguese governor of the Moluccas, Dom Jorge de Menzes, was apparently the first European to set foot on New Guinea when his ship was blown beyond Halmahera in 1526.[571] None of the earlier maps, however, includes the northern coast of New Guinea even after it was again touched upon by the Villalobos expedition in about 1545. The depiction of the Moluccas in these years was caught up in the demarcation controversies, and the cartographers seem to have specialized in catering to the positions taken by their sovereigns. The planispheres of Diogo Ribeiro prepared in 1525 and 1527 place the Moluccas in the Spanish demarcation following the opinion and judgment of Juan Sebastián del Cano.[572] Two atlases of about 1537 attributed to Gaspar Viegas locate the Moluccas in 145 degrees longitude and draw in the entire west coast of Celebes[573] —possibly on the basis of information obtained from the survivors of the Spanish expeditions. The anonymous chart of about 1535 incorporates materials from the Spanish voyages and is particularly clear on the area between the Philippines and the Moluccas. Not until the anonymous planisphere of about 1545 (now housed in the National Library in Vienna) is the representation of the Spiceries significantly improved and accurately drawn.[574]

The survivors of the Villalobos tragedy left the Spiceries in 1546 after their commander's death and three years later a number of them were back in Spain. One of their number, Father Cosmas de Torres, wrote a letter to Loyola and the Jesuits of Europe in January, 1549, from Goa telling of his voyage across the Pacific from Mexico to the Spiceries with the Villalobos fleet.[575] After almost eighteen months on Sarangani Island, he reports that they were forced to leave for the Moluccas because of their great losses through death. From April, 1544, to November, 1545, the remnant of the expedition stayed on Tidore Island.[576] Ultimately realizing that they would be unable to sail back to Mexico, they concluded a bargain with Fernão de Sousa de Tavora, commander of the Portuguese fleet, to take them to Goa. At Amboina in the spring of 1546 on the way to India, Torres met Xavier who so impressed the secular priest that he "soon wished to follow in his [Xavier's] footsteps...."[577]

[570] See *ibid.*, pp. 50–51.

[571] See Wichmann, *op. cit.* (n. 535), pp. 14–16, who contends that he visited the tiny port of Warsai on the small island of Wiak off the northwestern peninsula of New Guinea.

[572] Cortesão and Teixeira da Mota, *op. cit.* (n. 2), I, 99–101.

[573] *Ibid.*, pp. 117–21; actually their true location is further westward at about 128 degrees.

[574] *Ibid.*, pp. 155–57.

[575] Wicki (ed.), *op. cit.* (n. 80), I, 468–81. First published in *Copia de las cartas* (1565).

[576] For Gaetano's account of Tidore and the Portuguese establishment at Ternate *ca.* 1545 see Ramusio, *op. cit.* (n. 529), I, 417r and v.

[577] Wicki (ed.), *op. cit.* (n. 80), I, 475.

Torres realized his ambition in 1548 when he joined the Society of Jesus in Goa. His letter written in 1549 shortly before his departure for Japan was frequently published in Europe during the sixteenth century. Along with Gaetano's journal (published in Ramusio in 1550), it was one of the few printed accounts by a participant to report on the successes and failures of the Villalobos expedition. Ramusio's map incorporates many of the references which came into Europe before 1550 primarily through the accounts of the Spanish voyages.

It was not until after mid-century that Europe learned something in detail of what the Portuguese knew about the Spiceries. The *Book* of Duarte Barbosa, first printed by Ramusio in 1550, was accurate enough for its day (*ca.* 1518) but added nothing to what had become current through the accounts of the Spanish voyages. The best general survey of the Spiceries appeared in Barros' *Década* III, first published in 1563, just fifty years after direct information on the Moluccas began to trickle into Malacca from the letters of Francisco Serrão. That the Portuguese had long possessed detailed and accurate information on the Spiceries is clear from the evidence of unprinted maps and from the wealth of data in the unpublished portion of Pires' *Suma oriental* prepared in about 1515. If it is at all correct to talk about a studied policy of secrecy being followed by the Portuguese government during the sixteenth century, nowhere is it more apparent than in the case of the Spiceries. António Galvão's *Tratado . . . dos descobrimentos* appeared in Lisbon in 1563, the same year as Barros' *Década* III, but the reminiscences on his tenure (1536–39) as governor of Ternate were kept out of print by royal instructions. Even in the *Tratado . . .*, Galvão gives no systematic review of affairs in the Moluccas.[578] It is likely, however, that Barros in his capacity as official chronicler of the Portuguese discoveries in Asia had access to and incorporated material from Galvão's manuscript history into his own description of the Spiceries. From his own testimony we know that Barros consulted Galvão personally while writing on the Moluccas.[579] The historical period to which Barros' (and Castanheda's) work refers is, as in the rest of the *Décadas*, to the years before 1540.

The ancients, according to Barros, were ignorant about the physical features of the archipelago east of Sumatra and the Golden Chersonese. Ptolemy, after confessing his lack of acquaintance with it, nevertheless proceeded, according to Barros' understanding, to depict it in his *Geography*. Southward from the eastern extremity of Asia, the ancients erroneously postulated a huge peninsula which supposedly extended 9 degrees south of the equator. Ptolemy filled in this fabulous peninsula with equally imaginary rivers, bays, promontories, and cities, such as Cattigara. But since the Portuguese have navigated east of Malacca, it is now known that no great peninsula exists there and that this entire region is a sea dotted with many thousands of islands. In the midst of this maze of islands the Moluccas are to be found. They are located at three hundred leagues (1,200 miles) east of Malacca and south of the equator. Even as the

[578] See above, pp. 195–96.
[579] Cidade and Múrias (eds.), *op. cit.* (n. 39), III, 259–60.

crow flies, Barros underestimates the distance between the two places; he is also incorrect in putting the islands south of the equator. Actually most of the Moluccas are located north of the line, and the Portuguese fortress was on Ternate, the northernmost of all the Moluccas. It is hard to see how a scholar as well informed as Barros could have unintentionally committed these errors,[580] particularly as Pigafetta at an earlier date gives relatively correct latitudes for all five of the Moluccas.[581] It is possible that the Portuguese intentionally shortened the distance from Malacca to the Moluccas to keep information away from the Spanish which might have again led them to claim that the Spiceries lay within their demarcation.[582]

Barros describes the Moluccas, says that they are five in number, and tells us how they lie in a north-south line parallel to a large island located a short distance to the east. About sixty leagues (240 miles) in length, Batochina do Moro[583] (Gilolo or Halmahera) faces the western islands and enfolds them in three arms of land. The five smaller islands are called the Moluccas, a collective name comparable to the Canaries. Though he realizes that there are actually more than five islands which make up the complex of the Moluccas, Barros discusses only those islands to which the clove is native. These five clove islands are all within sight of one another and cover a complete distance from north to south of not more than twenty-five leagues (100 miles). In the native language the ancient names of the islands from north to south are: "Gape" (Ternate), "Duco" (Tidore), "Moutil" (Motir), "Mara" (Makian), and "Seque" (Bachan).[584] All of these islands are very small, the largest being not more than six leagues (24 miles) in circumference. Their coastal flatlands are narrow and the waters roundabout are filled with rocky reefs dangerous to the ships which try to approach or anchor off their shores.[585]

Nature has given the Moluccas little more than the clove. Climate and landscape are both unpleasant and unhealthy. Because of the equatorial location

---

[580] It is remarkable how the Portuguese of this period agree in misplacing the islands. Castanheda (in Azevedo [ed.], *op. cit.* [n. 79], III, 166–67) and Fróis (letter from Malacca, November 19, 1556, in Wicki [ed.], *op. cit.* [n. 80], III, 540) also locate the Moluccas just south of the equator. Notice also that on the Ramusio map Ternate is south and Tidore north of the equator. Xavier, however, is much more accurate than Barros on the distance to the Moluccas. In a letter from Goa (September 20, 1542) Xavier wrote to Loyola that "from this city of Goa it is 1000 leagues to Maluca . . . and it is 500 leagues from here to Malacha. . . ." (Schurhammer and Wicki [eds.], *op. cit.* [n. 93], I, 141). By simple subtraction it is easy to see that Xavier estimated the distance from Malacca to the Moluccas at 500 leagues (2,000 miles). For a contemporary complaint about Barros' strange inability to determine the exact location of the Moluccas see letter of Guillaume Postel to Abraham Ortelius, April 9, 1567 (J. H. Hessels [ed.], *Abrahami Ortelii et virorum eruditorum ad eundem et ad Jacobum Colium Ortelianum Epistolae (1524–1628)* [Cambridge, 1887], I, 43).

[581] Robertson (ed.), *op. cit.* (n. 136), II, 115.

[582] See Swecker, *op. cit.* (n. 11), p. 105, n. 1.

[583] Batochina equals "land of China" to Barros (Cidade and Múrias [eds.], *op. cit.* [n. 39], III, 262).

[584] What these names mean or what language they come from is not known. The same can be said for the modern names of these islands. See Crawfurd, *op. cit.* (n. 34), p. 283.

[585] Barros in Cidade and Múrias (eds.), *op. cit.* (n. 39), III, 257–58. For a description of the elevated coral reefs of Halmahera see Wallace, *op. cit.* (n. 94), p. 6.

of the islands, the sun is always near, even when at its northern and southern sol-
stices. Constant heat combined with high humidity encourages the growth of
heavy vegetation everywhere and produces clouds that hang near the tops of
the mountains. The moisture-laden air, so good for vegetation, is unhealthy for
humans. Most trees are never without leaves, though the clove puts forth its
leaves only every second year because the new growth is usually crushed at
harvest time. On the sides of the volcanic mountains of the interior, the atmosphere is healthier than in the marshy and disease-ridden lowlands. The soil on
all the islands is usually black, dry, and highly porous. No matter how much it
rains this thirsty soil (lava) seemingly absorbs all the water. Even rivers which
rise in the interior dry up before reaching the sea. Several of the islands have
active volcanoes, the most vital of these to the Portuguese being the one on
Ternate of which Barros gives a full description based on information received
from Galvão.[586] The clove islands are far from being self-sufficient in the
necessities of life. But nature has arranged it so that the islands supplement one
another by the things which they produce. Halmahera has no cloves but it has
plenty of foodstuffs to supply the islands where the cloves grow. Clay suitable
for pottery manufacture is found only on one islet, between Tidore and Motir,
which they call the "island of pots" (Pulo Cabale).[587] At the town of Gilolo on
the large island of Halmahera they make the sacks for shipping cloves. Supported
by the products of their neighbors, the five little islands produce the cloves sold
everywhere in the world for these trees are found nowhere else.

Millet and rice in small quantities are available in the Moluccas, but the diet of
the islanders is most dependent upon the products of the "sagum" (sago palm).
This tree, similar in appearance to the date palm, has fronds which are of a
darker green color, tenderer, and spongier. The trunk of the tree has leafy
branches at its top and on them grows a fruit, similar to cypress nuts, within
which one finds a powder. The trunk of the tree is a wooden shell in which
there is nothing but a mass of tender and moist pith. The natives extract the
moisture from the pith by letting it drip out overnight into a vessel. This
liquor is the color of whipped milk and they call it "tuaca."[588] Drunk fresh it
has a sweet and agreeable taste and the reputation of being healthful and fattening.
When cooked, this liquor can be converted into wine and vinegar. Once the
pith is well drained of its sap, what remains is used as flour from which to make
bread that is better than European biscuits. Two other trees, one of them being
the nipa palm, also yield bread, wine, and vinegar. Nothing goes to waste from
these trees, because the bark, fronds, and other remains are used for clothing,
shelter, and other purposes. A superior wine, ordinarily reserved for the nobles,
is distilled from large canes. The higher classes also live on the meat of pigs,

---

[586] Cidade and Múrias (eds.), *op. cit.* (n. 39), III, 258–59.

[587] *Ibid.*, p. 259; Barros explains that "Pulo" means "island" and "Cabale" means "pot." "Pulo"
is a Malay word usually applied to islands or islets. See Crawfurd, *op. cit.* (n. 34), p. 361.

[588] From Malay, *tuāq*, a term used throughout the eastern maritime world as far west as Madagascar.
See Dalgado, *op. cit.* (n. 53), II, 388.

sheep, goats, and birds. The insular animals, according to Castanheda, reproduce several times each year in this tropical climate. One of the finest delicacies is the meat of certain curious rabbit-like animals who carry their young in pouches.[589] Seafood and fish are both abundant and excellent, and more common in the diet than meat. The Moluccas appear not to be endowed with metals, though it is rumored that gold may be found there.[590]

The people of the islands are tawny in color and have long hair, robust bodies, and strong limbs. Surly of countenance, they grow grey early even though they often live to ripe, old ages. They are greedy, deceitful, and unpleasant, and are quick to learn everything. Nimble of limb and agile of body, they swim like fish and fight with the swiftness of birds. Whatever work is done in the fields or the marketplace is accomplished by the women. The men are lazy and indolent about everything but war. They are a hard people to control because they refuse to be convinced by means other than the sword. In war they are efficient and so cruel that fathers and sons sometimes fight against each other. The victors in battle cut off the heads of their enemies as trophies and hang them up by the hair. They have no trading junks because the foreign merchants call at the Moluccas for the cloves, their only export. Native warships are large, well made, and propelled by oars, some of them having as many as 180 oarsmen on each side. Evil and strife are endemic to the Moluccas, for the clove, though a creation of God, is actually an apple of discord and responsible for more afflictions than gold.[591]

Internal hostilities and the multiplicity of their languages seem to indicate that the inhabitants of the Moluccas are of diverse origins. In their everyday relationships with one another, these people are faithless, hateful, and constantly suspicious and watchful—not at all like the people of one nation. The languages commonly spoken in the islands vary widely, the speech of one place not being understood in the other.[592] Some form their words in the throat, others on the palate. If they have a common tongue through which they communicate, it is the Malay language of Malacca which was introduced by the Muslims to the nobility of the islands. Islam was reportedly accepted in Ternate a little more than eighty years before the Portuguese established a fortress there, or in about 1440.[593] Before this date, there are no historical records, only a few traditions preserved by word of mouth. During their pre-Muslim existence they had no written language, no calendar, and no weights and measures. Without knowledge

---

[589] Azevedo (ed.), *op. cit.* (n. 79), III, 168; a reference to the marsupial variety of *cuscus*, a kind of kangaroo. See the comments of Henry O. Forbes, *A Naturalist's Wanderings in the Eastern Archipelago* (New York, 1885), pp. 291–92.

[590] Barros in Cidade and Múrias (eds.), *op. cit.* (n. 39), III, 260–61.

[591] Barros in *ibid.*, pp. 261–62; Castanheda in Azevedo (ed.), *op. cit.* (n. 79), III, 168–69.

[592] A very astute observation since the languages of south Halmahera and the Moluccas are completely unrelated to the Indonesian languages, and their origin is still a mystery to students of comparative linguistics.

[593] Barros in Cidade and Múrias (eds.), *op. cit.* (n. 39), III, 263; Pigafetta (see above, p. 598) dates the introduction of Islam in Tidore about 1471. It is likely that Muslim merchants were active in Ternate before they penetrated Tidore.

of God and organized religion, they worshipped the sun, moon, stars, and earthly objects, even as the heathens living in the interior still do. The one tradition which all of them hold to firmly is the belief that they are not native to the islands but came originally from elsewhere.[594]

As elsewhere in the world, legends exist in the Moluccas which credit the rulers with divine origins. The "bestial people" of these islands, according to Barros, have such a legend about the descent of their rulers. The fable avers that in times past when the islands were governed by elders there was a principal elder named Bicocigara living on the island of Bachan. One day, while he was being rowed along the edge of the coast, the principal elder saw among some huge rocks a large thicket of *rotas* (rattan),[595] young canes used as rope by the islanders. Bicocigara, thinking these reeds especially fine, sent his men ashore to cut them down and bring them to the boat. On arriving at the place indicated, the men were betrayed by their own vision and could see no canes. In great indignation Bicocigara went ashore, pointed out the reeds to his servants, and commanded them to be cut down. Blood began to run out of the severed reeds and they noticed at the roots four eggs which looked like those of a serpent. A voice was then heard which told them to take the eggs from which would be born their princes. The eggs were carried home and stored in a closed and safe place until three princes and a princess were born from them. Accepted readily and enthusiastically by the people, one of the princes reigned on Bachan, another on "Butam," and the other in the Papuas (New Guinea), east of the Moluccas. The princess married the ruler of the Lolodas, islands west of the northern arm of Halmahera, and from this couple descended the kings of Halmahera. It is because of their firm belief in this creation story that the Moluccans revere as a shrine the place in the great rocks where the eggs were supposedly found.[596] From the viewpoint of the cultural and political unity of the Moluccas, it should be noticed that the action in this story takes place in various islands and that it was apparently accepted as the story of origins for all of them.

Barros speculates that the Moluccas, parts of them at least, must have been covered by the seas until fairly recent times. He arrives at this conclusion because the Portuguese in the islands find seashells in holes dug in the earth and even at the roots of trees. Such a deduction is reinforced by the absence of references in the oral tradition to a long history, and to the persistence of stories about originating elsewhere. When they first arrived in the islands, the Moluccans lived under the rule of their elders, in virtual isolation. Soon the islands were visited by the junks of three nations: China, Java, and Malaya. In some way the naming of the island of Batochina do Moro (Halmahera) seems to be associated

[594] Barros in Cidade and Múrias (eds.), *op. cit.* (n. 39), III, 261–62.

[595] See Scott, *loc. cit.* (n. 545), pp. 97–99.

[596] *Ibid.*, pp. 263–64. This legend is also told by B. Leonardo de Argensola in his *Conquista de las islas Malucas* (Madrid, 1609). See the reprint published at Saragossa in 1811, pp. 2–3. The probability is that he got this story from Barros because he cites the Portuguese chronicler on other matters having to do with the early history of the Moluccas.

with the arrival of the Chinese. Since "Bata" means "land," it could perhaps be deduced, Barros believes, that Batochina do Moro was the seat of a Chinese trading settlement and so was known in the Moluccas as "the land of China." It was only with the arrival of the Chinese that cloves became an item of international commerce and that they were used for something beside medicines.[597] The Chinese brought trading items and copper cash into the islands and carried out the cloves to the entrepôts of the East; from these marts they were transported to the rest of the world. The fame of this commerce increasing, the Javans soon began to come to the Moluccas. Following the decree of the Ming emperor forbidding venture overseas, Barros continues, the Chinese withdrew and the Javans became the masters of the clove trade for a time. With the founding of Singapore, and later Malacca, closer contact between the Malays and the Javans was established. It was not long until the Malays began to participate in the spice trade and until they appeared in the Moluccas. When the Muslims became involved in Eastern commerce, they brought their religion with them. The Muslims converted many Javans and Malays to the teachings of the Prophet, and they in turn helped to carry Islam to the Moluccas.[598]

Throughout history thirteen kings have ruled over Ternate and its dependencies. Tidore Vongue (also called Kĕchil or "Cachil"), the father of Boloife and the first to accept Islam, was apparently married to a Javanese noblewoman who helped to convert him. In 1520, when António de Brito arrived there, a minor of seven years was reigning, and, as we know from Pigafetta,[599] Tidore was in process of taking over the leadership in the archipelago's affairs. This usurpation was soon halted by the construction on Ternate of a Portuguese fortress and by the support which it lent to Ternate's position in politics and trade. The rulers of the Moluccas are all said to be Moors. They keep large harems and, along with their nobles who are called mandarins, dress in Malay style in rich silks decorated with gold and jewels. Castanheda describes at length their valuable arm-bracelets, earrings, and other personal adornments. These rulers receive no revenues from their subjects, are held in general esteem, and are considered divine by the common people.[600] Evidently the rulers of Ternate, as well as the dependent princes ("Sangages")[601] of the other islands, live entirely on the revenues derived from trade, imports, and middleman profits. It is clear from what all the writers report that negotiations for cloves went on directly between the ruler and the foreign merchants, and that the ruler acted essentially as an agent for both the buyers and the sellers of cloves.

The Portuguese and Malay merchants prefer to do their trading south of the

[597] Orta (in Markham [trans.], *op. cit.* [n. 359], pp. 218–19) reports that he also heard this.
[598] Barros in Cidade and Múrias (eds.), *op. cit.* (n. 39), III, 262–63.
[599] Above, p. 595.
[600] Castanheda in Azevedo (ed.), *op. cit.* (n. 79), III, 168–69.
[601] From Malay, *sangá-agi*, meaning "prince." Evidently it is also used to mean "vassal prince." See Dalgado, *op. cit.* (n. 53), II, 282–83.

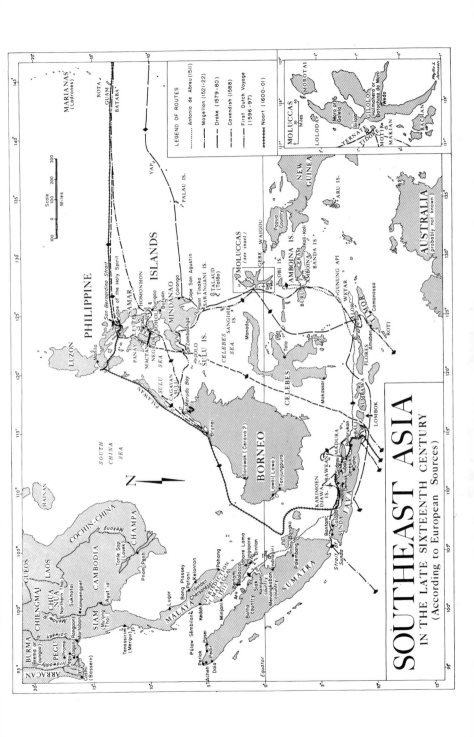

SOUTHEAST ASIA
IN THE LATE SIXTEENTH CENTURY
(According to European Sources)

LEGEND OF ROUTES

.... Antonio de Abreu (1511)

———— Magellan (1521-22)

— — — Drake (1579-80)

——·—·— Cavendish (1588)

– · – · – First Dutch Voyage (1596-97)

+++++++ Noort (1600-01)

MOLUCCAS

MARIANAS (Ladrones)

PHILIPPINE ISLANDS

LUZON

Manila

SAMAR

PANAY LEYTE

MACTAN HOMONHON

NEGROS BOHOL Butuan

MINDANAO

Zamboanga Caraga

Cape San Agustin

Point Tinaka

SARRANGANI IS.

TALAUD (Toloo)

SULU IS.

CELEBES SANGIHE IS.

CELEBES SEA

Manado

Tolo

CELEBES

Makassar

Comonassa

SOUTH CHINA SEA

HAINAN

COCHIN-CHINA

CHAMPA

CAMBODIA

Phnom Penh

SIAM

BURMA

PEGU

ARRACAN

LAOS

CHIENGMAI

CUEOS

CHUA

BORNEO

Brunei

Sarawak (Cerawa?)

Lawai (Lawe)

Tanjungpura

SUMATRA

MALAYA

MALACCA

Singapore

Palembang

Bangka

Strait of Sunda

Bantam

JAVA SUNDA

BALI

LOMBOK

SUMBAWA

FLORES

TIMOR

ROTI

AUSTRALIA (probably not known)

NEW GUINEA

ARU IS.

CERAM

AMBOINA IS.

BANDA IS.

GUNUNG API

WETAR

GEBE WAIGOU

OBI IS.

MOLUCCAS (see inset)

Scale

Miles

N

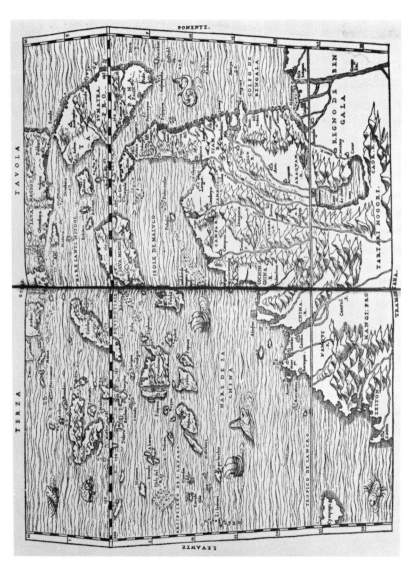

The map of southeast and eastern Asia in G. B. Ramusio's *Delle navigationi et viaggi* (2d rev. ed.; Venice, 1554), Vol. I.

The map of southeast and eastern Asia in Abraham Ortelius' *Theatrum orbis terrarum* (Antwerp, 1575). Courtesy of the University of Chicago Libraries.

The map of Sumatra in Ramusio's *Delle navigationi et viaggi* (2d rev. ed.; Venice, 1554), Vol. I.

The map of Java inserted into the Madrid edition (1615) of João de Barros'
Décadas de Ásia. Courtesy of the Cornell University Library.

Malayos

Ioann: à Doet fec:

Malachæ incolæ sermone et moribus quam reliqui Indi cultioribus et magis comes.

Inwoonders van Mallacka welcke alle andere Indianen in taele courtosije en amoreusheyt te boven gaen.

"Inhabitants of Malacca, who surpass all other Indians in courteous and amorous behavior." This and the illustration on the facing page are from Jan van Linschoten's *Itinerario* (Amsterdam, 1596). Courtesy of the Newberry Library.

Joannes à Doetc

Natives of Pegu, the Moluccas, and St. Thomas.

Alcune parole che vsano le genti della terra di Bressil.

Il lor formento che par ceci. Mahiz	
Farina	Hus
Vn hamo	Piuda
Coltello	Iacle
Pettine	Chignor
Forbici	Pirene
Sonagli	Itani maraca
Piu che buon Ium maras ghatum	

Parole del gigàte, ilqual presero appresso il fiume di s. Giuliano.

Capo	Her
Occhio	Other
Naso	Or
Supercilij	Sechechiel
Boccha	Piam
Dente	Sor
Lingua	Schial
Mento	Sechen
Pelo	Aschie
Gola	Ohumoi
Man	Chone
Palma	Caneghin
Dito	Cori
Orecchia	Saue
Mamella	Othen
Petto	Ochij
Corpo	Gechel
Gamba	Coll
Piedi	Tehe
Tallon	There
La suola	Perchi

Cuore	Cho
Huomo	Califchon
Acqua	Oli
Foco	Glialeme
Fumo	Iacche
Non	Chen
Si	Cei
Oro	Pelpeli
Azurro	Sechegli
Sole	Calipecheni
Stella	Setreu
Mare	Aro
Vento	Oui
Tempesta	Ohone
Pesce	Hoi
Mangiar	Mecchiere
Scodella	Elo
Et pronontiaua il tutto nella gola	

Parole che vsano gli habitatori del l'isola di Tidore.

Dio	Ala
Christian	Naceran
Turco	Rumo
Moro	Moseliman
Gentil	Cafre
Loro preti	Maulana
Huomo	Horan
Huomo sauio Horan pãdita	
Padre	Bapa
Madre	Mamaabui
Loro chiesa	Meschit
Figliuol	Anach
Fratello	Sandala

Suo auo	Mini C		
Suo focero	Mintuha		
Suo genero	Minante		
Moglie	Porampuam		
Capelli	Lambut		
Capo	Capala		
Fronte	Dai		
Occhio	Matha		
Supercilij	Chilai		
Palpebre	Chenia		
Naso	Idon		
Bocca	Malut		
Labra	Vebere		
Denti	Ciggi		
Gingiua	Ilti		
Lingua	Lada		
Palato	Langhi		
Mento	Agai		
Barba	Ianghi		
Mascella	Pipi		
Orecchia	Talinga		
Gola	Iaher		
Collo	Vidun		
Spalle	Balacan		
Petto	Dada		
Cuor	Atti		
Mamelle	Suffiu		
Stomacho	Parut D		
Corpo	Tundubatu		
Gambe	Mina		
Talon	Tumi		
Piede	Batis		
Suola	Empacachi		
Vnghia	Cucu		

NARRATIONE DI VN PORTOGHESE

Compagno di Odoardo Barbosa. qual fu sopra la naue
Vittoria del Anno M D X I X.

EL NOME Di Iddio & di bon saluamento. Partimmo di Siuiglia l'Anno M D X I X. alli x. d'Agosto con cinque naui per andar a discoprire l'isole Maluche, dõde cominciamo di nauigare da S. Lucar per l'isole di Canaria, et nauigammo per Lebeccio 960. miglia, onde ci trouammo a l'isola di Teneri fe, nellaquale sta il porto di santa croce in 28. gradi del polo artico

Et da l'isola di Tenerife noi nauigammo per mezzo giorno 1680. miglia donde ci trouammo in quatro gradi del polo artico.

Da questi quattro gradi del polo artico noi nauigammo per Lebeccio fino che ci trouam mo al capo di Santo Agostino, ilquale sta in otto gradi nel polo antartico donde habbiamo fatto 1100. miglia.

Et dal capo di Santo Agostino noi nauigammo alla quarta di mezzo di verso Lebeccio 264. miglia onde ci trouammo in vinti gradi del polo antartico.

Et da i vinti gradi del polo Antartico essendo in mare noi nauigammo 1500. miglia per lebeccio

Pigafetta's list of Malay words learned from the inhabitants of Tidore Island in the Moluccas. From Ramusio's *Delle navigationi et viaggi.*

Moluccas in the Banda Islands rather than going all the way to Ternate them-selves. The Banda Islands, sometimes called the "Nutmeg group," were first surveyed by De Abreu in 1511. He had evidently learned from the Javan and Malay traders at Malacca that cloves as well as the native nutmegs and mace could be purchased in the Bandas. The islands known collectively as Banda include, according to Barros,[602] the individual island of Banda with its port of "Lutatão" (Lontar), as well as "Rosolanguim" (Rosingain), Ai, "Rō" (Run), and Naira.[603] The island of Banda is a delight to see with its flat, horseshoe-shaped shoreline covered with shiny, sweet-smelling nutmeg trees. Its people are robust, white, and endowed with smooth, shiny hair. They are Muslims, though they have no kings but only elders as their governors. The men engage in commerce, while the women work in the groves cultivating the nutmeg and fruit trees of the island. All of the orchards are owned by the community and from June to September particular groups have the right to gather the harvest from assigned plots. The elders have a difficult time maintaining order, particularly in the seaports. The people of some of the neighboring islands specialize in piracy and prey upon the trade which centers at Banda.[604] While the Portuguese chroniclers give additional information on trading conditions both at Banda and in the Moluccas, they concern themselves primarily with Portuguese activities in the Spiceries. For the period after 1540, when the Portuguese chronicles cease, it is necessary to turn to the Jesuit letters and histories.[605]

Xavier visited and worked in the Spiceries for over one year (mid-February, 1546, to mid-April, 1547) of his eleven-year apostolate in the East. His first stop of any length was at Amboina where he spent over three months (February–June, 1546).[606] Then he lived through the summer of 1546 on the hot island of Ternate. In the middle of September he carried the gospel to the Moro Islands (roughly the northern arm of Halmahera and Morotai Island). After three months in these remote parts of the insular world, he started on the journey back to Malacca. He spent the first three months of 1547 on a second visit in Ternate while his vessel waited for the southwestward monsoon to blow it on the way back to Malacca.[607] Two of his letters of May 10, 1546, from Amboina were the first Jesuit letters from the Spiceries to be circulated in the sixteenth century. These letters were written after about three months of experience on the island.[608]

[602] Cidade and Múrias (eds.), *op. cit.* (n. 39), III, 266.

[603] For discussions of these identifications and a map see Leitão, *op. cit.* (n. 522), p. 49.

[604] For additional information on the Bandas see Castanheda in Azevedo (ed.), *op. cit.* (n. 79), III, 155–56.

[605] Maffei is very little help in this regard. His account (*op. cit.* [n. 98], I, 208–11) follows Barros closely and adds practically nothing. For the Jesuit letters from India see above, pp. 427–32.

[606] On his activities at Amboina see Wessels, *op. cit.* (n. 21), chap. ii; for a more nearly contemporary account see Guzman, *op. cit.* (n. 44), Vol. I, chap. xx. Also see above, pp. 281–82.

[607] Itinerary based on materials in Schurhammer and Wicki (eds.), *op. cit.* (n. 93), I, 339, 375, 348, 378, 384.

[608] Not published until Tursellinus' collection appeared in 1596; however, since they were the first letters from the Moluccas and widely circulated in manuscript and frequently cited in the six-teenth century, they will be discussed here.

Xavier apparently chose Amboina as his first stopover in the Spiceries because of what he heard in Malacca about its bright future in the Portuguese plan of empire. A regular port of call on the spice route, Amboina was the place where the fleets waited at anchor for several months to catch the monsoons to take them either to Ternate or Malacca. It was also the place where the crews of naval and trading vessels "relaxed" on board and ashore to the dismay of the natives and their own officials and priests. The Portuguese, who resided permanently in Amboina to service the fleets and to work in the spice trade, soon became involved in insular politics and civil hostilities. Many of them sided with the heathens of Amboina against their Muslim neighbors; in 1536, Portuguese sympathizers were sent to Malacca to request support for the *Oulisiva* (League of Nine), an alliance of states politically associated with Tidore and the pagans of Amboina and foe to the league of states headed by Ternate. It was at about this time also that certain heathen chieftains, desirous of having Portuguese aid, accepted Christianity. When Xavier arrived in the Spiceries, he found seven Christian settlements functioning on Amboina alone.[609]

Portugal's efforts to tighten its hold upon Amboina and the spice route brought a quick response from the Muslim merchant communities of Java and the Macassars. In 1538 a Javanese fleet attacked the Portuguese and their Moluccan allies at Amboina, and they were aided in this effort by several Muslim *kampongs* (villages) of Amboina. Once the invading fleet was beaten back, the conversions to Christianity became more numerous and the decisions of officials in Goa and Malacca came to have more meaning in Amboina. A particularly good example of growing Portuguese control is to be found in the case of Jordão de Freytas. This Portuguese, who visited at Ternate several times, had struck up a friendship with Tabaridji, the sultan of Ternate. When the sultan was summarily sent off to Goa in 1535 on a charge of disloyalty and treason to Portugal, Freytas visited him in prison and proceeded to convert him to Christianity. In gratitude to Freytas, the sultan bestowed Amboina and its environs upon him as a personal fief. This award was ratified in Lisbon, and Freytas was ordered to return to the Moluccas with Tabaridji to help re-establish him on his throne. Shortly before arriving at Malacca in 1545, the sultan died on board ship and by his will the throne of Ternate passed to the king of Portugal. Such dispositions were not recognized, however, by Hairun, who replaced Tabaridji as sultan of Ternate, and so conditions in the Spiceries became tenser than ever. Freytas sent his cousin to Amboina to construct a fortress on his property, and at this juncture Xavier decided to survey Portugal's latest overseas acquisitions as possible mission footholds.[610]

Shortly after Xavier's arrival at Amboina, the fleet of Fernão de Sousa da Tavora anchored there on the return from its expedition against the Spanish of

---

[609] See Wessels, *op. cit.* (n. 21), pp. 30–31.

[610] *Ibid.*, pp. 33–34. Xavier expected Freytas to take over Amboina personally in November, 1547, but in this hope he was disappointed. See Schurhammer and Wicki (eds.), *op. cit.* (n. 93), I, 340.

Villalobos' fleet. When the Portuguese fleet left for India on May 17, 1546, Xavier's letters to India and Europe went with it. For the enlightenment of his colleagues, Xavier explains that ". . . the region of Molucca is all islands, and, until now, no one has discovered a continent"[611] of the type postulated by Ptolemy. Seventy years before (*ca.* 1476), Islam was introduced into these islands and many who were originally heathens have since become Muslims. The gentiles and Moors hate each other, but fortunately the gentiles are still in the majority. The pagans resist accepting the teachings of the Prophet because the Muslims make slaves of them. The weather is temperate in the Spiceries but it often rains. The islands are so mountainous and so thick with vegetation that it is hard to journey through them. In time of war the people retire to these mountains which serve them as fortresses. No horses exist on the islands, and even if they did they would be of no use in getting about. Earthquakes are frequent and terrifying especially when one is at sea, for the ship shakes and seems to be running aground on rocks.[612] Volcanoes erupt with noise so loud that no amount of artillery fire could equal it and with impetus enough to roll huge rocks along. "In the absence of anyone who can preach the torments of hell in these islands, God allows hell to break open to the confusion of these infidels and their abominable sins."[613]

The depravity of these people is almost beyond belief and Xavier finds himself not bold enough to describe their wantonness in detail. He contents himself with condemning the infidels for their barbarism, treachery, and ingratitude, and concludes that they are worse than Negroes. The Jesuit has been told about islands where aged fathers are eaten at ceremonial banquets, a story which Varthema and Balbi respectively tell about the natives of Java and Sumatra, and which other European writers of the period recount about other remote places and distant peoples. On another island, possibly Halmahera, Xavier has been told that those killed in battle are eaten. Each island has its own language and on some of them almost every town speaks a tongue of its own. Malay is the only language spoken commonly throughout the region, and it is for that reason that Xavier translated certain sacred writings into Malay while he was in Malacca. No writings in the native languages exist. All the writing which is done is in Malay and in the Arabic alphabet and script. Xavier also tells of milking a male goat (*cabrón*) which had only one teat (the genitals?), an animal which was thought of as being so remarkable for the milk it continually gave that a Portuguese gentleman planned on sending one back to Europe.[614] Before departing from Amboina for Ternate, Xavier reports that he will be going to Moro (Galela),[615] where Franciscans from Ternate had earlier (1533–44) made many converts among the pagans. The Jesuit points out that nobody

---

[611] *Ibid.*, I, 328.
[612] *Ibid.*, pp. 331–33.
[613] *Ibid.*, p. 333.
[614] *Ibid.*, pp. 333–35.
[615] *Ibid.*, p. 325. Galela is located on the northeastern tip of the northern arm of Halmahera.

looks forward to a visit to this Ultima Thule of the Moluccas since its people are reputed to be treacherous and specialists in poisoning those whom they fear or dislike. While Xavier spent three months in this wild country, he seems to have written very little about it aside from mentioning his visits to the scattered Christian communities there, the primitive conditions of life, and the shortages of food and water.

The Jesuit letters written in the decade (1547–57) after Xavier's visit to the Spiceries are likewise not very illuminating. From India and Malacca the fathers comment in open astonishment about the great distance to the Moluccas, the difficulties of traveling there, and the slowness of communication.[616] Rumors, sometimes accurate, are relayed to Europe from the Jesuits in India about the hardships of life in the Moluccas, the ease with which the islanders are converted, and the addiction of the islanders to the use of poison as a political weapon. The serious lack of personnel and leadership in India itself from 1552 to 1556 and the consequent breakdown in communications is partially to blame for the dearth of reports on the activities of Xavier's successors in the Spiceries. Brother Aires Brandão writes from Goa in 1554 that there are only two fathers, João de Beira and Affonso de Castro, in the Moluccas and that they have with them two lay brothers, Nicolau Nunes and Francisco Godinho.[617] Early in 1555, Goa nonetheless learned from a letter sent by Cristovão de Sá, captain of Malacca, that great progress was being made in evangelizing the Moluccas. Meager as these notices are, they were published in Europe almost as soon as they arrived there and were even republished in following decades.

The first systematic description of the Moluccas prepared by a Jesuit was that contained in the letter of Brother Luis Fróis from Malacca to Portugal written in November, 1556.[618] The author received his information directly from Father Beira and Brother Nunes when they returned to Malacca to seek more missionaries for the Spiceries. Fróis' letter was first published in Europe in the *Nuovi avisi* of 1559 after being translated into Italian, revised, and edited by Polanco.[619] Like the Portuguese chroniclers, Fróis mistakenly puts "the fortress of Maluquo" (Ternate) one degree south, instead of one degree north of the equator. Hairun, ruler of Ternate and sultan of the Moluccas, is obedient to the Portuguese at the fortress and comes whenever he is called. He is kind to the Portuguese and eager to co-operate with them in order to retain their aid in

[616] Wicki (ed.), *op. cit.* (n. 80), I, 19, 24, 34, 43. The *Diversi avisi* (Venice), beginning in 1558, published portions from the letters of João de Beira (Feb. 25, 1549, Ternate to Goa, in Eglauer [trans.], *op. cit.* [n. 181], I, 123–25; Feb. 8, 1553, Cochin to Rome, in *ibid.*, I, 196–205), Manuel de Moraes (undated [1549?], Goa to Coimbra, in *ibid.*, I, 22–26), Affonso de Castro (Jan. 18, 1554, Ternate to Goa, in *ibid.*, I, 211–13; May 13 [1554?], Amboina to Goa, in *ibid.*, I, 278–81), and Antonio Fernandez (Feb. 27, 1554, Amboina to Goa, in *ibid.*, I, 214–17).

[617] Wicki (ed.), *op. cit.* (n. 80), III, 186.

[618] Written at the behest of Baltazar Dias (Malacca, Nov. 19, 1556) in *ibid.*, III, 522–64.

[619] A somewhat abbreviated translation of this into German is available in Eglauer (trans.), *op. cit.* (n. 181), II, 1–26. It is derived from *Diversi avisi* (Venice, 1559) and represents what was actually published in the sixteenth century. The European editors of the sixteenth-century edition telescope the explanations and omit a number of place names, but otherwise this is an accurate rendition of the original.

extending his own power over a constantly larger number of islands. While he is outwardly accommodating to the missionaries, he is secretly the enemy of Christianity and plots the persecution and death of the converts. In public he criticizes the followers of Islam and the teachings of the Prophet, but he resists conversion to Christianity himself because "he thinks it a severe hardship to leave his many women."[620] Still, he is not beyond hope, for he understands and speaks Portuguese well[621] and simply needs continuing attention. Xavier himself was not able to convert Hairun, though he did succeed in bringing a number of women from his family to Christianity. The most important of the royal converts was the queen, Dona Isabel,[622] mother of Sultan Tabaridji[623] and stepmother of Hairun. Better informed about the tenets of Islam than other members of her family, Xavier took advantage of Dona Isabel's theological turn of mind to convince her of the truth of Christian teachings. Had her baptized son returned safely from India, Fróis believes Ternate and its dependencies would quickly have become a Christian province. Now she is badly treated by her stepson who has confiscated her lands, and she receives very little comfort from the Portuguese officials who work with Hairun.[624] Nonetheless, nobody dares to harm her personally because she is virtuous and honest, from the best blood in the Moluccas, the mother of a former sultan and sister of a former ruler of Tidore (Rājā Emir who reigned from 1526–47), and venerated by the common people.

Troubles between the rulers of Ternate and Gilolo, according to Fróis, involved the Portuguese and the missionaries in insular wars during 1550–51. A land located seven leagues (28 miles) from the Portuguese fortress at Ternate on the island of Halmahera, Gilolo had maintained its own stronghold for seventeen years (or since about 1533). In that period the sultan of Gilolo had captured guns and artillery from the native Christians and turned them against the Portuguese and their converts. A great tyrant, many of the converts suffered martyrdom at his hands. Hostilities between Ternate and Gilolo which previously had been sporadic, began to be regular in 1549. A Portuguese fleet under Bernardin de Sousa, captain of Ternate, finally laid siege to the fortress of Gilolo. For three months (December 28, 1550–March 19, 1551) the sultan of Gilolo held out against the small but carefully trained group of Portuguese besiegers. Finally forced to capitulate, the king of Gilolo lost his title, acknowledged himself to be the vassal of Ternate, and paid tribute to the Portuguese. "They say," Fróis reports, "that he killed himself with poison. His son has succeeded him in the kingdom."[625]

---

[620] Wicki (ed.), *op. cit.* (n. 80), III, 540.

[621] Confirmed by Xavier's remark in his letter of Jan. 20, 1548 (Schurhammer and Wicki [eds.], *op. cit.* [n. 93], I, 386).

[622] Also known as Elizabeth Niachile Pocarago (*ibid.*, p. 126, n. 15).

[623] For his career see above, p. 610.

[624] Writing from Malacca in 1549 to Goa, Xavier asked that the Portuguese give her a pension and their unqualified support. See Schurhammer and Wicki (eds.), *op. cit.* (n. 93), II, 127.

[625] Wicki (ed.), *op. cit.* (n. 80), III, 543.

It is evident from the amount of material relayed to Fróis by Beira and Nunes that the missionaries to the Moluccas had spent a large part of their time following up work of evangelizing which had been undertaken earlier in Moro. From Fróis' letter we get for the first time an accurate description of what the Jesuits meant by the geographical term "Moro." Moro is twenty-five or thirty leagues (100 or 120 miles) beyond (i.e., north of) the town of Gilolo on Halmahera Island and is divided into two parts: Morotai and Morotia. The division called Morotai includes two islands which are respectively eight leagues (32 miles) [626] and three or four leagues (12 or 16 miles) from the island (Halmahera) on which Gilolo is located. The smaller of these is six or seven leagues (24 or 28 miles) and the larger is thirty-five leagues (140 miles) in circumference. Morotia is another large island which is said to have a circumference of 150 leagues (600 miles). From this description and from what can be inferred from other sources, Morotia seems in reality to be the northern promontory of Halmahera rather than a separate island. The two islands of Morotai probably refer to what we today call Loloda and Morotai which are located in the sea on either side of the tip of the northern promontory of Halmahera. [627]

Forty-six Christian communities, some of them with 700 to 800 inhabitants, are scattered along the coasts of these Moro territories. [628] The interior regions are peopled by barbaric pagans "who kill whomever they encounter to steal their clothes." [629] In the north of Morotai live white, unclothed savages who do not even know what weapons are. Others, of the same island, are peaceful, tattooed, well-formed, and similar in appearance to Brazilian Indians. [630] The tribal groups who live in these hinterlands are called the "Geilolos" (Gilolos), Ganes, "Bedas" (Wedas), Mabas, and "Bicholas" (Bitjolis). [631] The languages spoken in Moro are numerous, and within a distance of eight miles Nunes ran across languages as different from each other as French is from Portuguese.

From scattered references in Fróis' letter, it is possible to conclude that control of Moro was one of the issues in the war between Gilolo and Ternate. With the defeat of Gilolo in 1551, Ternate and the Portuguese apparently assumed uncontested suzerainty over this northern insular region. It also seems that in earlier times the kinglet of Loloda was the most powerful of the local rulers, and that the various chieftains of Loloda continued even while Portugal held sway in the area of Moro (1551–74) to be fairly independent of outside

---

[626] Wallace (*op. cit.* [n. 94], p. 244) puts Morotai Island twenty-five miles from the northeastern tip of Gilolo.

[627] For a map of the area with these names on it see Wessels, *op. cit.* (n. 21), end of volume.

[628] Wicki (ed.), *op. cit.* (n. 80), III, 548. The Jesuits in the Moluccas give 20,000 as the total number of Christian converts in Moro.

[629] *Ibid.*, p. 543.

[630] *Ibid.*, p. 546.

[631] These tribal groups exist today in the eastern and southern parts of Halmahera (*ibid.*, p. 543). Wallace (*op. cit.* [n. 94], p. 243) notes that in the nineteenth century the indigenous people of Halmahera were confined to the northern peninsula. Xavier (in Schurhammer and Wicki [eds.], *op. cit.* [n. 93], I, 380) mentions a group called the "Tavaros," possibly the Tabaru tribe of Halmahera, as being residents of the Moro area.

authority. The ruler of Tolo (in East Central Celebes), who supported Gilolo in its resistance to Ternate, likewise continued to be a thorn in the flesh of the missionaries. Occasionally the native Christians of Moro as well as the missionaries were personally attacked and their shrines and images desecrated. The converts would sometimes quarrel and fight with the pagans as each group sought to prove the greater merit and potency of its beliefs. The Jesuits were apparently forced to call upon their god to produce rain and other supernatural feats of the kind the pagans expected from their gods. Like most primitive peoples, the pagans of Moro have a vast pantheon of nature and familial gods. Spirits are everywhere at work and must be propitiated or exorcised. To frighten the spirits of the nether world and thereby prevent earthquakes and tremors, the natives beat the ground with sticks. They believe in forest nymphs (*charisique*) who damage their trees. Each individual, including the children, has his own god. Through this god, before whom ceremonies are performed, the individual makes contact with his ancestors. It is particularly difficult to convince the natives of the falsity of their beliefs in traditional gods and sorcery, because they do not possess the requisite vocabulary for the understanding and expression of religious ideas.

The Jesuits concern themselves considerably with the natural phenomena and environment of the Moluccas and Moro. Among other duties they bless the rice seeds of their converts before each planting and hold elaborate funeral services for native Christians. Aside from accommodating themselves to the practices and beliefs of these primitive agriculturists, the fathers note that the islands produce rice, ginger, and other foodstuffs. Fróis gives in some detail what can only be called a recipe for making sago bread, an item of paramount importance to the Europeans working and sailing in the Spiceries because it was the single most important food in their diet.[632] Wild chickens (*Magacephalon maleo*) in Moro lay large eggs which the natives gather and eat.[633] Crabs with claws larger than those of lobsters are trapped and eaten, but there is one black crablike creature which is deadly poisonous. The sea abounds in turtles which lay eggs, are themselves edible, and taste like mutton. Because the people of Moro have no cows on land, the Lord provides them with sea cows (manatees) which they catch in nets when the moon is low. The parts best for eating, and those which the Jesuits rate as good food, are the heads, necks, and teats.[634] The forests are alive with parrots which have no trouble imitating any language. On Ternate there are fantastic snakes (pythons) large enough to swallow a whole dog or goat, but which refrain from attacking people unless they are extremely hungry.[635]

[632] Wicki (ed.), *op. cit.* (n. 80), III, 544.

[633] For a thorough discussion of this mound-building bird of Celebes and the Moluccas see Scott, *op. cit.*, pp. 72–74.

[634] Wicki (ed.), *op. cit.* (n. 80), III, 545. The sea cow is called *duyong* in Malay. For discussion see Scott, *loc. cit.* (n. 545), XVII (1896), 135–37.

[635] Wicki (ed.), *op. cit.* (n. 80), III, 542. See Wallace (*op. cit.* [n. 94], p. 228) for his description of the python in Amboina which he judges is capable of "swallowing a dog or a child."

East of Morotai, Fróis reports, lies one of the largest islands of the area, the land of the Papuas.[636] The Jesuits learned of New Guinea from Papuan slaves in the Moluccas and from Castilians who had been there. A Spaniard who had been held prisoner in the land of the Papuas for ten or twelve years told the Jesuits in Ternate that the Papuas could be readily converted.[637] He reported that New Guinea is only seven or eight days distance from the Moluccas and that its people would welcome the Portuguese. The island is said to have seven hundred leagues (2,800 miles) of coast and to be located near to New Spain, possibly meaning that its eastern extremity lay close to what Fróis thought the Spanish demarcation to be. The island is rich in gold, its population is completely black, and many kings rule there. The natives, who look like Africans, are exceedingly clever, as evidenced by slaves working for the Portuguese, and show ability to grasp the essentials of the faith. Between Ternate and New Guinea countless other islands dot the sea and support people whose names are not known, except for the "Sumas" (in eastern Halmahera, now called Ngollopleppo), the "Gebes" (on Gebe island, east of Halmahera), and the "Gaiceas" (of Waigeu Island).[638] It can readily be seen from these observations that the Spanish informant of the Jesuits followed what has been the traditional trading route from the Malay world of the Moluccas to the Papuan world further to the east.[639] The Jesuits also heard from the Castilians about places to the north of the Spiceries where gold and cinnamon could be obtained called "Mindanoao" (Mindanao), "Tagima" (Tapima), and the "Xulas" (Sulu Islands).[640]

About lesser-known places in the Spiceries proper, Fróis comments on Celebes where the king of Manado[641] is a Christian and where the people are reputedly well disposed towards conversion. There is gold in this distant place, but not a single missionary. Southward from Manado are the Macassars where three Christian kings reign and uphold the faith even though no missionaries are now there to help them. The islands of the Amboina group contain many Christian communities and two churches.[642] All the inhabitants of Buru would become Christian if someone would go there to evangelize. The smallest island of the "Leasse" (Uliasser), probably Nusalaut, is entirely Christian, and "Loreçore" (Saparua), a cannon's shot away, has a number of older Christian communities and many recent converts. Before being drowned in 1554, Brother Antonio Fernandez baptized nearly thirteen hundred souls in Amboina

---

[636] Wicki (ed.), *op. cit.* (n. 80), III, 546–47.

[637] Possibly a sailor from the "San Juan" of the Villalobos expedition. In 1545, Ynigo Ortiz de Retes, the commander of the "San Juan," sailed along the northern coast of New Guinea as he sought for a passage back to Mexico. Here he fought several engagements against hostile natives. It was Ortiz who claimed the island for the king of Spain and gave it the name "New Guinea." See Wichmann, *op. cit.* (n. 535), pp. 23–28.

[638] Wicki (ed.), *op. cit.* (n. 80), III, 547.

[639] Cf. the sketch map of Wallace's voyage of 1860 from Waigeu to Ternate, *op. cit.* (n. 94), p. 411.

[640] Wicki (ed.), *op. cit.* (n. 80), III, 559–60.

[641] *Ibid.*, p. 559. Manado is at the extreme northern tip of this tentacled island and directly west of Halmahera.

[642] *Ibid.*, pp. 560–61.

and noted their names down on a register so that they would not be forgotten. Another nearby island is "Varanura" (Seram) where many still await redemption. After a fervent plea and exhortation to Europe for more missionaries, Fróis brings his letter to a close with the flat statement: "Europe has sufficient religious; the East hardly any." [643]

The cry for more workers in the Spiceries was to sound incessantly throughout the sixteenth century. Beira and Nunes, as a result of their visit to Goa in 1557, returned to the Moluccas at the end of the year with a company of nine (four fathers and five brothers), including themselves. More than one-fifth of all the Jesuits in the East outside of Goa (nine of forty-four) were in the Moluccas in 1557, and in the College at Goa lived one boy from Macassar and another from Amboina. [644] The Molucca mission, after a slow start, seemed to be on the verge of prospering, and in Europe several reports on its progress appeared in the *Diversi* and *Nuovi avisi* (Venice) of 1558, 1559, 1562, and 1565, in the *Epistolae Indicae* (Louvain, 1566), in the *Epistolae Indicae et Japonicae* (Louvain, 1570), and in the *Nuovi avisi* (Brescia) for 1571.

In a report written in 1559 addressed to the fathers in Portugal, Fróis includes an account of the conversion of the Sultan of Bachan and his subjects in the summer of 1557. [645] It appears that the sultan of this island group located "twenty leagues [80 miles] from Maluquo [Ternate] in the direction of Amboine [Amboina]" [646] was the nephew of Sultan Hairun. On a visit to Ternate the young ruler evidently eloped with his cousin, Hairun's daughter, and took her home with him. Shortly thereafter, the girl died in childbirth and the young husband became fearful of Hairun's wrath. To counter any moves which Hairun might make, the ruler of Bachan secretly sent an emissary to the Portuguese fortress at Ternate to ask for support and the dispatch of a missionary to his island. Father Antonio Vaz arrived at Bachan on June 23, 1557, and formally converted the young sultan and his advisers after a week of instruction. The Sultan, who had previously been a Muslim, was given the Christian name, John, since he was baptized on the feastday of Saint John (July 1). The newly

---

[643] *Ibid.*, p. 563. He estimates (*ibid.*, p. 561) that in 1556 there were probably 50,000 converts in Amboina and Moro, the two largest Christian centers in the Spiceries. At that time there were but two brothers in Moro, one father in Ternate, and nobody in Amboina. But it should also be recalled that there was a shortage of Jesuits everywhere in the East.

[644] See "Catalogue of the India Province" in *ibid.*, pp. 783–91. The boy from Amboina was the son of the Muslim ruler of Nusatelo (or Asilulu) of the Hittu peninsula of Amboina; the father was known as "a great persecutor of Christians."

[645] From Goa (November 14, 1559) and written at the behest of Quadros, the Provincial of India. In *ibid.*, IV, 347–50. It was published in Europe in 1562, 1566, 1569, and 1570. Notice arrived in Europe in this same letter of the conversion of the ruler of Timor and of the request sent by him to Malacca for the dispatch of a missionary to his island. For a much more detailed account of the mission in the Bachan archipelago see C. Wessels, "De Katholieke Missie in het Sultanaat Batjan (Molukken), 1557–1609," *Historisch Tijdschrift*, VIII (1929), 115–48, 221–45.

[646] For discussion of the eighty small islands of the Bachan archipelago, its population of less than 12,000 (1925), and its great store of sago see W. Ph. Coolhaas, "Mededeelingen betreffende de onderafdeeling Batjan," *Bijdragen tot de Taal-, Land- en Volkenkunde van Nederlandsch-Indië*, LXXXII (1926), 403–85. The young sultan evidently lived on the island of Kasiroeta at this time.

converted ruler then helped Vaz to destroy the mosque and accompanied him on a tour of the island. For four and one-half months Vaz instructed Sultan John and baptized men, women, children, and slaves. John, according to Vaz, is "a courteous and civil man, and, if he were a little whiter, would be taken for a Portuguese." After Vaz's departure, Brother Fernão d'Osouro stayed for a time at the side of the royal convert.[647] In the war which the chagrined Hairun launched against the Portuguese and Bachan, the young sultan remained steadfastly on the side of his Portuguese allies. Hairun's siege of the Portuguese fortress on Ternate cut off communications for several years between the missionaries in the Spiceries and their colleagues in Malacca and Goa.[648] Jesuits captured by the Moors were ruthlessly executed, a number of them suffering martyrdom in 1558–60. In 1559, Hairun himself was captured and held prisoner for a short time until he agreed to co-operate with the Portuguese. The Jesuits nonetheless continued to suspect his loyalty and to persist in believing that he was plotting treachery.[649]

The lengthiest letter written directly from the Moluccas, of those printed after reinforcements arrived in 1557, was from the pen of Father Pero Mascarenhas.[650] Dated from Ternate on November 12, 1564, this letter records both the victories and the defeats of the mission. Like most of the edifying letters, its theme is simple and direct: there would be more victories for the faith and fewer setbacks if more missionaries were available and if the Portuguese administrators would concern themselves to protect the Christians, would sublimate their personal desires for trade and wealth, and would consequently make fewer concessions to the stiff-necked Hairun. In May, 1563, Mascarenhas reports, Hairun outfitted an armada to attack northern Celebes and gave the command to his son, Crown Prince "Baba" (Bāb-Ullāh).[651] When the Jesuits at Ternate realized that an attack was being planned against the Christian rulers and converts at Manado, they determined to send Father Diogo Magalhães to prepare the Christians there for the expected onslaught. Hairun tried to prevent the dispatch of the Portuguese fleet, for he considered the rulers of these places to be his vassals. After some delay, the Portuguese fleet finally sailed with Magalhães aboard.

During the summer of 1563 the Jesuit father visited and made conversions at Manado, "Sichao" (Sangihe Islands), and at the towns dependent on Manado —"Bola" (Bolaäng), "Cauripa" (probably at the tip of the promontory), and

[647] Baltazar Dias to Miguel de Torre, Provincial of Portugal (Malacca, December 1, 1559), in Wicki (ed.), *op. cit.* (n. 80), IV, p. 483; Fróis to the Fathers in Portugal (Goa, December 1, 1560) in *ibid.*, pp. 741–42; Quadros to General Lainez in Rome (Bassein, November 28, 1561), in *ibid.*, V, 239.

[648] Fróis to Marco Nunes in Portugal (Goa, December 12 [?], 1560) in *ibid.*, IV, 835. D'Osouro was an illiterate, poorly prepared for this task, in Fróis' view, since he "barely knows how to recite the prayers."

[649] Manuel Teixeira to Marco Nunes in Portugal (Bassein, December 4, 1561), in *ibid.*, V, 316.

[650] Translated in Eglauer, *op. cit.* (n. 181), II, 279–90.

[651] The year before, in 1561, a similar fleet had joined with some Javan junks to besiege the Christian settlements on the northern coast of Amboina (Wessels, *op. cit.* [n. 21], p. 64).

"Totole" (Toutoli).[652] This northern coast of the northern promontory of Celebes lay between the Muslim kingdoms of Ternate and "Chigliguzarate" (unidentified) and seems to have had regular relations with Gilolo and Morotai on the opposite side of the Molucca Sea. It is likely that the peoples of this region also belonged to a group who are vaguely called "Batachinas" by the Portuguese and Jesuits.[653] A bellicose people, the subjects of the ruler of Manado were probably eager to accept Christianity in an effort to retain their independence from the more powerful Muslims who surrounded them. The island of "Sichao" is reported as having twenty-five thousand inhabitants, an army six thousand strong, and plentiful supplies of food and water.[654] The ruler of this island, shortly after Magalhães' stopover, personally visited the Portuguese fortress at Ternate.

In the Moluccas the Jesuits fear most the perfidy and machinations of Hairun and inveigh against the efforts which the Portuguese administrators and merchants make to appease him in the interests of trade. The Jesuits themselves continually concentrated their own attention upon converting and concluding alliances with his political and hereditary enemies. In 1564, a few days before Mascarenhas wrote his letter, the Jesuits baptized a male cousin of the ruler of Tidore, an influential and wealthy nobleman "whose conversion will, we hope, help to promote that of the whole of Tidore." [655] This event occurred at a time when the Sultan of Ternate was trying to dethrone his seventeen-year-old rival at Tidore. Hairun, who must have been as outraged with the Jesuits as they were with him, began in 1564 to make overtures to appease Mascarenhas. This transformation is brought about, Mascarenhas thinks, by Hairun's fear that the Jesuits will finally manage to bring Tidore to Christianity and that the Portuguese will then switch the center of their mercantile activities to the rival island. In an interview with Mascarenhas, Hairun agreed in November, 1564, to give the Jesuits freedom to preach in his realm and to attend their services himself in the company of his sons. While pleased by this turn of events, Mascarenhas concludes that the wily Sultan knows that "if the king of Tidore accepts the faith and he rejects it, he [Hairun] has nothing more to hope for from the viceroy [Henrique de Sá] and everything to fear." [656] For the moment the Jesuits seemed to have matters under control at Ternate; and their Christian ally, the ruler of Bachan, meanwhile protected the Christian communities in Amboina from Muslim reprisals by stationing his fleet in nearby waters.[657]

But Mascarenhas is describing the calm which precedes a storm. Early in 1565

---

[652] Xavier (Schurhammer and Wicki [eds.], *op. cit.* (n. 93), II, 113) mentions Toutoli as one of the places to be evangelized. For a general review of this mission see C. Wessels, "De Katholicke Missie in Noord Celebes en de Sangi Eilanden, 1563–1605," *Studiën,* CXIX (1933), 365–69.

[653] Also see Mascarenhas in Eglauer (trans.), *op. cit.* (n. 181), II, 327. For a map of the Minahasa part of Celebes see Wallace, *op. cit.* (n. 94), p. 189.

[654] Based on Magalhães' letter from Manado of Aug. 5, 1563, which is included in Mascarenhas' letter of Nov. 12, 1564, as translated in Eglauer (trans.), *op. cit.* (n. 181), II, 280–84.

[655] *Ibid.,* p. 286.

[656] *Ibid.,* p. 289.

[657] Wessels, *op. cit.* (n. 21), p. 64.

the Christian communities in the Amboinas were pillaged, burned, and their people killed and scattered by the combined forces of Ternate and the Muslim Javans.[658] The Portuguese commandant at Ternate meanwhile, much to the indignation of the Jesuits, decided not to interfere at Amboina. A large fleet carrying more than one thousand men was shortly thereafter, in 1566–67, outfitted at Goa to recapture the Moluccas. It left Malacca in August, 1567, under the command of Gonçales Pereira Marranaque. He plotted his course to the Moluccas around the north of Borneo, probably to seek out the Spanish of the Legaspi expedition who were thought to be violating the Portuguese demarcation. The fleet did not arrive in the Spiceries until 1568 and Marranaque still continued to be more interested in the Spanish than in straightening out the affairs of the Moluccas. In 1569, however, he led an expedition against the Muslims in Amboina accompanied by levies furnished him by Bachan and Tidore. Here, after driving the Javans and local Muslims into the interior, he built a strong, palisaded fortress. In the meantime, in 1568, Diogo Lopez de Mesquita had arrived in the Moluccas, accompanied by Mascarenhas, to take over as the new captain of Ternate.

In the early months of 1569, in this atmosphere of new hope and optimism, letters were written from Ternate by two old hands, Nicolau Nunes and Mascarenhas. Two years later, both letters appeared in Italian translation in the *Nuovi avisi* then being published at Brescia. Nunes, the senior member of the mission and personal acquaintance of Xavier, writes that the Moluccas promise now to be the most fruitful vineyard in which the Jesuits toil.[659] While most of the mission stations are located only in the coastal towns of Ternate, Bachan, Celebes, and the Moro Islands (notice the absence of Amboina from this list), the Muslims can certainly be annihilated in these islands "if more workers become available." Magalhães still works with success in Celebes, now being at Tolo in the eastern and central part of the island. Nunes himself is in Morotai at the city of "Sequita" (unidentified) and is aided by Brother Antonio Gonçalvez who recently visited the nearby island of Rau. Churches have been built in almost all the Christian settlements in Morotai. Great progress is likewise being recorded in Bachan by Fernão Alvares, whose converts are better able to grasp and understand Christian teachings than the more primitive pagans of Moro. Besides these heathens there are many others, particularly the Papuans, who are eager to have the faith brought to them. On one occasion, when in Bachan, Nunes saw some visiting chieftains from New Guinea who expressed the desire to become Christian like their host.

Mascarenhas, shortly after arriving at Ternate, accompanied an expedition which was sent in September, 1568, to help restore the Christian king of "Sion" (Sião or Siam in Lower Macassars) to his possessions in northern Celebes. In a

---

[658] In an official report (Goa, November 25, 1565) from Quadros to General Lainez, the Provincial of India observes: "The fathers have been expelled from Amboina by the Moors who have taken over the islands and the 70,000 Christians in them." See Wicki (ed.), *op. cit.* (n. 80), VI, 493.

[659] Eglauer (trans.), *op. cit.* (n. 181), II, 317–22.

letter written shortly after his return to Ternate from this expedition [660] Mascarenhas explains that the subjects of the king of "Sion" joined in the general
revolt of 1565 against the Portuguese. The king with his family were thereafter
forced to flee to Ternate for protection. It was apparently the arrival of Marranaque's fleet which enabled the Portuguese to delegate a task force to accompany
the deposed ruler on the return to his homeland. Word had been received in
Ternate, previous to the departure of the expedition, that the king would be
welcomed back by his own people. Upon arriving at Manado, Mascarenhas
learned, however, that only half of the king's territories were willing to acknowledge him and that he would probably have to fight to regain control over the
others. After delivering the king to "Sion" and making a mild display of their
arms, the task force had to depart in order to rendezvous with the rest of the
Portuguese fleet. The king, Mascarenhas, and two Portuguese aides were left
behind and they then took sanctuary in a village near "Sion." Upon hearing
of the Jesuit's presence, envoys came to him from the king of "Sanguim"
(in the Sangihe Islands), to request baptism for their sovereign.

On the feast of St. Francis (October 4), Mascarenhas, accompanied by eight
ships and the king of "Sion," left for and arrived at "Sanguim." He was then
taken to the residency and principal city of "Calanga" (Kalama?) where he
stayed for several days, just long enough to baptize the royal family and nobles
of both sexes, to erect a cross, and to begin construction of a church. Thereafter
the expedition began its return to the lands of the king of "Sion"; on November
2 Mascarenhas was evidently dropped off at the city of Manado. After ten days
here, the Jesuit went on to Bolaäng to pick up a youthful convert whom
Magalhães had left there. Finally, he arrived at "Cauripa" where the king of
"Sion" was scheduled to meet units from the Portuguese fleet which would
help him quell those territories still in revolt. Though the expected aid failed to
appear in January, 1569, two armed Portuguese vessels (probably manned by
freebooters) ultimately arrived on the scene and their captain offered his ships
and men to the king. After a siege of several days, these forces captured and
occupied two strategic centers and the king of "Sion" then felt that he was in
command of the situation. When Mascarenhas left for Ternate in February,
1569, he took with him the king's oldest son, a nine-year-old boy, to be brought
up as a Christian under the Jesuits.

The forecast of Christian victories and future conquests in these two letters of
1569 was overly optimistic. The government of Diogo Lopez de Mesquita at
Ternate quickly ran into new trouble with Hairun and the Muslim alliance which
he commanded. Mesquita, vexed by the craftiness of Hairun and perturbed by
internal questioning of his own policies, agreed in 1570 to a conference with
the Sultan. At this meeting Hairun was brutally stabbed to death by the nephew
of Mesquita at the instigation of his uncle. This act put Bāb-Ullāh into power
on Ternate, and he at once took an oath of vengeance. War broke out in various
places between the Portuguese and the confederation of Muslim rulers, and the

[660] Dated March 6, 1569, from Ternate. See *ibid.*, pp. 322–30.

fortress at Ternate was put under siege. For nearly five years the Portuguese withstood the siege, but their fortress finally fell in 1574. The Christian communities, many of which were located in places subject to Ternate, were doomed. The only place to hold out against the forces of Bāb-Ullāh was Amboina, and refugees from the other places poured into it. Finally, in 1578, the Portuguese regained enough strength to return to the clove islands and to build a fortress at Tidore, the island which had traditionally fought against the extension of Ternate's influence. For the period from 1571 to 1578 not a missionary letter from the islands is extant, a reflection of the almost complete annihilation of the Christian enterprise in the Spiceries.[661] In Europe, nothing at all was published by the Jesuits on the Spiceries during the last generation of the sixteenth century,[662] except for the reprinting of earlier materials. Even Guzman, who gives a summary of Jesuit activities in the Spiceries in his *Historia de las missiones* (1601), records nothing about events there for the years after 1570.[663] The thick veil of silence covering the Jesuit writings is probably to be accounted for by the political and religious difficulties as well as by the internecine differences which plagued the Europeans in the Moluccas during the last generation of the century.

The only substantial, eyewitness record of the changed situation in the Moluccas was printed in 1600 in Hakluyt's *Principal Navigations* (III, 730–42). It is entitled *The Famous Voyage of Sir Francis Drake into the South Sea . . . begune in the yeere of our Lord 1577*, and is probably a compendium produced by Hakluyt himself on the basis of several manuscript accounts written by participants in Drake's voyage.[664] From *The Famous Voyage* we learn that Drake arrived in the Moluccas on November 14, 1579, almost two years after his departure from Plymouth. While coasting off the island of Motir on the way to Tidore, Drake's vessel was hailed by some *praus* from Ternate which had officials aboard. The Englishman, who probably had known before leaving England about Ternate's earlier alliance with Portugal,[665] had to be convinced by the Ternate spokesmen who came aboard that the situation had changed and that he would be accorded a friendly reception by Bāb-Ullāh, now the enemy of Portugal. Drake, finally resolving to approach Ternate rather than Tidore, anchored in Bāb-Ullāh's harbor on the following day. He sent the Sultan a

[661] Wessels, *op. cit.* (n. 21), p. 90.

[662] *Ibid.*, p. 9.

[663] *Op. cit.* (n. 44), I, 178–88. This is particularly striking, because his information on many other places, such as south India, is very current. The first seventeenth-century book to deal with this period in detail is Bartolomé Leonardo de Argensola, *op. cit.* (n. 596).

[664] There is some question when this account was first printed, but by 1600 it existed in a number of published versions in English, Dutch, and German. For its publication history and authorship see Henry R. Wagner, *Sir Francis Drake's Voyage around the World, Its Aims and Achievements* (San Francisco, 1926), pp. 238–41.

[665] Contrast the statement (*ibid.*, p. 177): "When Drake left England, it is hardly likely that he had sufficient knowledge of political conditions in the islands to induce him to seek any one in particular." Such a conclusion hardly seems justified in the light of what Englishmen could readily have known from printed materials alone about political conditions in the Moluccas.

velvet cloak as a token of his peaceful intentions and a message which indicated that he had come to trade and nothing else. A response quickly came from shore that the Sultan would be happy to trade and that "he would yeelde himselfe, and the right of his Island to be at the pleasure and commandement of so famous a Prince...."⁶⁶⁶ Though it is unlikely that Bāb-Ullāh actually offered vassalage to England, the East India Company later claimed that this "verbal treaty" gave England certain rights in the Moluccas.⁶⁶⁷

Drake's vessel, the "Golden Hind," was shortly thereafter towed into a safer haven by four large *praus* sent out to it. The Sultan himself then came out to the ship accompanied by his retinue. This royal procession is described in some detail in *The Famous Voyage*, and Bāb-Ullāh is depicted as a tall man who was greatly delighted by the music which he heard aboard the "Golden Hind." After the Sultan's departure, provisions were sent to the ship from shore along with a quantity of cloves. Not long thereafter the Sultan, who had promised to return to the ship, sent his brother instead and requested Drake to come ashore. Fearing treachery, Drake declined the invitation and sent a number of his men to the beach in company with the ruler's brother. The English delegation was taken to the royal residence where a thousand persons were assembled to see them. Here they were received in state by the elders, and evidently the Sultan himself appeared on the scene. After this reception, Drake decided to leave Ternate with his cargo of provisions and cloves in order to be on his way to distant England. The observations which the Englishmen made at Ternate add nothing of significance to what was already available in other European sources. Probably the most valuable remarks are those which have to do with the dress and display of the court and the descriptions of the *praus* which came out to the ship. On a silver cup, which Queen Elizabeth is said to have presented to Drake in 1580 on his return, there is engraved the scene of the four *praus* towing the "Golden Hind" into the roads of Ternate, an indication of the great importance which the queen attached to the establishment of relations with the Spiceries.⁶⁶⁸ The *mappemondes* published after the circumnavigation of the world by Drake and Cavendish include geographical data on the Moluccas and Celebes acquired during these voyages.⁶⁶⁹

8

THE PHILIPPINE ISLANDS

Claims have repeatedly been advanced that, long before Magellan reached the Philippines in 1521, they were visited by European travelers and merchants. Vague and unidentifiable references in the writings of Marco Polo, Odoric of

⁶⁶⁶ From text of *The Famous Voyage* as reprinted in *ibid.*, p. 279.
⁶⁶⁷ See *ibid.*, p. 182.   ⁶⁶⁸ *Ibid.*
⁶⁶⁹ *Ibid.*, pp. 405–37. For the Spanish view of Drake as the first of the "heretical pirates" to invade the Iberian world in the East see Argensola, *op. cit.* (n. 596), pp. 104–9.

Pordenone, and Varthema have been pounced upon in vain attempts to prove that these early authors touched upon the Philippines in the course of their travels.[670] That Ibn Batuta made a halt in the Philippines in the mid-fourteenth century when his ship was driven off course by a typhoon seems to be a more firmly founded conjecture.[671] It is possible that Francisco Serrão, who had been sent out by Albuquerque to reconnoiter the trade routes and who had been shipwrecked in 1512, may have gotten to the island of Mindanao.[672] Other Portuguese ships in these early years may also have been wrecked, or may even have called intentionally at certain of the southern Philippine Islands. It is well known that later Portuguese vessels on their way to the Spiceries were blown beyond the Moluccas and thereby discovered a number of other islands in their vicinity. When Magellan arrived at Malhón Island (more commonly Homonhón)[673] in what is now called the Gulf of Leyte, he was told by the natives that they had already seen others of his kind.[674]

These earliest contacts with the outside world notwithstanding, the Philippines were first discovered, in any meaningful sense of the term, by the Magellan expedition. Europe quickly heard about the islands uncovered by the Spanish from the published writings of Maximilian of Transylvania (1523) and Pigafetta (*ca.* 1525). A truncated Italian version of the Pigafetta story appeared at Venice in 1536.[675] Nothing more is learned about the later Spanish experiences in the islands until the publication of Oviedo's Book XX in 1548. Two years later Ramusio republished Maximilian and the truncated version of Pigafetta, and published for the first time Pires' short account (prepared *ca.* 1515) as well as the report by Juan Gaetano on the Ruy Lopez de Villalobos expedition (1542–43) which sailed from Mexico to the Philippines.[676] A few additional details on the Spanish activities in the western Pacific were incorporated into Gómara's *Historia* published in 1552. Accounts of later events in the Philippines, after the

---

[670] Alfredo Gumma y Marti, "El archipiélago Dondiin, el nombre de Luzon y los origenes del Christianismo en Filipinas," *Boletim de la real sociedad geografica* (Madrid), XXXIX (1897), 21–46; also Austin Craig, *Pre-Spanish Philippine History and the Beginnings of Philippine Nationalism* (Madrid, 1935), pp. 91–101. The evidence advanced is not substantial enough to support these conjectures.

.[671] Zaide, *op. cit.* (n. 208), p. 119.

[672] A. Galvão in Bethune (ed.), *op. cit.* (n. 524), pp. 117–18. For an exposition of the theory that Magellan himself had secretly visited the Philippines from Malacca in 1512 see C. M. Parr, *So Noble a Captain* (New York, 1953), p. 328.

[673] See Andrew Sharp, *The Discovery of the Pacific Islands* (London, 1960), p. 13. Alternative names for Malhón are Homonhón and Jomonjol. See U.S. War Department, Bureau of Insular Affairs, *Pronouncing Gazetteer and Geographical Dictionary of the Philippine Islands* (Washington, 1902). At present Homonhón is a barrio (pop. 1,960) of the municipality of Guinan (Samar Province).

[674] See Cortesão (ed.), *op. cit.* (n. 46), I, 133–34, n. 2.

[675] Italian version translated from the original French summary of *ca.* 1525. The part on the Philippines is in *Delle navigationi et viaggi*, I (Venice, 1554), 389v–400v. It is this Ramusio text which was translated by Richard Eden into English in *Decades of the Newe World* (1555) and republished by Purchas in 1625. The complete Pigafetta manuscript did not see print until 1800; the modern, authoritative edition is Robertson (ed.), *op. cit.* (n. 136), I, 99–193; II, 13–25. The most significant omissions in the texts published in the sixteenth century are: certain miraculous events, stories of sexual practices, some place and personal names, and the list of Bisayan words.

[676] Gaetano's itinerary was probably written in 1546 or 1547; it was addressed to the Emperor Charles V.

Spanish conquest began in 1565, are included in the histories of China by Escalante and the Augustinian, Mendoza. These works, supplemented by incidental data in Linschoten,[677] constitute the narrative accounts published during the sixteenth century. Though the Jesuits arrived in the Philippines in 1581, a survey of the letters printed in the sixteenth century shows that they were extraordinarily silent about their early activities in the islands. The first book published by a member of the Philippine province of the Society appeared at Rome only in 1604.[678]

The Philippines were not slow to appear on European maps after the return of Magellan's crew to Europe. An anonymous chart, prepared in about 1522 and attributed to Pedro Reinel, includes the inscription "Islas s. Lazaro," the name given by Magellan to the Philippines in honor of St. Lazarus on whose feast day the expedition jubilantly sighted the mountainous archipelago.[679] Other data provided by Juan Sebastián del Cano were incorporated into the anonymous planisphere of 1527 attributed to Diogo Ribeiro, the first cosmographer of the *Casa de Contratación* in Seville.[680] Particularly striking are the additions on an anonymous chart of about 1535 which delineate the southern Philippines and name particular islands. Cebu and Negros are shown, and Mindanao is correctly depicted as the largest and southernmost of the islands.[681] The delineation is improved upon in subsequent representations and a map published in 1554 by Ramusio includes not only the individual islands mentioned above but also the inscription "Filipina," a name which was given by Villalobos to a single island in 1543 [682] and which quickly became the official designation for the entire archipelago shortly after the prince for whom it was named became King Philip II.

The paucity and slightness of the published materials, whether maps or narratives, contrasts sharply with the importance which certain of them have had for the historiography of the pre-Spanish period of Philippine history. Almost no native writings of the pre-conquest period are extant, and significant archeological remains and inscriptions are few.[683] Aside from the European sources, the historical records of the pre-Spanish period are limited to scattered references in the sparse annals of the neighboring insular areas and in the Chinese histories. Given the poverty of indigenous sources, the firsthand observations of a Pigafetta or the secondhand account of a Maximilian of Transylvania no longer seem so slight. Consequently, historians of the Philippines have long looked upon these two early European tracts as sources of focal

---

[677] Linschoten's account (in Burnell and Tiele [eds.], *op. cit.* [n. 25], I, 123–24) is extracted from Mendoza, but has also a few personal comments on the veracity of the Spanish account.

[678] Pedro Chirino, *Relación de las islas Filipinas i de lo que en ellas an trabaido los padres de la Compañia de Jésus* (Rome, 1604).

[679] Cortesão and Teixeira da Mota, *op. cit.* (n. 2), I, 35–36.

[680] *Ibid.*, pp. 99–101.

[681] *Ibid.*, pp. 123–24.

[682] This map was probably drawn by Giacomo Gastaldi. See Carlos Quirino, *Philippine Cartography* (*1320–1899*) (2d rev. ed.; Amsterdam, 1963), p. x.

[683] Zaide, *op. cit.* (n. 208), pp. 40–41.

importance which they have systematically combed and recombed for each tiny fragment of specific information. They have somehow not been so thorough in their survey of the materials in Oviedo and Ramusio which are also important for the pre-conquest period.

The historian of the Spanish debut on Philippine soil (from 1565 to 1600) has available, by contrast, an abundance of material. He has a few printed sources from the last generation of the sixteenth century; the published materials, however, become numerous only after 1600. He can consult also a substantial number of sixteenth-century documents, most of which have been collected and published only within the last century.[684] What is missing so far is a synthesis of the voluminous materials contained in the great source collections in print and in the archives. No detailed and satisfactory history of the Philippines exists for either the pre-conquest or the Spanish period. In part, because of the difficult source problem, a new approach to the history of the Philippines has been tried in recent years which stresses working carefully back from the present into the past. Called ethnohistory for want of a better name, it seeks to bring the disciplines of anthropology and history into closer collaboration in an effort to integrate and evaluate the growing corpus of primary material with the aid of contemporary archeological, linguistic, and native testimony.[685]

Like a number of other insular peoples, natives of the Philippine Islands were first "discovered" by the Portuguese in the Strait of Malacca. Pires, who wrote in about 1515 on the basis of information available to him in Malacca, refers to the "Luções" (Luzones) as an insular people who live "ten days' sail beyond Borneo."[686] The merchants and sailors from Luzon, as seen from Malacca, trade in both Borneo and in the new Portuguese colony. They are mostly heathens, and they are little esteemed in Malacca. Still they are strong, industrious, and given to useful pursuits; in many of their ways they resemble the people of Borneo and these two groups are treated as being from one place in the Malacca community of foreign merchants. In their own country, the "Luções" have plenty of foodstuffs, wax, honey, and gold of a very inferior grade. They have no king, but are governed by a group of elders.[687] It is only in recent years that they have begun coming to Malacca. Around 1515 about

---

[684] For a review of the manuscript and printed sources see John L. Phelan, *The Hispanization of the Philippines: Spanish Aims and Filipino Responses* (Madison, Wis., 1959), pp. 199–210; for a survey of the manuscript sources on trade at Seville see Pierre Chaunu, *Les Philippines et le Pacifique des Ibériques* (Paris, 1960); for the Jesuit materials see H. de la Costa, S. J., *The Jesuits in the Philippines* (Cambridge, Mass., 1961), pp. 629–33.

[685] The University of Chicago project on the Philippines headed by Fred Eggan is an outstanding example of this new approach. For example, see Eggan *et al.*, *The Philippines* (Human Relations Area Files [4. vols.; New Haven, 1955]).

[686] Cortesão (ed.), *op. cit.* (n. 46), I, 133. This is the first reference to Luzon in European literature. By 1563, on the basis of reports from a Portuguese who evidently got to Luzon in 1545, the name "Luçoes" begins to appear on maps (*ibid.*, n. 2).

[687] A vague reference to the *barangay*, a unit of settlement and government normally ruled over by a *datu* or *raha* and a council of elders; this small community organization survives today in the islands as the barrio. The term *barangay* is also used to refer to the ships in which the original settlers are presumed to have come to the islands. Zaide, *op. cit.* (n. 208), pp. 67–68.

five hundred "Luções" are reported to reside in "Mjjam" (Minjani),[688] a town on the western side of the peninsula between Malacca and Kedah. This group includes a number of important merchants who would like to trade at Malacca, but who cannot get permission to leave Minjani because that town is still secretly supporting the Malay sultan in his fight against the Portuguese.[689]

Upon arriving in the western Pacific, Magellan first landed in the Ladrones (Marianas) and touched on its southernmost islands of Guam and Rota.[690] While Maximilian reports that these islands are uninhabited, Pigafetta from his own experience there paints a fascinating word picture of the islanders. They live in freedom with no lord over them and no formal religion. In appearance they are tawny, well-formed, and as tall as Europeans. They wear what is fairly common tropical dress—small palm-leaf hats, long hair and beards, and very little else. They subsist on a diet which includes coconuts, batatas or sweet potatoes, birds, flying fish, bananas, and sugar cane. Primitive as they are, the women remain indoors and spend most of their time weaving palm leaves into mats, baskets, and other household necessities. Their wooden houses are covered with planks and banana leaves and are well furnished with palm mats. They sleep on soft and good beds of shredded palm straw. The only arms which they carry are spears with points of fishbone. For their only recreation they take excursions in their little black and red boats which resemble the gondolas that ply between Fusine and Venice. When in the water themselves, the islanders swim and leap about like dolphins. From the bewilderment which they exhibited on seeing Europeans for the first time, Pigafetta concludes that the islanders must formerly have believed that they themselves were the only people in the world. The natives excel so in thievery that Magellan in reprisal burned their houses and killed a few of their men. From their skill in stealing, the commander called their islands the archipelago of *Ladrones*, the Spanish word for "thieves." The later accounts of the Ladrones (which sometimes actually refer to islands in the Marshall group rather than in the Marianas) are essentially in agreement with Pigafetta's. In 1565, Legaspi formally claimed the Ladrones for the crown of Spain, but the Spanish were not able to annex them for another century. It is probable, however, that by 1600 all of the Ladrones from the Maug group to Guam had been sighted or touched upon by the Spanish in their search for trans-Pacific passages between Mexico and the Philippines.[691]

While taking fresh water aboard in the Ladrones, Magellan learned from the natives about an island further to the west called "Selani" where he could

---

[688] Pires in Cortesão (ed.), *op. cit.* (n. 46), I, 107, n. 2.

[689] *Ibid.*, p. 134.

[690] Maximilian (in Coote [ed.], *op. cit.* [n. 463], 126–27) refers to "Inauagana," the major city on Guam's northern coast, and to "Acacan," the watering-place at the western end of Rota, an island north of Guam. For confirmation of these identifications see Sharp, *op. cit.* (n. 673), pp. 5–6. For a summary of all the Pacific discoveries made by Magellan and his survivors see *ibid.*, p. 11.

[691] *Ibid.*, p. 86.

obtain all the provisions which he required.[692] On March 16, 1521, at a distance of three hundred leagues from the Ladrones, the Spanish sighted the mountains of Samar in the Philippines, and on the following day went ashore on the uninhabited islet of Homonhón just to the south of Samar. Here, while resting and taking fresh water aboard, the Spanish were visited by nine natives from a neighboring island. The natives being friendly, Magellan gave them a few trinkets in exchange for food and a jar of arrack. Through sign language, the natives let the Spanish commander know that they would return in four days with coconuts, rice, and other provisions. This reference to coconuts gives Pigafetta an opportunity to discourse at length on the numerous virtues of the coconut palm; his description is based not only upon his stay at Homonhón but obviously on his total experience in the East.[693] In any event, the natives returned to Homonhón as they had promised, and informed the Spanish through signs about the neighboring islands and their products. The Spanish, from their base at Homonhón where they stayed for one week, explored the neighboring islands and found them to be inhabited by semi-nude heathens whom they described as being dark, fat, and painted, and as having goats, fishing nets, and an assortment of metal weapons and large shields. These people, in Pigafetta's view, are clearly more sophisticated, friendlier, and better armed than the primitive residents of the Ladrones. Not only do they know how to use metal in the manufacture of weapons, they also decorate their spears with gold—one of several optimistic signs that the hopeful Spanish immediately noticed about the presence of gold in the Philippines.[694]

Refreshed and revictualed the Spanish sailed southwestward for three days and anchored off Limasawa, a small island south of Leyte. The flagship was soon approached by a small boat with eight men aboard. Magellan's slave, a native of Sumatra, addressed them in Malay. Though they readily understood him, they were at first unwilling to board the ship. After Magellan had thrown them a few trinkets, the natives rowed away to notify their chief (*datu*) of what they had seen and heard. Two hours later, two large boats called "balanghai" (*barangays*)[695] approached Magellan's ship; in the larger one of these the chief himself sat under an awning. Henrique, Magellan's slave and interpreter, talked with the ruler from a distance. After a while a number of the natives were sent aboard the ship while their chief remained in his *barangay*. Satisfied that the Spanish were friendly and trustworthy, the chief himself came aboard on the next day. After presents were exchanged and a banquet eaten, Magellan had the interpreter tell the chief that he wanted to be his blood brother. Kolambu,

[692] Maximilian in Coote (ed.), *op. cit.* (n. 463), p. 127. This is possibly a reference to a port on the southwest side of the island of Leyte. Maximilian, who omits mention of the first landings in the Philippines, says that the expedition was driven by storms to "Massana" (Limasawa), a little island south of Leyte.

[693] All of this is reproduced in Ramusio, *op. cit.* (n. 529), I (1554), 393r and v. See also Robertson (ed.), *op. cit.* (n. 136), I, 99–103.

[694] Robertson (ed.), *op. cit.* (n. 136), I, 103, 109.

[695] See above p. 626n.

as the chief is called, and Magellan sealed their friendship by a blood compact (*kasikase*), the first recorded one in Philippine history. Then the commander of the Spanish expedition put on a display of his rich cargo and his military might. He frightened the natives by discharging the ships' guns and rendered the chief almost speechless by having an armored soldier take blows from three men armed with swords and daggers without being wounded. The interpreter-slave then relayed to the chief Magellan's studied opinion that one such armored man was probably worth more than one hundred of the native's unarmored retainers. When Kolambu concurred, Magellan informed him that he had two hundred such armored men in each of his ships. After Magellan showed him the ship's instruments and explained how they enabled the Europeans to sail out of sight of land for many days, the overawed chief agreed that Pigafetta and another of the ship's company might go ashore with him.[696]

When the Europeans and Kolambu reached the beach, the chief lifted his hands towards the sky in thanksgiving and then turned to his two strange companions. Pigafetta and his colleague were led by the hand to a bamboo awning under which a large *barangay* was sheltered. The party sat down in the stern of the boat to converse by signs in the presence of the royal guardsmen. Soon a plate of pork and a large jug of wine were brought in. Each bite of meat was accompanied by ceremonial wine drinking. Before the chief took the cup, he raised his fist toward the sky and brandished it at his companions. After he had taken the cup to drink, he flung out his left fist so sharply and abruptly that Pigafetta thought for a moment that the chief meant to strike him. When the European came to realize that the chief was merely offering a friendly toast, he replied in kind.[697] Once these ceremonies ended, the Europeans presented the chief with a number of the gifts which they had brought ashore with them. In the meantime the Italian wrote down the terms which the natives were using; their astonishment was obvious when he was able to read their words back intelligibly from his phonetic transcriptions.

After a supper of pork and rice, the Europeans were taken to the chief's abode. It was "built like a hayloft and was thatched with fig and palm leaves."[698] Since this house rested on wooden stilts, it had to be entered by climbing up ladders. Once inside, the Europeans sat down beside the chief on a bamboo mat and were served a dish of fish and ginger. The interior was lighted by torches made from tree gum wrapped in palm and banana leaves. The chief's son joined the party and Pigafetta's companion soon became intoxicated from the overindulgences of the day. The chief indicated by a sign that he would retire for the night, and he left his son to entertain the reveling Europeans. The young men finally slept for a few hours, their heads resting on pillows made of leaves. At dawn, the chief awakened the Europeans and sent them back to their ship. They were accompanied to their ship by Kolambu's brother, Siaui, the ruler

---

696 Robertson (ed.), *op. cit.* (n. 136), I, 111–13.
697 On ritual drinking see Phelan, *op. cit.* (n. 684), p. 23.
698 Robertson (ed.), *op. cit.* (n. 136), I, 117.

[629]

of Butuan and Surigao in northeastern Mindanao, who was then visiting and hunting on Limasawa.[699]

From Siaui the Europeans learned through their interpreter that chunks of gold the size of walnuts and eggs are found in Mindanao by sifting the earth.[700] The chief's dishes and part of his house are reportedly made from gold. Even on his very imposing person, the chief gives evidence of great wealth. Atop his long black hair, he wears a covering of silk, and two golden earrings are fastened in his ears. His body is wrapped in a sarong of cotton cloth embroidered with silk. Around his waist hangs a dagger with a long golden shaft which protrudes from a scabbard of carved wood. Even his teeth look as if they are edged and inlaid with gold. Tattooed all over and highly perfumed, Siaui is regarded by Pigafetta as the "finest looking man that we saw among those people."[701]

After Siaui's visit to the fleet, Magellan apparently decided that it was safe for a large body of men to go ashore to hear mass on Easter Sunday. Both of the native rulers participated in the ceremonies, the first recorded Catholic rites held on Philippine soil. When communion had finally been taken, Magellan put on a fencing tournament to entertain the chiefs. Then he had a cross brought forward which, he explained through the interpreter, he would like to set up on a high place as a symbol of his appearance in these islands. Should other Europeans chance to visit Limasawa, he reassured the natives, they would recognize the cross and would likewise behave in a friendly manner. The cross, the natives were told, would also protect them from the elements if they would make their obeisances to it every morning. Magellan also inquired about their own beliefs and learned that they were not Moors but heathens who worshipped a god in the skies called "Abba."[702]

After this short digression on religious matters, Magellan inquired why there was so little food on Limasawa. Kolambu explained that this was not his home island, but just a retreat where he came to meet his brother and to hunt. On the afternoon of Easter Sunday, the cross was planted with due ceremony on the highest peak of the island. Magellan then made further inquiries of his hosts about the best place to find provisions. He was told that there were three nearby islands—"Ceylon" (Panaon, south of Leyte), "Zuba" (Cebu), and "Calagham" (Caraga)—where they might find stores, but that Cebu was the largest and the one with most trade. Kolambu offered to show the Europeans the way to Cebu himself if only they would wait two days until he could complete the rice harvest and attend to his other affairs. To facilitate matters some of the Europeans helped to harvest the rice and Pigafetta evidently tried

---

[699] *Ibid.*, p. 119. Maximilian (in Coote [ed.], *op. cit.* [n. 463], p. 127) describes Kolambu as being the ruler of three islands, possibly including therein the territories governed by his brother.

[700] On gold production see Conrado Benitez, *History of the Philippines: Economic, Social, Cultural, Political* (Manila, 1954), pp. 55–56; also Zaide, *op. cit.* (n. 208), p. 17.

[701] Robertson (ed.), *op. cit.* (n. 136), I, 119.

[702] A Bisayan word for the supreme being; for a list of the other names under which the supreme being is known in the Philippines see Juan Roger, *Estudio etnologico comparativo de las formas religiosas primitivas de las tribus salvajes de Filipinas* (Madrid, 1949), p. 67.

bartering with the natives while taking a few notes on their customs. He remarks particularly on their nudity, tattoos, habit of chewing betel, and on Limasawa's products.[703]

Finally, the rice being harvested, the fleet of Magellan escorted by Kolambu's ships set sail for the northwest. On their way to Cebu they passed five places: "Ceylon" (Panaon), Bohol, "Canighan" (Canigao, southwest of Leyte), "Baybai" (Bayban on the west central coast of Leyte), and "Gatighan" (Apit or Himuquetan?).[704] In the vicinity of these islands they saw all sorts of wild fowl and huge bats.[705] Since Kolambu's *barangay* had great difficulty in sailing as fast as the European ships, they were forced to wait for him near the three Camote Islands to the west of Leyte. Contact being re-established, Magellan took Kolambu and several of his chieftains aboard the flagship and set his course directly for Cebu.

On Sunday, April 7, 1521, the Europeans entered the port on Cebu's eastern coast. As his three vessels approached the city, Magellan ordered them to strip their sails down, as if preparing for battle, and to fire all their artillery. The people on shore, who must have been puzzled and perplexed merely by the sight of three strange, ominous-looking vessels, were almost thrown into panic by the sound of the artillery bursts. Once anchored in the harbor, Magellan sent a representative and his interpreter ashore to confer with Humabon, the ruler of Cebu. After reassuring the chief that the guns had been fired as a token of peace and friendship, the interpreter told the questioning Humabon that his master was in the service of the greatest king in the world and was on his way to find the Moluccas. Magellan, Humabon was told, had come to Cebu, on the recommendation of the ruler of Limasawa, to exchange goods for provisions.

While responding in a friendly fashion, Humabon firmly announced that all foreign ships were required to pay tribute before engaging in trade. To prove this fact, the ruler brought forward a Muslim merchant from Siam who had arrived just four days earlier in a junk loaded with gold and slaves. He was now doing business at Cebu after having paid the required tribute. The interpreter insisted, however, that his master, as the agent of the greatest king in the world, would pay no tribute and threatened hostilities unless his demands were met. The merchant from Siam then erroneously informed the chief that the Christians were the same as those who had conquered Calicut and Malacca and that it would be advisable to trade on their terms. After agreeing to discuss the matter with his advisers, Humabon was visited by Kolambu who evidently reassured him about the intentions of the Europeans. The ruler of Cebu thereupon agreed to negotiate the next day with the intruders from afar.[706]

Formal negotiations were carried on at first between Humabon and his

---

[703] Robertson (ed.), *op. cit.* (n. 136), I, 128–29.

[704] *Ibid.*, pp. 129, 256–57. For a listing of old place names in the Philippines see Quirino, *op. cit.* (n. 682), pp. 67–72.

[705] Bats are very numerous in the Philippines. At dusk, clouds of "flying foxes," huge fruit bats, often darken the sky. See Eggan *et al.*, *op. cit.* (n. 685), pp. 44–45.

[706] Robertson (ed.), *op. cit.* (n. 136), I, 133–35.

chiefs on one side and Magellan's notary and interpreter on the other. Fearful that the European wanted to make him a vassal, the ruler of Cebu was reassured that Magellan had no such intention and that he wanted "only to trade with him and no others."[707] As a testimony of their mutual good faith, Humabon suggested that he and Magellan should exchange drops of blood from their right arms as well as presents. On the following morning (Tuesday, April 9, 1521), Kolambu and the Muslim merchant went to the ships to tell Magellan that the king of Cebu was collecting provisions and that he would send his representatives to make peace arrangements in the afternoon. The delegation of chieftains who appeared later on that day was led by Humabon's nephew and heir. Asked if they came with full powers and the authority to speak publicly, the natives answered in the affirmative. In the discussion which followed, Magellan inquired about their succession practices and lectured to them about peace and Christianity. The purpose of his digression into Christian ideas was obviously to find out something about their own beliefs and their possible attitude towards conversion. Though he counseled them not to accept Christianity and his peace offering through fear, he promised that if they became converts he would leave a suit of armor with them and that they would be everlastingly free from the torments of spirits and devils. Peace vows being concluded, the pact was sealed with embraces and an exchange of gifts.

Pigafetta and the interpreter accompanied the Cebuan delegation ashore to thank Humabon officially for his gifts. They found the chief seated before his "palace" on a palm mat in the midst of a great number of people. A short, fat man marked with tattooings, Humabon wore only a loin cloth, an embroidered scarf on his head, a necklace, and two large gold earrings encrusted with precious stones. In front of him on another mat were two porcelain dishes of turtle eggs which he was eating and four jars of palm wine which he was sipping through straws. After officially extending their commander's thanks for his gifts, the representatives of Magellan clothed Humabon in a Turkish-style yellow and violet silk robe, red cap, and strings of glass beads which Magellan had sent him as presents. After sampling the turtle eggs and sipping the palm wine, Pigafetta and his companions went off with the chief's nephew to a party at his house. Here, while they ate dinner, they were entertained by native musicians and naked dancing girls.[708]

Their negotiations complete, the Europeans began on Wednesday (April 10, 1521) to bring merchandise ashore to exchange for provisions and other local products. The beginning of trade gives Pigafetta an opportunity to discourse on a number of local customs. He notices that commercial rules are studiously followed and that they have accurate weights and measures of their own

---

[707] *Ibid.*, p. 137.

[708] *Ibid.*, pp. 139–47. Much of the description of this gay party (*ibid.*, pp. 146–47) is given only in summary in the version printed by Ramusio (*op. cit.* [n. 529], I, 396v). Evidently these and similar descriptions of frivolity were purposely deleted or abbreviated by the sixteenth-century publishers of Pigafetta.

type.[709] In their houses, which are built on stilts, they have separate rooms, and under their houses they keep pigs, goats, and poultry. Beautiful large shellfish called "laghan" (*lagan*)[710] which are good to eat are found on Cebu. It is said by the local people that if a whale swallows one of them alive, the *lagan* will come out of its shell and kill the whale by eating the heart. In the official trading which began on Friday (April 12, 1521), the Europeans exchanged iron and other metals for gold, and their smaller and less valuable items for rice, meat, and other foods. Magellan evidently had to give orders to his gold-hungry men that they should not spoil the trade in gold for others by giving too much in exchange for it.

In the meantime preparations were being completed for the formal cere-monies by which Humabon, Kolambo, and their wives and retainers would publicly become Christians. Apparently it had been arranged in Magellan's negotiations with the Cebu delegation that baptismal services would be held on Sunday, April 14. Earlier in the week the land in the public square had been consecrated by the ship's chaplain preparatory to the burial of two sailors who had died after arriving in Cebu. On Saturday, April 13, a platform was erected in this consecrated square and it was decorated with hangings and palm branches to lend as much solemnity and pomp as possible to the chiefs' acknowledgment of the Christian god. On Sunday morning, the program began with the appear-ance on the beach of Magellan and forty men from the ships. As they landed, all of the ships' guns fired a salute. They were led in procession by the royal banner of Spain and two armored soldiers. After a formal exchange of greetings, Magellan and Humabon, each with his chief attendants, ambled to the platform to take their places. While conversing with the chief, Magellan learned that some of Humabon's subordinates were unwilling to accept Christianity. With this revelation all pretenses were dropped. The Portuguese Magellan, who had long before learned how to mix force with persuasion, threatened to kill and take other reprisals against the reluctant chiefs. At the same time he reassured Humabon that he intended to make him, as a Christian lord, into the supreme and unchallenged ruler of the entire region. Without further ado a large cross[711] was raised in the center of the square and the natives were told that they were to destroy their old idols and to kneel before the cross each morning. Instruction being over, Humabon and his principal retainers were baptized and given Christian names. Before mass was sung that morning, five hundred men were baptized. After lunch the royal ladies and their attendants likewise accepted baptism. Counting men, women, and children, eight hundred[712] souls came to Christ on that notable Sunday in Cebu;[713] ironically, in Germany, Martin

[709] For comment and names see Zaide, *op. cit.* (n. 208), p. 92.

[710] Robertson (ed.), *op. cit.* (n. 136), I, 149; 261.

[711] This cross and some sacred images are still preserved in Cebu as religious relics. See Zaide, *op. cit.* (n. 208), p. 139, ns. 59 and 61.

[712] Robertson (ed.), *op. cit.* (n. 136), I, 155.

[713] Maximilian (Coote [ed.], *op. cit.* [n. 463], p. 129) notes that the numbers baptized during Magellan's entire sojourn in Cebu totaled 2,200.

Luther was preparing for his appearance two days later (April 16, 1521) before Charles V and the Diet of Worms.

After these first mass baptisms, people from other parts of Cebu and neighboring islands also accepted Christianity. The Europeans, presumably acting in the name of the Christian king of Cebu, had no hesitation about burning down a village on a neighboring island when its people refused to acknowledge the authority of Humabon. Magellan himself went ashore daily to hear mass in the temporary chapel constructed of tree branches and sails.[714] On these occasions he talked with Humabon about Christianity and the need for spreading it to the neighboring islands. He also called in the chiefs of the city and the island and required them to swear obedience to Humabon. In turn, Magellan required Humabon to take an oath of fealty to the king of Spain. After warning all the Cebuans that their oaths could not be broken except on pain of death, Magellan presented the chief with a red velvet chair. Humabon replied that he was having bejeweled golden earrings, arm- and ankle-bracelets, and other precious adornments made for Magellan to wear. The Portuguese navigator, who was apparently not averse to decking himself out as a heathen prince, chided the new converts for not burning their idols as they had promised to at the time when they had become Christians. They responded that their idols were then being propitiated in behalf of an aristocrat who was seriously ill. Magellan told them that the patient would recover quickly if only he was baptized. When all turned out as Magellan had predicted, the hold of Christianity became correspondingly stronger than ever and the new believers systematically began to destroy their old shrines and images.

Magellan's swift successes soon led him to take the step which ultimately brought about his death and the downfall of his Christianizing effort. Maximilian of Transylvania summarizes the project as follows:

Magellan seeing that this island [Cebu] was rich in gold and ginger, and that it was so conveniently situated with respect to the neighboring islands thought that it would be easy, making this his headquarters, to explore their resources and natural productions. He therefore went to the chief of Subuth [Cebu] and suggested to him, that since he had turned away from the foolish and impious worship of false gods to the Christian religion, it would be proper that the chiefs of the neighboring islands should obey his rule; that he had determined to send envoys for this purpose, and if any of the chiefs should refuse to obey his summons, to compel them to do so by force of arms.[715]

While a number of neighboring chiefs readily acquiesced, Mactan, an islet near Cebu, refused to submit. It was clearly Magellan's policy whatever the opposition might be, to elevate Humabon from his position of *datu* of a large *barangay* (community) to that of a vassal king dependent upon Spain.[716]

The resistance to Magellan's demands was kept alive on Mactan by a chief called "Cilapulapu" (Lapu-Lapu). He continued to defy Spain and Cebu even after one of his villages had been burned by the Europeans and after another

---

[714] *Ibid.*, p. 128.   [715] *Ibid.*, p. 129.
[716] Phelan, *op. cit.* (n. 684), p. 16.

Mactan chieftain (Zula) had agreed to submit.[717] In his determination to force Lapu-Lapu's surrender, Magellan led a contingent of Europeans and Cebuans to Mactan. The European commander, who apparently hoped to impress Humabon with the effectiveness of European arms and tactics, ordered the Cebuans to remain off shore in their *barangays*. With about fifty men he waded ashore to attack the fifteen hundred warriors of Lapu-Lapu who waited in battle order. The odds being about thirty to one, the superiority of European armor, weapons, and tactics did not shine forth on that day (April 27). Lapu-Lapu's warriors won the engagement and before sunset Magellan himself was dead, a number of his men were wounded, and the entire expedition was shorn of its prestige in the eyes of the natives.[718]

It was not long thereafter before Humabon, possibly in connivance with Magellan's interpreter-slave, turned against the Europeans.[719] He tricked a number of them into going ashore by inviting them to a banquet at which he was supposed to deliver the jewels earlier promised to Magellan. Twenty-seven Europeans were massacred at the banquet, and the men who remained behind on the ships, hearing the din of battle, pulled up anchor and sailed away from Cebu on May 1, 1521. Pigafetta himself escaped the massacre because he had stayed on shipboard to nurse a wound received in the Mactan engagement. It is probably this injury which is responsible for the fact that Pigafetta lived to tell his story about Magellan's exploits.

From his twenty-five days of experience in the harbor and on the shore of Cebu, Pigafetta observed a number of native customs and recorded his impressions of them. His attitude towards the island and its people is interested and objective, especially if it recalled under what harsh condititions he and his companions were forced to flee. As he sees the Cebuans, they are people who love "peace, ease, and quiet,"[720] devote themselves to the joys of the flesh, maintain strange customs filled with superstitions, and live "in accordance with justice."[721] In common with the peoples of the Malay archipelago, some of them understand the Malay language of commerce, chew betel, and keep a principal wife and as many others as they desire.[722] As a rule the Cebuans of both sexes wear nothing but loin cloths. Males of all ages have their sexual organs "pierced from one side to the other, with a gold or tin bolt as large as a goose quill."[723] Whenever the Europeans go ashore, they are wined and dined

717 Pigafetta in Robertson (ed.), *op. cit.* (n. 136), I, 163, 171.

718 For the Philippine nationalist view on the "battle" of Mactan see Zaide, *op. cit.* (n. 208), pp. 140–42. Monuments to both Magellan and Lapu-Lapu stand on Mactan today. For the details of the battle see Pigafetta in Robertson (ed.), *op. cit.* (n. 136), I, 171–79.

719 For Pigafetta's theory, see *ibid.*, I, 180–81; essentially the same story, with a few variations, is told by Maximilian. See Coote (ed.), *op. cit.* (n. 463), pp. 131–32.

720 Robertson (ed.), *op. cit.* (n. 136), I, 149.

721 *Ibid.*, p. 147.

722 Polygamy seems not to have been widespread among the natives of the Philippine Islands; its practice was largely confined to the Bisayan Islands where it was probably introduced by Muslim traders from Borneo and elsewhere in southeast Asia. See Phelan, *op. cit.* (n. 684), p. 18.

723 Pigafetta in Robertson (ed.), *op. cit.* (n. 136), I, 167; cf. similar practices attributed to the Peguans (above, p. 553).

at banquets which last for five or six hours. Wine always flows freely,[724] but the meats which they serve are half-cooked and very salty to the European palate. At fiestas the Cebuans play music on stringed instruments and metal gongs.

Pigafetta describes in some detail two of their religious ceremonies. The first has to do with the sacrifice of the hog in a ritual performed solely by elderly women.[725] After the ceremonial killing of the animal, its blood is smeared on the heads of the men in the assemblage. Only the women are invited to eat the ceremonial dishes of rice, millet, and roast fish which are used in these rites.[726] Whenever a chief dies, the Cebuans follow equally curious mourning and burial customs. The corpse is put into a box over which a kind of canopy is erected. One of the women in attendance ceremoniously and slowly cuts off his hair while the principal wife lies down on top of him. Ceremonies are performed over the dead chief's body for five or six days at the end of which time the box with the deceased in it is covered with a wooden lid and buried.[727]

Cebu produces many types of meat, fish, and seafood as well as a long list of fruits and vegetables.[728] Most interesting are Pigafetta's references to bananas as long, delicious figs and to *mangcas* (breadfruit), a fruit which resembles the cucumber on the outside and the pulp of which tastes like chestnuts.[729] Maximilian describes how sago is obtained and prepared in Cebu, and even sends a specimen of this strange type of bread to his father, the Cardinal of Salzburg.[730]

Pigafetta evidently collected, while in Cebu, his list of Bisayan words, as well as details on the geography of the archipelago. For the instruction of those who will go there in the future, he notes that Cebu itself is a large island located at 10 degrees north latitude and 164 degrees east of the line of the demarcation.[731] Its port is served by two entrances, one to the west and the other to the east-northeast. The island of Mactan, where Magellan died, is close by and helps to protect the harbor.

After fleeing from Cebu in their three ships, the survivors of the Magellan expedition took refuge temporarily on the island of Bohol. Here they burned one of their ships because there were too few crewmen left to sail all three. From

---

[724] The Bisayans also had a reputation with subsequent Spanish commentators for being heavy drinkers. See Phelan, *op. cit.* (n. 684), p. 23.

[725] Ritual sacrifices were usually performed by elderly women known as the *babaylan* or the *katalonan*, a professional priestly caste. See *ibid.*, p. 24. This was an agricultural fiesta called *Mang-mang*. See Roger, *op. cit.* (n. 702), p. 145.

[726] Pigafetta in Robertson (ed.), *op. cit.* (n. 136), I, 163–67. For a similar description of this sacrificial ceremony see Blair and Robertson (eds.), *op. cit.* (n. 475), V, 172.

[727] Robertson (ed.), *op. cit.* (n. 136), I, 169–71. For a summary of death rites as described by a number of other observers see Roger, *op. cit.* (n. 702), pp. 125–35.

[728] Robertson (ed.), *op. cit.* (n. 136), I, 183.

[729] *Ibid.*, II, 149. The *mangcas* are fruits known scientifically as *Artocarpus integrifolia* or commonly as breadfruit. In Malacca and India they were called *jambos*. See Orta's description in Markham (trans.), *op. cit.* (n. 359), pp. 235–37.

[730] Evidently it had been used as a staple on the "Victoria." See Coote (ed.), *op. cit.* (n. 463), p. 128.

[731] Pigafetta placed the Philippines about 25 degrees farther to the east than they actually are. For the calculations which show his error see Quirino, *op. cit.* (n. 682), pp. 18–19. This may have been an intentional error, since it is hard to believe that Magellan would have been so far off in his reckoning.

Bohol they proceeded to the southwest along the island of Panglao where they saw Negritos living. Finally they came to a large island which Maximilian refers to as "Gibeth" (Quipit), a place which is actually on the extreme northwestern coast of the Zamboanga Peninsula on the island of Mindanao.[732] Its main port is "*Chipet*" (Quipit), an excellent harbor which he located at 8 degrees north latitude and 167 degrees east of the demarcation line. The *datu* of Quipit, Kalanao, concluded a blood compact with the Europeans, and Pigafetta, presumably because he was something of a language student and because they had lost Magellan's interpreter-slave, went ashore alone to visit with the ruler. After a long row upriver, Pigafetta arrived at the *datu*'s residence. Here, he observes, the eating and drinking customs and ceremonies are the same as those followed at Limasawa. He explains how they cook their rice so that it "becomes as hard as bread,"[733] a mode of preparation which he alleges to be general throughout the region. He spent the night with one of Kalanao's chieftains, and the next morning went roaming around the island. In the course of his wanderings, he noticed that gold was more abundant than food. Then after a simple noonday meal of rice and fish, he went to visit Kalanao's principal wife who lived at the top of a high hill. While he saw gold here and elsewhere on his excursion into Mindanao, he observes that the natives care very little about it and that they have no iron tools with which to dig it. Here he also learned that two days' journey to the northwest is located another large island called "Lozon" (Luzon).

But Luzon was not in the direction that Pigafetta and his companions were headed. In their search for the Moluccas they took a south–southwest course from Quipit into the Sulu Sea. Finally they landed on the sparsely inhabited island of "Caghaian" (Cagayan de Sulu) located at 7.5 degrees (actually at 7 degrees) north latitude. The few residents of this island were Muslim exiles from Borneo who lived in virtual nudity.[734] Since little extra food was available in this primitive place, they took a west-northwest course to "Pulaoan" (Palawan), a large island located at 9.3 degrees north latitude and 171.33 degrees from the demarcation line. Here, at last, they found the food supplies which they were looking for and so they called it "the land of promise."[735] They quickly concluded a blood compact with the local ruler and then began to look around.

The people of Palawan labor in the fields and fish in the seas. From their rice they make a distilled wine which Pigafetta considers to be stronger and better than palm wine. They value particularly products made of metal, such as brass rings, chains, bells, knives, and copper wire. They raise and train large cocks which they pit against each other in fights upon which they bet. Pigafetta was particularly intrigued with their blowpipes and poisoned arrows and so he

---

[732] Quipit (now spelled Kipit) is the name of both the river and town.
[733] Robertson (ed.), *op. cit.* (n. 136), II, 17.
[734] *Ibid.*, p. 21.
[735] *Ibid.*

describes them in some detail. Once their two vessels were loaded with provisions and water, the Europeans left Palawan for Borneo.[736]

From the end of July to the beginning of November, 1521, after they visited Brunei, Pigafetta and his companions roved the Sulu Sea seeking to find their way to the Moluccas. Pigafetta, who continued his observations under all conditions, remarks in interesting detail on the marine life of the Sulu Sea, noting the presence of crocodiles, gigantic oysters, and horned fish.[737] Not having enough men, ships, or arms to risk encounters with the rulers of the larger islands, the Europeans raided the small, sparsely populated islands and pirated unprotected vessels at sea.[738] In their frenzied search for food, water, and a pilot to guide them to the Moluccas, they finally found themselves back at Quipit in Mindanao. Then they sailed southwards around the Zamboanga Peninsula to the Jolo group of the Sulu archipelago before going into the Moro gulf. Finally, after turning northward again and landing in southwestern Mindanao near Zamboanga, they found cinnamon but apparently no pilot or provisions. From here they continued sailing to the northeast; en route they captured a party of Mindanao chieftains. On the advice of the leader, a man who knew the seas, the Europeans changed their course to the southeast. On the island of Sarangani, just south of the Mindanao cape, they finally captured two pilots who knew the route to the Moluccas.

Except for their brief visit in Borneo during July, the Magellan expedition was in the waters or on the islands of the Philippines for about seven and one-half months.[739] The first three and one-half months (March 16–*ca.* July 1, 1521) were spent threading their way through the central Philippines from uninhabited Homonhón in the east to Palawan in the west. The return visit (July 30–*ca.* November 1, 1521) brought them to a great number of islets in the Sulu Sea, to the Sulu archipelago, and to northern and southern Mindanao. In their travels through these regions, the Europeans saw Bisayans, Moros, Negritos, the "sea-rovers" known as *Sámal Laut*,[740] and some cannibals.[741] In the period after its hasty departure from Borneo, the expedition was seriously handicapped by a lack of leadership and discipline. While resorting to hit-and-run tactics, the Europeans were often forced to seek refuge in remote places. During their two extended visits the Europeans learned a bit about several of

---

[736] See above, pp. 580–83.

[737] Robertson, *op. cit.* (n. 136), p. 47. He also comments on "walking leaves," insects which resemble leaves (*Phyllium orthoptera*).

[738] The Europeans, like many native groups around the Sulu Sea and in the insular areas southwest of Mindanao, resorted to piracy as a means of livelihood. On the organization of piracy in these regions see J. Franklin Ewing, S. J., "Notes on the Tawsug of Siasi in Particular, and the Moros of the Southern Philippines in General," in Fred Eggan (ed.), *Papers Read at the Mindanao Conference* (Mimeographed; Chicago, 1955), I, 100–107.

[739] Robertson (ed.), *op. cit.* (n. 136), II, 45–61; for an analysis of Pigafetta's sketches of the various islands see Quirino, *op. cit.* (n. 682), p. 18.

[740] For description of these people who were then apparently near Zamboanga in Mindanao see Robertson, *op. cit.* (n. 136), pp. 53, 204.

[741] Called "Benaian" by Pigafetta (in *ibid.*, pp. 57, 204).

the levels of civilization in the pre-Spanish Philippines. More specifically, the account of Pigafetta shows that he grasped many details about local products, trading practices, and native languages. Although the natives are depicted as living in primitive conditions, the authors are also aware of the existence of the indigenous traditions and exhibit an understanding for their similarities and differences from place to place.⁷⁴²

The "Victoria" entered the port of San Lúcar de Barrameda in Spain on September 6, 1522, after completing the first circumnavigation of the world. She had aboard a rich cargo of spices from the Moluccas and twenty-one survivors—eighteen Europeans and three East Indians.⁷⁴³ During the following several years, thirteen other survivors made their way back to Spain by various routes. In the meantime the returned Europeans were feted and welcomed in Spain and throughout Catholic Europe. The great losses to the first expedition were conveniently attributed in official circles to the wrongheadedness of Magellan, even though Pigafetta defended his policies stoutly.⁷⁴⁴ Since the cargo of the "Victoria" yielded enough to pay for the entire expedition, the Spanish and Charles V hastened to prepare new fleets to follow in Magellan's wake. In quick succession three expeditions were sent out under Loaisa (1525), Cabot (1526), and Saavedra (1527). The first expedition got into the Philippines and the Moluccas, but was unable to return across the Pacific and so it ended in the Spiceries. Cabot did not even get around South America. Saavedra's expedition, which was sent out from Mexico by Cortes, suffered the same fate as the Loaisa enterprise. In 1530, after the conclusion of the pawning arrangements at Saragossa (1529),⁷⁴⁵ the Spanish refugees in the Spice Islands surrendered to the Portuguese. These survivors, among them Andrés de Urdaneta from the Loaisa expedition, were sent back to Europe via India and the Cape of Good Hope. By 1536 most of them were back in Spain.⁷⁴⁶

The Spanish, in the meantime, were not entirely happy about their monarch's decision to halt the expeditions to the Moluccas. Complaints were heard in the Cortés of Castile,⁷⁴⁷ and independent plans were being laid in the New World, especially by missionaries, to foster new Pacific expeditions. Oviedo, who was official chronicler of Charles I, was in the thick of these controversies both in Spain and Mexico. Book XX of his *Historia general y natural* . . . , which first appeared in 1548, recounts the history of Spain's Pacific voyages from 1519 to 1529. On the three voyages which followed Magellan's, he derives his information from the survivors. While in Santo Domingo in 1539, he

⁷⁴² For a Portuguese view of the Magellan expedition see Castanheda in Azevedo (ed.), *op. cit.* (n. 79), III, 160–64.
⁷⁴³ The eighteen Europeans, whose names are all known are the only survivors ordinarily mentioned; the three East Indians (probably Malays) are not named. See Zaide, *op. cit.* (n. 208), p. 149, n. 19.
⁷⁴⁴ Juan Sebastián del Cano, whom Pigafetta does not even mention, is usually given responsibility for the discrediting of Magellan.
⁷⁴⁵ See above, p. 118.
⁷⁴⁶ Zaide, *op. cit.* (n. 208), pp. 158–59.
⁷⁴⁷ Swecker, *op. cit.* (n. 11), p. 181.

interviewed two survivors of the Loaisa fleet, Andrés de Urdaneta and Martin de Islares, who were then on their way to Guatemala.[748] It is from these experienced observers, as well as from official sources, that the Spanish "chronicler of the Indies" and contemporary of Barros, derived most of his information on the Ladrones (Marianas), the Philippines, and the Spiceries to the southeast.[749]

While Oviedo's description of the Ladrones[750] corresponds in general with Pigafetta's, the Spaniard adds new dimensions to the picture. He evidently learned about these islands from his informants in New Spain who in turn had gotten their information on them from Gonçalo de Vigo, a Galician and a deserter from the Magellan expedition who was picked up by the sole remaining ship of Loaisa's fleet in 1526. This man, who had spent five years in the Ladrones, was subsequently of great use to his fellow Spaniards because he knew both the language of the islands and commercial Malay. Through Vigo, it was learned that the Ladrones include thirteen islands which run in a north-south direction as far north as 21 degrees north latitude.[751] The first of these islands to be sighted after a Pacific crossing is one called "Botaha," possibly a reference to the island south of Gaum which appears on later maps as "Bataba."[752] Aside from the generalities of insular life also noticed by Pigafetta, Oviedo points out that the people of the Ladrones have no livestock for meat and no metals with which to make tools and weapons. Even birds are not numerous, for, aside from a few sea gulls and pelicans, they have only small birds like turtledoves. These little birds are kept in cages where they are made to fight one another in a sport similar to the quail fights enjoyed by the Italians. The Ladronese themselves work and fight with instruments of stone, bones, and extremely hard wood. They make canoes and boats of many different kinds, which Oviedo describes. Most noteworthy among their social customs is the freedom which young bachelors enjoy in consorting with married women.

On October 2, 1526, fifteen days sail from the Ladrones, Loaisa's ship entered the harbor of "Viçaya" (Bicaio?)[753] near the southeastern tip of Mindanao. For thirteen days it stayed near the beach in an effort to get provisions and water. A landing party was then dispatched inland to see what could be found. After roaming about aimlessly for a long time, the Spaniards finally sighted a canoe in the bay. Vigo tried to hail its occupants in the Malay language, but they were not able to understand him. So the Spaniards got into their ship's boat and followed the canoe upriver to a center called "*Vendanao*" (Mindanao itself or Magindanas in present-day Cotabato province). Here they found some

---

[748] *Ibid.*, pp. 195–96; also see De los Rios (ed.), *op. cit.*, (n. 298) pp. 58–59. Urdaneta himself wrote a brief report for King Charles I in 1537. For an English translation of this narrative see Sir Clements Markham (trans. and ed.), *Early Spanish Voyages to the Strait of Magellan* (London, 1911), pp. 41–89.

[749] For his materials on the Spiceries see above, pp. 600–601.

[750] De los Rios (ed.), *op. cit.* (n. 298), pp. 60–62.

[751] Urdaneta (in Markham [trans. and ed.], *op. cit.* [n. 748], p. 51) says in his report that they extend from 12 degrees to 19 degrees north latitude.

[752] See Sanson's map of 1692 prepared for Louis XIV.

[753] Cf. below, p. 641.

natives who could understand and speak Malay. Though they were treated hospitably at first, the atmosphere of cordiality soon changed. On their initial effort to trade their merchandise for provisions, they met with delay and excuses. In an effort to get at the root of the problem, Vigo was sent a short way into the interior to interview their chieftain. Here he was asked if they were *Faranguis* (Franks or Portuguese), and the Galician interpreter assured him that they were not. The chieftain said that he knew that trouble began whenever these *Faranguis* appeared and that he was gratified to learn that the Spaniards also opposed them.[754] Still, he was not sufficiently reassured to allow peaceful trading. His men repeatedly tried to seize the Spanish ship and its boat. And they often tried at night to cut the ship's cables. While they failed in these actions, the Spanish were equally unsuccessful in getting the provisions which they badly needed after their long voyage across the Pacific. From here the Spanish sailed along the coast of Mindanao to the southernmost tip of the island at a place called "Baguindanao" (Banajan?).[755] Then they tried to sail northwestward to Cebu, which they knew about from the Magellan expedition, but were forced southward by contrary winds. They finally anchored on October 22 off the northeastern shore of Talão (Taland) Island, an islet "almost midway" between Mindanao and Ternate in the Moluccas. At this place they were well received, acquired all necessary provisions, and refurbished the ship.[756]

Mindanao, according to Oviedo, has a circumference of about three hundred leagues (1,200 miles) and belongs, he erroneously believes, to the Celebes archipelago. From the information gathered by the Spanish along the eastern and southern coasts, he concludes that the island is divided into six provinces: "Baguindanao" (Maguindanao), "Paraçao" (unidentified), "Bituan" (Butuan), "Burse" (unidentified),[757] "Viçaya" (southeastern coast?), and "Malucobuco" (Malibog?).[758] From the southernmost tip of Mindanao (Point Tinaka) it is possible to see many islands,[759] three of which are named "Sandinguar" (Sampantangu?),[760] "Carraguan" (Sarangani),[761] and "Sanguin" (Sanguir).

[754] De los Rios (ed.), *op. cit.* (n. 298), p. 63; this is perhaps an indication of the fact that Portuguese freebooters were active in the Philippines before 1526, or merely that news of their depredations elsewhere had reached eastern Mindanao.

[755] Possibly the old name for Point Tinaka. See Felipe Bravo, *Diccionario geográfico, estádistico, histórico de las islas Filipinas* (Madrid, 1850), II, 320. It is more likely, however, that it refers to "Maguindanao," an older form of Mindanao, and the name of the sultanate which then controlled the southern half of the island.

[756] De los Rios (ed.), *op. cit.* (n. 298), p. 64.

[757] Oviedo (*ibid.*, p. 14) refers to "Burse" as a territory rich in cinnamon; it is possibly in the western part of the island.

[758] Malibog is the name of a river which debouches on the eastern coast. See Bravo, *op. cit.* (n. 755), II, 203.

[759] For a similar but more extended list see Pigafetta in Robertson (ed.), *op. cit.* (n. 136), II, 57.

[760] Sampantangu is a point on the southern coast, but it is the only other name in this area which resembles "Sandinguar." See Bravo, *op. cit.* (n. 755), II, 421.

[761] This island was also visited by the Magellan crew (above p. 638) and in 1578 by Francis Drake (Sharp, *op. cit.* [n. 673], p. 49).

The people of Mindanao are clever, bellicose, and treacherous, even in their relations with one another. Under cover of night, while some tried to cut the ship's cables, others sought to sell gold to the crew. The tribes of one part of the island are almost constantly at war with one another. For this reason arms are normally carried at all times by everyone including the children. Around their waists they wear dagger-like blades. They never go anywhere without their shields, and their lances are like the harpoons used for killing tunny, only more elegant and finished.[762] To all these parts each year come the junks of China to exchange their silks, porcelains, and finely wrought brass and wood items for gold, pearls, and slaves.[763]

Mindanao and its environs were also visited by the Villalobos expedition in 1543. The official report on this voyage was written in 1547 or 1548 by the pilot Ivan Gaetan (beginning with the reissue of 1588 the editor writes Juan Gaetano) and was printed in Ramusio as early as 1550.[764] While noting that this island is usually called "Vendenao" (by Oviedo, for example) Gaetano gives it the better spelling of "Migindanao." Reportedly, Villalobos named this island "Cesarea Caroli" in honor of his king and emperor.[765] "This island," writes the pilot, "is very large, and after circling it we found it had a circumference of 380 leagues [1,520 miles], and had its greatest extension from east to west while stretching in a north-south direction from 11.5 degrees to 5 or 6 degrees north latitude."[766] While circumnavigating Mindanao, the Villalobos expedition saw many different peoples, both Moors and heathens, as well as divers kings and dignitaries. Like Oviedo, Gaetano notices that all the people are well clothed, and he observes that they wear sleeveless robes called *patolas*,[767] the rich having theirs made of silk and the rest of the people having theirs made of various types of cotton cloth. In addition to the offensive and defensive weapons noticed by Oviedo, Gaetano remarks that in places where the Muslims do business the natives also have small pieces of artillery. The island has numerous wild animals, such as pigs, deer, and buffalos.[768] Its people cultivate chickens, rice, and palms. Since they raise no wheat, they make something resembling bread from either rice or sago. The island is rich in ginger, pepper, and gold. Along its westernmost cape (Zamboanga) cinnamon grows, and the Portuguese sometimes touch there when they go to the Moluccas.

---

[762] For a brief account of weapons in use among the Bogobos and Colu Mandaya tribes of southeastern Mindanao see Fay-Cooper Cole, "Cultural Relations between Mindanao Regions and Islands to the South," in Eggan (ed.), *op. cit.* (n. 738), pp. 4, 6.

[763] Oviedo in De los Rios (ed.), *op. cit.* (n. 298), 64.

[764] *Op. cit.* (n. 92), I, 416r–417v. It is entitled "Relatione di Ivan Gaetan pilotto Castigliano. . . ." For a short biographical sketch of Gaetano see Zaide, *op. cit.* (n. 208), p. 160, n. 16.

[765] Zaide, *op. cit.* (n. 208), p. 161.

[766] Ramusio, *op. cit.* (n. 92), I, 416r. It is actually between 5 degrees and 10 degrees north of the equator and its irregular coastline is estimated as being about 1,600 miles.

[767] This is a Portuguese version of Kanarese, *pattuda*, meaning "a silk cloth." See Yule and Burnell, *op. cit.* (n. 218), p. 520. For modern dress of the Bogobos see Cole, *loc. cit.* (n. 762), pp. 4–5.

[768] Probably the carabao. On the fauna of the Philippines see Eggan *et al.*, *op. cit.* (n. 685), pp. 43–50.

Villalobos, after encircling the island, laid over for three or four months in 1543 at an unpopulated place near Point Tinaka to refurbish his ships and to refresh their crews. Then he sailed southward to the nearby islands of "Sarangã" (Sarangani) and "Candigar" (Sampantangu?)[769] which are just two miles apart. There, Gaetano reports, they found a pirate's lair and he describes in some detail the raiding ships. Not being able to provision his ships at these small islands, Villalobos sent a ship northwards to forage for food. The "San Juan" under the command of Bernardo de la Torre skirted inhospitable Mindanao (later writers allege that the Portuguese had conspired with the natives of Mindanao not to give supplies to the Spaniards)[770] and finally landed at an island called "Tendaia." Modern scholars disagree as to whether this island was Samar or Leyte, but Samar appears to be the more likely identification.[771] Gaetano reports that the heathens of this island treated them with great kindness and that they quickly got together a cargo of provisions and fresh water. In gratitude, the Spanish gave the name "Filipina" to this island. On Ramusio's map, first published in 1554, the name "*Filipina*" appears beside a long, narrow island which is roughly in the position occupied by Samar and Leyte.[772]

In 1577, Escalante's *Discurso de la navegacion* . . .[773] appeared at Seville and its last chapter contains a brief discussion of the "Islands of the West which we call the Philippines."[774] Twelve years earlier the Legaspi expedition had begun to set up a permanent Spanish establishment in the Philippines without regard for the Portuguese claim that these islands were within their demarcation.[775] Still, in Escalante's book there is no mention of Legaspi's activities in the islands or of the foundation of Manila on the island of Luzon on June 24, 1571. Escalante, like Oviedo, is inclined to think of the Ladrones and Mindanao as satisfactory but undistinguished stopovers on the way across the Pacific to the Moluccas. But, since he is primarily concerned with China in his *Discurso* . . . , he merely mentions the proximity of Luzon to Canton, its overwhelmingly Moorish population, and its gold production.[776] Clearly, from this book, one obtains the notion that Escalante and his informants had little concern for the Philippines themselves, but thought of them mainly as way stations on the sea track to richer places.

---

[769] Cf. above, p. 641.

[770] Zaide, *op. cit.* (n. 208), p. 161. The Portuguese came from the Spice Islands to southeastern Mindanao to obtain gold and recruits for their activities in the Moluccas. They apparently touched frequently on Sarangani Island. For references see Castanheda in Azevedo (ed.), *op. cit.* (n. 79), IV, 382–83, 388, 522–23.

[771] For a short rundown of the views of a number of authorities see Zaide, *op. cit.* (n. 208), p. 161, n. 21; for a convincing identification with Samar see Blair and Robertson (eds.), *op. cit.* (n. 475), III, 193; 316. Also see Quirino, *op. cit.* (n. 682), p. 72.

[772] For a similar description of the Villalobos expedition see Galvão in Lagoa and Sanceau (eds.), *op. cit.* (n. 525), pp. 275–77.

[773] For further discussion see below, pp. 742–43.

[774] Carlos Sanz (ed.), *Primera Historia de China de Bernardino de Escalante* (Madrid, 1958), p. 94. Incidentally, the Portuguese authors refer to the Philippines as "the Islands of the East."

[775] A number of Spaniards accepted the Portuguese claim, including the pilot and mission leader of the Legaspi expedition, Father Urdaneta.

[776] Sanz (ed.), *op. cit.* (n. 774), p. 99.

It was from the reports of his fellow Augustinians [777] and from the Franciscans who endeavored to penetrate China in 1577 that Mendoza received most of the information on the Philippines printed in his popular *Historia . . .* (1585). Like Escalante and the missionaries themselves, Mendoza was mainly preoccupied with China. But, the Augustinian historian, like his fellows in the field, digressed sufficiently from his primary interest to inform Europe about a score of years (1565–85) during which the Spanish and four of the religious orders established themselves in the Philippines. As the backdrop for these movements, he sketches in many new details about the islands, particularly with regard to Luzon and its immediate neighbors.

Like the other Spanish authors, Mendoza commences his discussion with the Ladrones where the galleons from Acapulco first drop anchor after being out of sight of land for forty days. [778] His description of the people and their customs parallels Oviedo's, but the Augustinian includes only seven or eight islands (instead of thirteen) as lying within the archipelago. The friar, like Pigafetta and Oviedo, notices the freedom with which young bachelors, according to their customs, visit married women with the knowledge and consent of their husbands. [779] Over these islands there reigns no central political or religious authority. Consequently, the islanders are often at war with each other, particularly when a Spanish fleet appears with goods to exchange for food and woven mats. The inhabitants of the Ladrones prize iron and glass products much more highly than silver or gold. Nobody knows what these people believe in because no European has been in the islands long enough to learn the language. [780] Mendoza's informants believe that the language could be learned easily [781] and the people be readily converted from their heathenish idolatry if only a few missionaries and soldiers could be spared from Spanish enterprises elsewhere. It is thought, avers Mendoza, that these gentile people are descended from the Tartars for they have many similar ceremonies and customs. Moreover, they buy iron from the Spaniards to sell it to the Tartars who come there to trade. Evidently, these Tartars, to which he refers, were merchants from either Japan, the Liu-ch'ius, or China.

The Spanish, in Mendoza's words, sail due westward from the Ladrones for almost two hundred leagues (800 miles) to a strait called "of the Holy Ghost" [782] and through it they enter into the archipelago. Composed of an infinite number of islands, the archipelago stretches, by his naïve geography, in a semicircle from the Moluccas to the strait at Singapore. Manila, the Spanish political and

---

[777] The Jesuit procurator sent from Mexico to Rome in 1577 was under orders from his provincial congregation to collect data on the Philippines, especially from the Augustinians. See De la Costa, *op. cit.* (n. 684), p. 5.

[778] Mendoza in Staunton (ed.), *op. cit.* (n. 394), II, 253–57.

[779] Cf. their remarks (above, pp. 627, 640).

[780] Evidently Mendoza had never heard of the Galician, Gonçalo de Vigo, who remained there for five years between the Magellan and Loaisa expeditions (above, p. 640).

[781] Mendoza (in Staunton [ed.], *op. cit.* [n. 394], II, 256) gives two words of the "native" language.

[782] *Ibid.*, p. 258. This is the strait between Samar and southern Luzon now known as Bernardino Strait. The northeastern cape of Samar was long known as the Cape of the Holy Spirit.

ecclesiastical capital, he locates with precision on the island of Luzon at 14.25 degrees north latitude. The countless islands of the archipelago are almost all inhabited by "natural people," a minority (400,000)[783] of whom have been brought within Manila's jurisdiction. When the Spanish explorers first arrived in the islands, political anarchy reigned throughout the archipelago. But, according to Mendoza's view of history, the war of all against all was a fairly recent condition. In earlier times, China had ruled the islands until its emperor decided to give them up of his own free will—a reference to the decision of the Ming emperors in the early fifteenth century to prohibit overseas activities. Left to their own devices, the natives reverted to brutish ways and went about recklessly killing and enslaving one another.[784] But God, in his divine wisdom, provided a remedy by leading the missionaries to the islands where, by evangelizing, they helped Him restore peace, order, and justice.[785] Had the Spaniards not come when they did, the hapless natives would have fallen to Islam through the proselytizing activities of Muslims who regularly came to the Philippine Islands from Borneo.[786]

The religion of the Tagalog people of Luzon, where the early Augustinians and Franciscans were most active and effective, prescribes worship of the sun, moon, other natural phenomena, and numerous idols.[787] The most revered of their idols is one called *Batala*,[788] who is traditionally superior to the other gods even though the natives seem unable to give any satisfactory explanation as to why he alone occupies the supreme position. The gods, called "maganitos,"[789] are honored at sumptuous festivals known as "magaduras."[790] The priestesses who preside at the sacrificial ceremonies are called "holgoi"[791] and Mendoza characterizes them as witches held in high esteem for their ability to talk with the devil and perform feats of sorcery. Throughout Luzon soothsayers enjoy a high reputation and the common people are acutely sensitive to portents and signs. The natives of the Ilocos region of northern Luzon, who were pacified by Legaspi in his expedition of 1572, are said to worship the devil as compensation for the vast stores of gold which he has given them.[792] While the missionaries make great progress in the islands, Mendoza points out that their numbers are too few, particularly as new islands are being discovered almost daily.

When the Philippines were first discovered, they were reputed to be

---

[783] *Ibid.*, p. 263.

[784] While denouncing native slavery, Mendoza lashes out against the Spaniards in the islands who continue to maintain it. On slavery in the pre-conquest period see Lasker, *op. cit.* (n. 427), pp. 36–41.

[785] For a similar rationale by a modern author see De la Costa, *op. cit.* (n. 684), pp. 18–19.

[786] Mendoza in Staunton (ed.), *op. cit.*, II, 260–61.

[787] *Ibid.*, pp. 261–63.

[788] Correct. See Zaide, *op. cit.* (n. 208), p. 78.

[789] The spirits were called *anitos*, and the religious sacrifices honoring them were called *maganitos* (*ibid.*, p. 79).

[790] Unidentified.

[791] Unidentified.

[792] A reference to the gold mine rites of the Igorotes, who believed that the gold belonged to the *anitos* (spirits.) See Roger, *op. cit.* (n. 702), p. 151.

unhealthy and hence unfit for colonization.[793] Experience, however, soon disproved this belief as the islands were quickly found to be both healthy and habitable for Europeans. Mendoza gives a long list of the products of Luzon, and remarks on the inexpensiveness of all native products there. Like so many other commentators, Mendoza dwells at great length on the countless uses which are made of the palm tree and its products. Though the islanders have no olive oil or wine made from grapes, they have satisfactory substitutes in linseed and flaxseed oil and in palm wine. Every year more than twenty junks from China bring beautiful silk and cotton textiles in all colors, gunpowder, and saltpeter, and luxury items of brass, copper, and carved wood. Close to the city of Manila on the other side of the Pasig River from the Spanish settlement there is a colony of Chinese. Most of the Chinese are artisans (shoemakers, tailors, blacksmiths, and goldsmiths), merchants, or functionaries, and all have accepted the official Christianity of the city. It was the easy conversion of these overseas Chinese which reinforced the missionaries in their hope of converting mainland China even though they well understood that they were strictly forbidden to go there by Chinese law. It was with the help of the Manila Chinese that the missionaries were able to translate into Spanish the Chinese materials used by Mendoza in preparing his work on China.[794] Even though the Spanish missionaries were finally thwarted in their efforts to evangelize on the China mainland, they succeeded at Manila in making a few beginnings towards the understanding of Chinese culture.

Very little was known in Europe about southeast Asia before 1500 except for the names and the major products of a few of the leading continental states and chief islands. With the passage of another century, thanks to the chroniclers, officials, explorers, and missionary reporters, a substantial amount of information had been printed on every major country and island from Burma to Indochina, the Philippines, New Guinea, and the Marianas. Much additional data had also been siphoned into Europe which did not see print for reasons of secrecy or merely because they were considered too repetitive or inconsequential. While Malacca was the center of trade and information for the entire region, the Europeans have little to say about Malaya after Albuquerque seized the entrepôt. Java, Borneo, and Sumatra, probably because they were Moorish strongholds, are likewise slighted by the European authors. The Portuguese and Spanish chroniclers summarize in their narratives what was known in Europe by mid-century about Siam, Burma, Indochina, and the Spiceries. Most of what was published about the Philippines and New Guinea came from the Spanish explorers. The Jesuit letters are especially valuable for Malacca and the Spice Islands. They have only incidental references in them to the continental states where the Jesuits were conspicuous by their absence, and to the Philippines where they were less influential than the Spanish Franciscans and Dominicans.

---

[793] Mendoza in Staunton (ed.), *op. cit.* (n. 394), pp. 264–66.
[794] See below, pp. 747–48.

Nevertheless, most of what was known in Europe about the activities of the mendicant and preaching orders in southeast Asia was relayed through the Jesuit letters. All of this information, scattered and questionable as some of it undoubtedly is, remains valuable to modern scholarship because of the dearth of native sources, the unreliability and lack of regard for accurate dating in those that exist, and as supplements to the precise annals of China.

The European observers, especially Barros, sought to learn about the pre-European history of the region from local informants. They record whatever they were able to learn from the oral traditions, whether mythical or factual, about the origins and development of Burma, Siam, Cambodia, Sumatra, the Moluccas, and the Philippines. Many of them studied the native languages and were therefore able to supply commercial, religious, and administrative terms, especially in Malay, Javan, Bisayan, Mon, Thai, and Cambodian. Some of the missionaries tried to obtain examples of local literature, and both lay and ecclesiastical writers comment on the existence of books in Burma, Siam, Cambodia, and Cochin-China. Had Pires' account of Java been published, Europe would have also known about the existence of Javanese writings. Xavier deplored more than once the absence of a native literature in the Malay language of the archipelago; this lack he attributed to the fact that the Malays had but recently learned to write their language in the Arabic script of the hated Muslims. The Europeans are almost unanimous in expressing their admiration, mixed sometimes with wonder and disgust, for the religious architecture and sculptures which they saw on the continent.

Impressed from the beginning of their adventure in southeast Asia with the universal importance of China and the Chinese, the Europeans point repeatedly to evidences of China's prominence in southeast Asia's past. The Javans, because of their skill and ingenuity, are supposed by Barros to be related historically to the Chinese. According to Burmese tradition, the origin of Burma is linked to a Chinese woman. Siam, the greatest state of the region at the beginning of the sixteenth century, continues to be a vassal of China. Cochin-China is allied economically and by marriage to Peking. Chinese products are noticed in the marts of remote Chiengmai, and the primitive Laotians conduct forays over China's borders. Halmahera, which is also called Batochina do Moro, is believed to have had early and intimate contacts with Chinese traders. Malacca was a vassal to Peking and appealed to China for help against Albuquerque. Sumatran tradition has it that the Chinese at one period controlled the commerce of the straits. Mendoza surmises that the Philippines were ruled by the Chinese before the Ming emperors decided to prohibit overseas ventures in the fifteenth century.

The Europeans show less consciousness about the impact of Hindu culture and political activity in southeast Asia. This is in part because they do not associate Buddhism with India proper, only with Ceylon; it is also because of the prominence during the sixteenth century of Muslim traders from Gujarat and Hindustan whom they often classify as "Arabs." Still they relate certain southeast Asian customs to what they know about India: eunuchs are as important at the court of Pegu as they are at Bengal; succession in certain Sumatran ports is by assassination, similar to practices reported to be characteristic of Bengal; Klings from the Coromandel coast are highly regarded in Siam as soothsayers and sorcerers; in a number of places they note that the natives, like those of Malabar, worship each day the first thing which they see in the morning —even in distant Cambodia. While the Europeans talk mainly about the non-Muslim parts of Java, they strangely show no appreciation for Java's historical relationship to Indian culture.

The hatred of the Europeans for the Muslims and their competition with them for trade leads the writers of the sixteenth century to overestimate the relative importance of the Moors in southeast Asia. Such an emphasis was inescapable inasmuch as both groups were active in the port cities and neither was able to penetrate the hinterlands effectively. The Portuguese chroniclers almost audibly give a sigh of relief when they are able to point out that the Muslim merchants are not nearly so influential on the continent as they are in Malacca and the archipelago. The missionary writers, who are themselves propagating trade along with Christianity, see clearly that the faith of the Prophet is being extended continuously by Muslim merchants, sailors, and religious teachers. The Christian writers, both lay and ecclesiastical, almost never forget to record what they know about the introduction of Islam in each place about which they discourse. They bring out clearly that after the fall of Malacca the major centers of Islam were located in the islands of Sumatra, Java, Borneo, and the Moluccas. Until 1570 the Portuguese, often to the dismay of the Jesuits, collaborated in the Moluccas with the Muslim rulers of Ternate. And, it was firmly held by most of the Spaniards, perhaps as a rationale for their own military activities, that the Philippines would gradually have been taken over by Muslims based on Borneo if the Christians had not forcefully penetrated the archipelago before them. While belligerently hostile to everything Moorish, the missionaries admit grudgingly the potency of Islam as a unifying and civilizing force in the archipelago. In fact, it might be observed that the tactics followed by the Portuguese and the Christian missionaries show more than a little resemblance to the pattern of conquest, conversion, and king-making followed by the Muslims.

The continental states are depicted as having independent but similar political, social, and military systems. In all of them the king is an absolute monarch who is the proprietor of the land and the arbiter of every man's destiny. The rulers of Pegu, Siam, and Cambodia claim suzerainty over their smaller neighbors or over one another. These rulers derive most of their revenues from internal taxes and wars, though they strictly regulate and exact tribute from international trade as well. In the case of Siam, it is clearly brought out that the aristocracy is rewarded for service by grants of lands—though such rewards are never given in perpetuity. The lower classes in these countries, aside from those who participate in and service trade, seem clearly to be dependent upon agriculture, especially rice cultivation. The quiet labors of peace time are frequently interrupted by the numerous wars on which these rulers embark as they seek to subdue their neighbors. The continental wars, in which many Portuguese participated, clearly involve huge movements of people since everyone was liable for military service and since it was commonly the practice to raze a captured city and to depopulate it by scattering the inhabitants or by carrying them off into exile.

In religion and social usages the continental states likewise exhibit similar lineaments. They are all great, heathen states where neither the Muslims nor the Christians can make many converts. While not clear on the history or the doctrines of Buddhism, the Europeans are fully aware of its predominance and are conspicuously impressed by its magnificent temples, stupas, and sculptured images. They also understand that there exists a close association between the ruler and the religious establishment. The hierarchical organization of Buddhism, especially the existence of vast numbers of mendicant and cloistered monks who live by rule, reminds them of the religious system of Catholic Europe. Many of the Europeans credit the clergy of these countries with preserving native traditions, cultivating learning, and carrying on the works of education and social service. Still, despite the architectural magnificence of their religious establishments and their concern over what are admittedly constructive activities, the Buddhist monks are castigated for their unrelenting devotion to superstition and error. While much of this hostility was undoubtedly genuine, the reader of the European works frequently comes away with the impression that heathen practices are denounced as much out of convention as conviction.

The insular world east of Malacca has a life of its own which has little relationship, except for trade, to what is transpiring on the continent. Here there are no great, heathen states with strength enough to resist Portuguese-Christian expansion. Wherever the Europeans meet prolonged and bitter opposition, it is spearheaded (except for the defense of Mactan in the Philippines) by the uncompromising Moors. Almost universally the Moors, sometimes followed or supplanted by the Christians, occupy and control the coastal territories. The rulers of the port towns involved in the spice trade seem to live almost entirely from their levies on commerce, the sale of ship's provisions, and their profits as middlemen. In the hinterlands, which the Europeans know mainly by report, live the people who preserve the heathen past in their beliefs and practices. As a rule the primitive natives are not described as "noble savages," though Maximilian of Transylvania and Oviedo are inclined to laud the natives of Borneo, probably without basis, for their devotion to a peaceful, unspoiled life. Other Europeans, on the contrary, stress the poverty, filth, and abhorrent practices of the primitive islanders even when noting that they are sometimes friendly. The Christian writers are especially shocked by the prevalence of cannibalism in Sumatra, the Spiceries, and the Philippines. They are likewise indignant about the widespread use of poison and inveigh against other forms of treacherous behavior. Most of them are obviously awed by the vast area over which the islands lie scattered, and show special gratitude to the Malay language for giving them a medium through which to communicate with very different peoples in so many widely scattered places. The writers actually in the field, particularly the Jesuits, seem to be overwhelmed by the diversity of human forms, colors, abilities, and languages to be found in the islands. Some of them try to record the names (ancient as well as contemporary) of towns, mountains and rivers, tribal designations, and the words for everyday items of food, shelter, and commerce. Despite such brave efforts, the Europeans, merchants and soldiers as well as missionaries, seem to be stunned by the magnitude of the task confronting them in the archipelago. Camoëns gives expression to this feeling of dismay when he sighs: "Nations of thousand names and yet unnamèd." [795]

[795] Canto X, line 126.